PUNCH
AT THE
THEATRE

FIRST PUBLISHED IN 1980 BY ROBSON BOOKS LTD.,
28 POLAND STREET, LONDON W1V 3DB.
COPYRIGHT © 1980 PUNCH PUBLICATIONS LIMITED.

British Library Cataloguing in Publication Data
'Punch' at the theatre.
      1.   Theatre - Anecdotes, facetiae, satire, etc.
      2.   English wit and humour.
      I.   Morley, Sheridan
      827'.8'080355   PN.6231.T57
      ISBN 0-86051-102-2

Designed by Glyn Rees
Research by Susan Jeffreys

Printed in Hungary

Edited by Sheridan Morley

Robson Books

CONTENTS

Old Lady (turning to neighbour, during last Act of tragedy).
"EH, MISTER, BUT THEM 'AMLETS 'AD A DEAL O' TROUBLE IN THEIR FAMILY!"

INTRODUCTION
Sheridan Morley

When PUNCH first began going to the theatre (in the year of its birth, 1841) Henry Irving was three and Sarah Bernhardt wasn't even born, let alone wooden-legged. The going rate for a thousand-word review was seven shillings, and for that the critic was expected to sharpen his own quills. We're none of us getting any younger, but mercifully the money has improved a bit and, as the magazine's fifteenth drama critic (give or take a few who couldn't stand the pace or the plays and dropped out well before their third **King Lear**) I feel the time has come to put some of our theatrical past on display.

The magazine had taken its name from one of the earliest forms of local street theatre, and in the first sixty years of its life over five hundred plays and sketches by PUNCH writers saw the lights of some stage somewhere. The first editor, Mark Lemon, once toured as Falstaff (no padding) and President Lincoln was unfortunately assassinated while watching the play of a later PUNCH editor, Tom Taylor. He (Taylor, that is, not Lincoln) often took part in Victorian benefit nights, on stage alongside such other members of the PUNCH table as Shirley Brooks and George du Maurier who of course wrote **Trilby,** thus allowing Sir Herbert Beerbohm Tree to establish the true definition of overacting.

Since that time we can also claim George and Weedon Grossmith, an editor (Francis Burnand) who founded the Cambridge ADC, and the memory of an earlier writer, Thackeray, who toured with his own lecture show, though an unkind friend told him that what he really needed was a piano.

In this century PUNCH once (albeit briefly) staged its very own London revue, and our dramatists have included A.A. Milne, A.P. Herbert, P.G. Wodehouse, John Van Druten and Jeremy Kingston, while Basil Boothroyd once wrote for Sid Field. Much of that will emerge from the pages which follow, though it should perhaps be added that of the present resident editorial staff, no less than 25 percent carry Equity or Musicians' Union cards.

Not that this is therefore an inside job; seldom if ever can a single magazine have regarded the theatre with such a constant and consistent mixture of love and loathing, and my sole regret after several happy weeks in the archives is that I haven't found space for it all. I'd like, for instance, to have included the anonymous reviewer who found Ellen Terry "unpromising," and the one who spent an entire notice of Gielgud's first Hamlet debating the merits and demerits of tights.

I'd also have liked to include more of the signed reviews of such distinguished postwar predecessors of mine as Eric Keown and B.A. Young but, forced to establish rules for elimination, I settled for only including weekly notices where either the play or the leading players were of over-riding interest because of what happened to them later. From the wealth of early material, I have tried to choose what best illustrates the eccentric realities of Victorian and Edwardian Theatre in this country; the later material has been selected on a more (though unashamedly) personal basis of favouritism.

To all our contributors here, artists and writers alike, and to all the people they caricatured or reviewed I am deeply grateful; but above all to William Hewison who for the last twenty years has virtually alone kept the art of theatrical caricaturing alive, and who moreover endures having to go to the theatre with me once a week.

"...Nice to see them swotting for their finals."

8

THEATRE NOTES.
THE MAN IN THE PIT.

THE difficulties of theatrical management are notorious. It has constantly been proved that there is no season of the year which is favourable for the production of a play. In the long winter months people do not want to leave their cosy homes; when spring comes, with Daylight Saving, the people are busy in their gardens or idling on the river; in the hot summer they do not want to be cooped up in a stuffy theatre; in the treacherous autumn months, when the first colds begin, they are afraid of draughts, and then too, having just finished their holiday, are hard up and are settling down to work. Just before a holiday season they are saving up their money, and just after a holiday season they have no money left. During the week they are too tired or busy to go to the theatre, and over the week-end they are out of town.

The principal enemies of the theatre are stated to be:—

1. Very good weather.
2. Very bad weather.
3. General Elections.
4. By-Elections.
5. Municipal Elections.
6. Books.
7. Papers.
8. Films.
9. The Wireless.
10. Dancing.
11. Dining.
12. Pubs.
13. Puritans.
14. Cabarets.
15. Concerts.
16. Dog-Racing.
17. Dirt-Tracks.
18. Boxing.
19. Bridge.
20. Political Meetings.
21. Parliament.
22. Clubs.
23. Cocktail-Parties.
24. Billiards.
25. Chess.
26. The Entertainment Tax.
27. Poverty of the Intelligent Classes.
28. Stupidity of the Wealthy Classes.
29. High Rents.
30. Low Brows.
31. Sickness.
32. Strikes.
33. Scarcity of backers.
34. Interference of backers.
35. American competition.
36. British competition.
37. Cost of production.
38. Cost of seats.
39. Monday.
40. Friday.
41. Sunday.
42. The Censor.
43. The Critics.
44. The Actors.
45. The Playwrights.

In spite of these difficulties it is admitted that one or two theatres do still contrive to keep open, and that a few scattered citizens do still attend the play.

5 December 1928

"I've seen every performance. I'm a throat specialist."

9

MAIDEN SPEECH

Westminster. The House of Lords. Enter several Lords. They dispose themselves loosely about the Chamber. To them, enter LORD OLIVIER.

LORD OLIVIER

My lords, it doth compassion most entice
Which, like a mole, can crawl into the ear
And there, as precious Hector's brother's son
Did, from the moment that he blood-bound sprang,
Untimely born, into this keening world,
Work to the general detriment of all,
And bring direction into several doubt,
That we assembled peers, liege to our Queen
(Who late at Ascot hath so bravely borne
Herself, the very stallions did weep)
That we, I say, should take such little count
Of Section Nine, Clause Four, Amendment Six,
Which touches us most close, and in that touch
Rubs on our bias, so our line unlined
Is yet relined to lie not where it lies.
And thus I cannot, while these poor bones breathe,
Stand idly by as some ignoble hand
Tears down the horse-trough close by Walham Green
And, ere the ravished grass has scarce resprung,
Puts up the James P. Funt Memorial Bench.

LORDS

Oh!

LORD OLIVIER

I see you catch my trawl! But not my trail,
Or, rather, trial, since trolling makes it so:
I hold no enmity against this Funt,
Whom legend and the Plumbing Trades Gazette
Hold that he served the Walham Council well,
Keeping her drains and sewers free from taint,
Despatching all towards that mighty sea
That rings this island with its fluent steel,
For only seventeen pounds four a week.
But shall we, like the pig, stare at the Sun
Until, grown blind, we cannot see the Moon?
(Enter Lord Kilburn)

LORD KILBURN

Hear! hear!
(Falls asleep)

LORD OLIVIER

My thanks, good Cousin Kilburn, and methinks
My thanks bespeak bespoke respect. And yet,
Ere Sirius 'gins to drag his draying drogue
One more full course across the Heaven's dark dyke…

THE LORD BISHOP OF FOWCESTER

He's piss'd!
(Dies)

LORD OLIVIER

…Strong sinews, mallets, picks, and all the bleak
Accoutrements of Public Works shall join
And wrench this piteous horse-trough from the sod…

THE DUKE OF NORFOLK

Wash your mouth out!

LORD OLIVIER

…And wrench this piteous horse-trough from the earth,
Disbowelling Nature's bosom, like the whelk
Which wreaks its evil in the roots of yews,
Until…
(Alarums without. Sennets. Keatons. Enter LORD GOODMAN, scant of breath)
How now, brave peer! My lords, this good man sent
By me to ascertain the latest drift
At Walham Green, is now return'd. I trust
What news?

LORD GOODMAN

It's a diabolical liberty! You wouldn't credit it!
(Hands over letter)

LORD OLIVIER

What treachery is this? What foul misdeed
That threats the very passage of the Sun?
My lords, the evil Scroop, Clerk of the Works
To Walham Council, hath with twenty men,
Rough Irish mercenaries, by this account,
Ridden to Walham Green and there encamped!
Their tinny huts already fright the grass,
Their braziers taunt God's chilblains with their coals,
And e'en this second, iron clangs on stone,
In vile defiance of Amendment Six,
By which we lords, empowered by our Queen,
Have sought to stay its dark destructive blows!
(A peal of bells without)
It is the call to arms! Come, let us…

LORDS

Lunch! Lunch! It's sausage toad today!
(Exeunt, variously running and hobbling)

LORD OLIVIER

O, naughty Lords! Is England come to this?
Towed by a sausage to a harlot's kiss?
(Exit, removing mascara)

A.C.

FLATTERY IN SHOWBUSINESS
Keith Waterhouse

Hamlet, in Act III, Scene ii of *Everyman's Dictionary of Quotations*, sounds off at great length about the trouble with actors. Suit the action to the word, he tells them, the word to the action; with this special observance, don't ham it up.

I doubt very much whether Shakespeare himself ever spoke to his players in this peremptory fashion. Imagine—if he'd interrupted the final dress rehearsal to give the two gravediggers all that stuff about speaking no more than was set down for them. They might have said nothing at the time, but the business with Yorick's skull would have gone for nothing come opening night. What more likely happened is that Will let them play the scene through, and then he put his arms around the two of them and said: "Boys, you were fantastic! Marvellous! And that mother-in-law gag you worked in—wow! But boys, believe me, you're killing your exit. Supposing we try it this way..." Then he stomped home in a foul temper, sharpened a quill and worked all night doing a quick rewrite. "Hey, Hamlet—I know this gives you an extra speech to learn, but I think you'll agree it strengthens the part. It's sort of

Sweet Thing (to total stranger sitting in front). "DON'T YOU FIND IT AWFULLY HOT?"
Stranger. "YES, VERY."
Sweet Thing. "WELL, YOU WON'T SOON, AS I'VE DROPPED AN ICE-CREAM INTO YOUR HAT."

advice to the players kind of thing—you know, a send—up of the whole business…"

The principle on which the theatre survives is that flattery is the father of invention. There is no aspect of theatrical industry—rewriting the play overnight in a hotel bedroom, learning a revised second act between matinée and evening performance, building a new set by Tuesday—where the oil-can is not passed liberally over the cogs as an automatic preliminary. Actors praise each other unstintingly in the knowledge that flattery is the one sure antidote to the galloping insecurity which is the profession's industrial disease. Directors dish it out or withold it, like nannies with the barley sugar. Impresarios use it to tempt good actors into bad parts and, with the subtle grace of a coal lorry going down into second gear, to ease bad actors out of good parts. "Frankly, and speaking as a friend, I don't think this play will do anything for your growing reputation…"

In the theatre, the art of flattery has as many themes as it has variations. I was sitting in a theatrical club one night in the company of television director who was very drunk indeed. An actor wandered in and the director immediately congratulated him on his performance in *Rosencrantz and Guildenstern are Dead.*

The actor thanked him but regretted that he was not in that particular play.

"*Othello*, then? Did I see you in Olivier's *Othello?*"

The actor said that he had never worked for the National Theatre.

"But I've seen you in something—I remember I was very impressed. Very impressed indeed. Very, very impressed in—"

The actor said that as a matter of fact he had done nothing except one week in a radio serial for the past nine months, and that he was working at the moment in the groceries department of Harrods.

The TV director snapped his fingers.

"*That's* where I've seen you!" he exclaimed. "*And you were bloody marvellous!*"

And it wasn't such a gaffe as all that. What my friend instinctively understood, even with the best part of a quart of whisky inside him, was that in his circle flattery is the easiest, and sometimes the only method of communication. Like convicts banging on water pipes with their tin mugs, people in the theatre use flattery to talk to each other when there are no easier means available.

An actor and an actress meet on a film set. They have not seen each other for two years—they may indeed be total strangers. Before the morning is out they will be in bed together with a microphone boom over their heads, playing a love scene. How can they strike up this necessarily affable relationship except by buttering one another up? "I thought your Ophelia was the most moving thing I have ever seen" may not be how Stanislavski envisaged an actor getting into the right mood, but Stanislavski wasn't working to a budget.

From the other side of the footlights, flattery in the theatre still has a reputation for being slightly less subdued than Niagara Falls. It would be refreshing to report that "*Dah*ling you were *mah*vellous!" went out with "Anyone for tennis?" but, at present, there is little evidence that the theatrical revolution has got as far as the dressing-rooms. The first-night telegrams still bristle with superlatives, the bouquets roll in from Constance Spry and Moyses Stevens, the stone corridors ring with congratulations, the kissing never seems to stop. The justification is that however much the theatre may have changed, a first-night is still the culmination of a ludicrous journey into the unknown—a moon landing without (unless you count the Manchester try-out) the instruments having been tested. It's the nearest thing anyone is likely to see, now

"We had Oscar Wilde today, sweetie."

13

that the Brotherhood of the Flagellants is out of fashion, to a fit of mass hysteria. How, in this atmosphere, can you tell somebody that he was rather good?

It may be because flattery is dispersed in this reckless way that the theatre has very little left over for its most profitable purpose of self-advancement. Most of the actors I know would starve rather than tell a writer or director that they would love to be in one of his plays. It also seems to be a convention that while a producer may tell an actor at length how much he admired his work, the actor—possibly because he doesn't want to interrupt—doesn't usually reciprocate. This uncharacteristic reticence can be overdone. I can remember a brilliant character player in a provincial repertory company complaining that, no matter how good his notices, no producer ever offered him work in the West End. He was brooding on this mystifying state of affairs when there was a knock on the door and a distinguished Shaftesbury Avenue impresario, a man of great influence and corresponding dignity, entered. "Hello, fatty!" hailed the actor with genuine delight. He has still to make his West End début.

I hope I haven't given the impression that it is only he who plays the king who needs his ha'porth of adulation. Flattery is the mainline drug of the theatre—there is no one connected with that ridiculous institution who does not need his fix. I was once sitting is a restaurant with the cast of a new play; the first-night had gone well and we were waiting up for the notices. All but one, it transpired, were excellent—but it happened that the author of our one bad notice was sitting a few tables away from us. It also happened that he had a carbon copy of his review in his inside pocket, and he felt moved to come across and read it out to us. He paused after each scathing sentence, and the reading—interrupted as it was by cries of "Why don't you——off!"—took a long time. I wondered, in the ensuing gloom, what had motivated this display of sadism.

It was only later, when the favourable notices came in, that I was able to think about our intruder more charitably. He was *proud* of his review. He had polished each phrase, honed up each little bit of invective. Possibly under the influence of a good dinner, he thought that we would appreciate and applaud the quality of his writing.

All he wanted was a little flattery.

"If you ask me even the applause was simulated."

HERO-WORSHIP.

Henrik Ibsen. "AND ALL THIS IN HONOUR OF MY CENTENARY!"

THEATRES FOR LONDONERS.

THE new managerial system of running the same pieces for several years (a system utterly detrimental to dramatic literature and to theatrical art) has produced the natural effect. There is no wrong without a remedy. The Lovers of the Drama (a distinct class from the people who will go anywhere, provided a door is opened) have made representations to the country managers and to the railway authorities, and the result is that special Theatrical trains will start from London, so as to enable the Playgoer to go to the Play in towns where the performances are occasionally changed. The managers at Bath, Bristol, Dover, Brighton, Margate, and many places within easy reach have come into the scheme; and as the trains will be very fast, and the prices very low, Londoners will at last be enabled to see a play now and then. The arrival of the trains will be telegraphed to the theatres, and the overture will begin the moment the visitors are seated. The return transit will be equally well arranged, and people will be at supper in town earlier than they could be if they sat out a London bill. The remedy was absolutely necessary, if the educated classes were not to be allowed to lose all their taste for the theatre, and the actors to lose all their chance of study and improvement.

16
April
1864

MARCEL MARCEAU

Who broke into Duncan's room? Who covered up the Banquo caper? Is Macduff telling the truth? Where was Malcolm? Is the King of Scotland a crook? Here at last are

The Macbeth Tapes

prepared and edited by HANDELSMAN

I

MACBETH
Is this (inaudible) I see before me,
The handle toward my hand? Come, let me clutch thee!
I have thee not, and yet (inaudible).
I go, and it is (unintelligible).
Hear it not, Duncan, for it is (inaudible).
That summons thee to heaven, or go (expletive).

II

MACBETH
Was it not yesterday we spoke together?
(CHARACTERIZATION OMITTED)
It was, so please your Highness.
MACBETH   Well then, now
(Inaudible) predominant in your nature
That (unintelligible) common eye
For sundry weighty reasons.
2nd (CHARACTERIZATION OMITTED)
   We shall, my lord,
Perform what you command us.
MACBETH
Your spirits (unintelligible) flight,
If I find heaven, must (inaudible) tonight.

III

MACBETH
Which of you have done this?
LORDS   What, my good lord?
MACBETH
Thou canst not say I did it. Never shake
Thy (characterization omitted) locks at me.
ROSS   Gentlemen, rise.
His Highness is (inaudible).
LADY MACBETH
   Sit, worthy friends.
My lord is often (unintelligible).

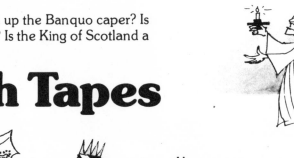

IV

MACBETH
How now, you (background interference) hags,
What is't you do?
3rd WITCH
Scale of dragon, tooth of wolf,
(Unintelligible) gulf,
(Technical disturbance) hence,
(Harmless ethnic inference).
Purposes so far from laudable,
Something (expletive)(inaudible).
MACBETH
Then live, Macduff. What need I fear of thee?
But yet I'll (unintelligible) be.

V

LADY MACBETH
Out, (characterization omitted) spot!
Out, I say! Who would have thought
the old man to have had so much
(unintelligible) in him? What, will
these hands ne'er be (inaudible)?

VI

MACBETH   I will not yield,
To kiss the (unintelligible) feet,
Though Birnam Wood be come to Dunsinane,
And thou opposed, being of no (inaudible),
Yet I will (18 minute hum). Macduff
And (tape ran out) that first cries "Hold, enough!"

VII

MACDUFF   Hail,(gap)!Behold where stands
Th'(inaudible)'s (characterization omitted) head.
MACBETH
This newest crisis hath me near defeated!
I'll tough it out, and (expletive deleted).

17

NO WREATHS FOR SHAFTESBURY AVENUE
Eric Keown

Once again—as often happens in the silly season when there are no spectacular poisonings or stranglings—the word "crisis" is being bandied around the theatre, because lately fourteen new plays in London flopped within two months. To this latest bout of hysteria there are three very short answers: first, that the Chairman of Keith Prowse reports his ticket sales up by four per cent on 1959, itself a boom year; second, that at the moment of writing at least eleven of the thirty-eight theatres on the London list are doing standing-room-only business; and third, that these eleven include the Duchess, with *The Caretaker*, Harold Pinter's wild but brilliant play in the vein of Godot. No one could pretend the West End theatre is in the best of health—so far as I know it never has been—but tears are out of place. The theatre in the provinces is another matter.

A high proportion of the recent failures should never have been allowed to get within a mile of the stage. Blame the managers? It is easy to do this, but we must be careful to distinguish between them. In London they fall roughly into three groups. (1) The few long-established managers at the top, often controlling a number of theatres. These are on the whole men of taste and integrity, who do their best to strike an intelligent compromise between art and their pockets, and sometimes contrive to satisfy both. They are too shy of experiment and the classics, but seldom give us a bad play. Their success works in a spiral, enabling them to afford the best actors and producers, who in turn attract the best playwrights. (2) Their eventual successors, a group of younger men of similar calibre, but probably more limited means, who are in the process of learning their job the hard way. Already we owe to them some of the brightest items in the London list. (3) The lunatic fringe, victims of stage-fever with little qualification, whose ineptitude insults the public and does the theatre a great disservice. When, as recently happened it adds to an abnormal run of flops (some of which came from good stables, which are bound to slip up now and then), the damage is apt to continue in a chain-reaction; the vacuum is filled in a panic by plays that would normally not have a hope of reaching London, and for a time the stability of the whole section of the theatre may be affected.

It is hard to see what can be done about this last type of manager. Whenever a limping little comedy gets the bird it is really he and his moronic backers who should be booed, and not the wretched cast who have been doing their best to mitigate the play's horrors.

Remember also that managers are working in financial circumstances that would strike the leaders of any other industry as fantastic. The relevant figures (taken from Richard Findlater's excellent book, *The Unholy Trade*) are that in the last eighty years theatre rents have increased by as much as ten times and production costs by six, while the price of most seats has only doubled. Apart from the sharp increase in taxes, this means that managers would be justified in charging at least three pounds for a stall. Imagine the outcry if they did.

The cost of putting on even a modest play in the West End with one set has risen to approximately £5,000-£6,000 (in America to nearer £50,000) of which actual production costs will be £3,500-£4,000. With full houses and a very fair wind a manager can get home in as soon as three to four weeks, but this level of expense is no encouragement to him to nurse an ailing play in the hope of recovery.

I am glad to see that no bricks have been thrown at actors during the latest controversy, for there is no doubt whatever that the standard of acting on all fronts has never been higher in this country. We have a dazzling top drawer of classical actors and actresses, and it is a pity that we cannot find enough new plays that match up to their talents.

There has always been a shortage of good new plays. At the moment we have six in the West End of which we may be reasonably proud: *Ross, A Passage to India, A Man for All Seasons, Rhinoceros, The Caretaker* and *Roots*. We cannot expect often to do better than that.

The poetic drama that showed such promise ten years ago, led by Fry and Eliot, has rather fizzled out, and the focus of interest now seems to be on the new school of inconsequence, owing something to Samuel Beckett and headed by Harold Pinter, N. F. Simpson, John Mortimer and Ionesco in translation. I find it enormously encouraging for the future that Simpson's *One Way Pendulum* should have run five months in the West End, and that Pinter's play should be following its example.

The angry young men, I am convinced, were no more than a flash in the pan of mediocrity; most of their pot-shots at the Establishment missed, anyway. We can look for plays with far more constructive social comment from men like Arnold Wesker, whose *Roots* analyses cleverly the loneliness that education can bring in a working-class family, and does it without self-pity.

The gravest shortage to-day appears to be in what may be called the Rattigan group, those traditional dramatists who bother about being craftsmen. Examples are Wynyard Browne, N. C. Hunter and Peter Ustinov. There is always room in London for plays like *A Question of Fact, A Day by the Sea* and *Romanoff and Juliet,* but the supply is terribly limited.

The public will always flock to that kind of play, but in other respects its taste has changed considerably in the last few years. It seems as if, unexpectedly, television is a good influence. In the late 'fifties it began to produce a choosier audience (just as the talkies did in the 'thirties) by educating people in the drama, and by drawing off the lazier elements; also by providing so much light entertainment it has made the public hungry for something different in the theatre. It may well have signed the death warrant of comedies about stockbrokers' wives having rural fun in cottages with drink trays and French windows, and of farces in bedrooms with five doors and no steady tenancy. (It is interesting to note that the French equivalents still thrive in Paris, where TV was late in arriving.) If these old favourites go, unmourned by many, they will leave a big gap and offer great chances to more original minds. Another type of play that may be doomed on the stage through its familiarity on TV is the crime thriller.

All managers report their audiences to be younger and quicker on the ball. I am sure this goes back to the astonishing revival in the better theatre that was one of the surprises of the last war (in contrast to the fluff-and-leg shows that were the chief recreation of the first one); and that a lot of the credit for it must also go to Stratford and the Old Vic. One is crammed all summer, the other all winter; this must be making a difference. It may be that London audiences will grow smaller; there is little doubt they will be more intelligent, and that is the surest guarantee for the future.

But the theatre in the provinces is, alas, in a much worse way. Consider these shocking facts. In the whole of Great Britain there are now fewer than forty touring dates left. This summer Newcastle and Leicester, both cities with over a quarter of a million inhabitants, *have no live theatre at all.* The so-called repertory theatres have dropped to roughly sixty, of which only about half are putting on good stuff. Last summer every rep in the country took a terrific beating, and the fact that it is happening again this summer suggests causes deeper-rooted than good weather. Clearly TV keeps the less enterprising at home. Holidays abroad eat into box-office figures. Audiences are at last losing patience with the shabbiness and discomfort which is all many reps can afford to give them. But when we have said all that, managers still do not think

we have arrived at the full answer. A mystery remains, which they are desperately trying to solve.

One thing that sticks out is that the non-profit-making reps, which include the most enlightened, are not being helped as much as they should be by their municipalities. The Local Government Act of 1948 empowered local authorities to spend up to 6d. in the rates on the arts and entertainment, including non-commercial reps. Very few give more than a small fraction of a penny to their rep, though there are shining exceptions, such as Canterbury. The best of the non-profit-making reps could not survive for long without the annual grants from the Arts Council, which keep about twenty of them just at subsistence level. Councillors maintain an old-fashioned shyness over spending public money on culture; when it comes to the test of another election they still believe something solid like a public lavatory is a more telling recommendation. If playgoers in the provinces would only combine to make candidates' lives a misery over the sixpenny rate, the reps would be a lot safer.

As it is, they are alarmingly rocky, and it is saddening to think of dead theatres all over Britain and of how much talent the West End has owed to the reps. Small comfort to remember that France and America, the countries closest to us in the theatre, have no reps to lose.

July 20, 1960

27 February 1864

PANTOMIMIC ATROCITIES IN 1864

SIR — Pantomimic atrocities this year are greater than has ever been known before. The poor babies have been principally the sufferers. As many as 2,753 have fallen victims to the severity of the season since last Boxingnight. Two perish nightly at Drury Lane Theatre. Their cries before receiving the last spoonful of pap have generally been of the most heart-rending description—so much so, as to have made the heart of MR. MALTHUS out-Herod HEROD himself in leaping with joy, if he could only have heard them. This "murder of the innocents," far from being visited with shouts of indignation, is hailed every evening with the most joyous peals of laughter, more especially be the female portion of the theatrical community. No measures have yet been taken to put a stop to this fearful increase of pantomimic infanticide, though we cannot help thinking it must tend eventually to harden the hearts of the spectators. Not even a single inquest has been held upon their mangled bodies; in fact, the only persons who have sat upon them have been the Clown and Pantaloon, who have taken the most malicious delight in falling upon them one after another, with all their might. An elderly gentleman has been blown nightly from a gun. It is now known what particular offence he has committed, but he has been thrust into the mouth of the gaping Armstrong, without so much as his name or address being asked, and in an instant stuck against all parts of the building.

Four dozen charity boys have been forced into cisterns, and, the lid being instantly put on, have never appeared on the surface again. Policemen, too, have been the favourite objects of ill-treatment. They have been subjected to every form of indignity; been cuffed, pelted, kicked, bonnetted—but all things considered, have borne it with considerable good humour. Every kind of practical joke has been practised upon them, and amongst others that of throwing them into a hot cauldron, apparently for no purpose other than that of changing their colour from blue to red. This, we are credibly informed, is only a playful allusion to the crustacean tribe to which they are popularly supposed to belong. No deaths have fortunately resulted from this culinary practice, but still the inhumanity of the proceeding cannot be too loudly condemned.

The red-hot poker, also, has this year been most freely used, but we have not heard of any fatal cases that have occured from the liberal application of it. Beyond making the patient jump and howl a little, it does not seem to inflict much injury. However, the Legislature should look to it. I remain, yours respectfully,

A SOFT-HEARTED PHILANTHROPIST

COME BACK MAX MILLER

cries Barry Took
after every Royal
Performance

When the first Royal Variety Performance took place on 1st July, 1912 at the Palace Theatre, Shaftesbury Avenue, a notable absentee from the bill was the delectable Marie Lloyd. She was not included by the organisers on the grounds that her performance might be offensive to Royal ears. One would have thought that King George V and Queen Mary were made of sterner stuff.

But if the Royals were robbed of Marie, they were treated to a gallimaufry of variety stars, including Chirqwin the white-eyed Kaffir, Barclay Gammon and a grand piano, and Paul Cinquevelli—"The Human Billiard Table." In spite of the decline, in fact the almost complete disappearance of the Music Hall, since 1912, Variety's big night hasn't altered much. Today the saying "Variety is dead and television is the box they put it in" has never been more true. Only rarely is anyone on the show who is not an established TV name, and the purpose of the exercise seems to be to provide an even longer and duller TV spectacular than usual.

The priorities were underlined last year when Mary Hopkin declined to appear because she was recording her own television show that night. She was replaced in the programme by Sandy Powell—which was "let them eat cake" with a vengeance. Whatever the particular skills and attainments of both artistes, it's difficult to see the reasoning that led to replacing a girl singer in her twenties with a 70-year-old North Country comedian, doing a burlesque of Arthur Prince and Jim. Perhaps Mary Hopkin had something up her sleeve we didn't know about. Was she going to sing "Those Were The Days" while smoking a cigar and drinking a glass of water? Did one of the organisers inadvertently say Sandy Powell when he really meant Sandie Shaw? *Was* it Sandie Shaw all the time?

I don't suppose we will every know—as I suppose we will never really know how the cast of a Royal Command Variety Show is assembled. It's pleasant to imagine the Royal breakfast table on a bright September morning and the small cry of delight as Her Majesty the Queen opens her morning mail. "I say, it's a letter from that nice Mr. Delfont. He's asking who we fancy for this year's Variety Show. Now don't all ask at once…" It doesn't seem very likely, does it—and yet the bill gets put together somehow. A cynic might say—anyhow. The ingredients are now traditional.

There must be a young, unknown comedian who will steal the notices and it's obligatory to have an established star who misjudges his material and is greeted with stony silence. There has to be a folk troupe. The top of the bill must be flown in specially from America and be suffering all too obviously from "Jet Lag," and every year the show must overrun.

As an outing, I reckon the Royal Variety Show falls somewhere between the Cup Final and the Royal Command Film Performance. On one hand it is indoors but on the other you can't sit in the dark and doze

THE ELLEN TERRY MEMORIAL

THE objects of the promoters of this Memorial, on whose committee Mr.Punch has the honour to be represented, are:—

1. To acquire Small Hythe Place, the Tudor house which was ELLEN TERRY'S home for the last twenty-five years of her life, and endow it with an income sufficient to put it in good repair, preserve it, keep up the garden, and pay the salary of a custodian, one of whose duties will be to show the house to visitors who may be expected from all parts of the English-speaking world.

2. To keep two rooms much as they were in her lifetime, preserving the atmosphere of simplicity which faithfully reflects her character and taste.

3. To devote another room to the purposes of a Library, chiefly of books relating to the drama and the theatre, of which ELLEN TERRY'S own collection will be the nucleus, and a Museum of theatrical relics of historical interest.

4. To adapt the Barn adjoining the house, a fine outbuilding of the same date, to the purpose of a "Barn Theatre," where it is hoped to institute an Annual Dramatic Festival on a small scale during the week in July in which the anniversary of ELLEN TERRY'S death falls.

For these purposes a sum of £15,000 is required, the greater part of which will be used as an Endowment Fund. Mr.Punch begs that all those among his readers who loved ELLEN TERRY'S art and personal charm wil take this opportunity of paying a tribute to her memory. It is hoped that the sum needed may be raised by February 27th, her birthday. Gifts should be sent to the Hon. Treasurer, ELLEN TERRY Memorial Fund, 56, Manchester Street, London, W.1.

---

off during the dull bits. Films and football are easier to manage than variety and I suspect that the final make-up of the bill rests in the hands of a small group of men dedicated to the memory of the Empire—the Hackney Empire. These men are the last survivors of a dying race—"the tribe that hides from men" someone has called them. They are Variety Agents. (Many of them are related and all work for the same organisation in spite of what it says on the brass plate outside their respective offices). All are fiercely independent of each other but all share a common belief—you can't beat a live show if it's booked by them. In the sense that royalty is a family business that the outsider can only occasionally break into; these men are royalty. The business and its traditions are passed down from father to son, from uncle to nephew.

Like royalty, their power nowadays is symbolic rather than real and only manifests itself on rare occasions—one of these occasions is the Royal Variety Performance. As with royalty, one can only guess at the dialogue of their most intimate councils—but let's have a guess anyway.

The scene, an imposing office-cum-boardroom, the decor an intriguing mixture of Louis Quatorze, Habitat and Old Times Furnishing Company. The men sit around an impressive board table, the discreet lighting reflecting impartially off its polished surface and their heads. These men have grown bald in the service of Variety and baldness, actual or incipient, is to them what haemophilia or the Hapsburg Lip is to other dynasties. To make it simpler, I've called them all Lou so as to differentiate from Lew who is a different kettle of fish entirely. The first Lou speaks.

1st Lou: Well, to start off with, we don't want a repetition of last year.

2nd Lou: What do you mean?

1st Lou: Well you know as well as what I do that when the galaxy of stars is introduced to her gracious Majesty, the twits must not speak until they are spoken to.

4th Lou: Are you perchance referring to my boy, Jim Muffcock?

1st Lou: Yes. Your boy, Jim Muffcock.

4th Lou: Well, he's young, he's enthusiastic.

1st Lou: He's a burke.

4th Lou: So—he's an enthusiastic burke.

2nd Lou: What did he say?

1st Lou: Say? He told her gracious Majesty the one about the two niggers in the fish shop.

4th Lou: Well, what about your boy, Samoy Tuft. Two years ago *he* said, "It's a bloody shame they closed the Sheffield Empire, your majesty." That's nice language in front of royalty.

1st Lou: Well it *was* a bloody shame about Sheffield Empire. Besides, even Prince Philip swears.

3rd Lou: Well, who was it introduced Glenn Campbell to the Queen as Englebert Humperdinck?

1st Lou: Well she didn't know he wasn't.

2nd Lou: Neither did Engelbert.

3rd Lou: No, but I think Glenn Campbell did. You could tell by his eyes.

2nd Lou: Temperamental bloody performers. They're all the same.

1st Lou: Well anyway—that's all in the past now. What about this year?

2nd Lou: Well, I think that in the past we've tried for too much. I mean, six hours straight off is enough to try the patience of Golda Meir. I think it should be eight good acts. Acts that really know their stuff. Say—Enid and Edna Runcible ("Tapping their way to the top"). Tiny Alf ("the looney on a unicycle"). The Exploding Grobstocks, Manny and Sherma ("Doves of all nations"), Tonia the Giraffe, Aldrich and Oakley ("in sentimental mood"). Kamikasi and Partner and Ninette.

3rd Lou: Wait a minute, they're all your acts.

2nd Lou: So? I had them in Yarmouth this summer—they broke all box office records.

The other Lous turn on their friend and there is a brisk exchange of views.

1st Lou: Gentlemen—gentlemen, language. Look, let's examine the thing from the point of view of The Royal Family. What are they? What can we assume they'll enjoy? Let's analyse it. H.R.H. H.M. the Queen is a patron of the arts and badminton. Her husband, the Prince Philip, Duke of Edinburgh, is a navy man, Their son and heir, Charles, is a revue performer of no mean calibre, viz. appearing in a dustbin in a university revue. Next, their daughter Anne is an ace horsewoman. So far so good, but where are we going to find a sailor who does a satirical act with a horse? But let us look at it from another point of view. Her Majesty is concerned about unemployment and the Common Market. She understands the needs of old people and the desires of the young. She responds to the plight of underdeveloped nations, is alert to the East/West detente, is conscious of Britain's role in the world and above all, she is alert to the need for world peace.

3rd Lou: So?

1st Lou: With al that on her mind, she's not going to give a monkeys about who's on this year's Royal Variety Show. Right, we'll go round the table—Who do you fancy?

2nd Lou: Eric and Ernie.

3rd Lou: Mike and Bernie.

4th Lou: Mike and Albie.

5th Lou: Cilla.

6th Lou: Lulu.

7th Lou: Nina.

8th Lou: Des.

9th Lou: Les.

10th Lou: Danny.

11th Lou: Dickie.

12th Lou: Ronnie.

13th Lou: Frankie.

And so on—until this year's bill is finally decided and presented, with a suitable loyal address, to Bernard Delfont.

At least, this is what appears to happen. In some inscrutable way that no one has ever been able to fathom, the Royal Variety Performance turns what should be a happy, convivial occasion into an affair in comparison with which an amputation without anaesthetic would seem a lighthearted romp.

Perhaps if Marie Lloyd had been included in the first Command Performance her irreverence and high spirits would have created another, jollier, precedent. But alas, history shows you don't get into the New Year's Honours List by larking about.

"Ooh, he's changed his act because he the Queen's crazy on animals…"

Rehears
for The C

in the august preser
BILL TIDY

"Supposed to be a British Show, and for them big bleedin' American names

een

"Let's get this presentation line up sorted out.
Who wants to be the Queen?"

"That one's out for a start."

to go

"We don't want to upset anyone.
Personally I think he's showing
too much."

"C'mon! Mr Delfont says someone's
got to share a dressing room with him!"

SEARLE'S-EYE VIEW
As the imagination sees them, and as the camera does

Eugene Ionesco

26

John Osborne

Harold Hobson

N.F. Simpson

DOWN PERISCOPE! UP CURTAIN!

A group of "long-haired strolling players" are to board the Royal Navy submarine *H.M.S. Andrew,* **which will carry them on a goodwill tour of the south coast of England. They will give "myth and magic" shows ashore and create "a happy circus-like atmosphere." The crew's morale went "shooting up" at the news.**—*Daily Telegraph.*

Excerpt from the diary of Lt. "Dicky" Bracebright, of Her Majesty's submarine Egregious, *first of the new "Trend" Class.*

Monday, August 21, 1972: Put in at Falmouth to pick up Greenwich Village Liquid Theatre "C" Company for goodwill cruise. A right rum lot. Much stroking and pawing everywhere and too many avowals of friendship for my liking. Skipper had his ankle felt and has been acting strangely. The Ministry of Defence says it's all good training—but training for what?

Tuesday: *Egregious* alerted to watch out for Sir Francis Chichester, rumoured to have slipped his doctors and put to sea again. Crew too heavily engaged with Liquid Theatre to keep proper watch. Picked up two or three fat women on lilos five miles out of Exmouth and handed them over for stroking. All hands stroked fast but none stroked faster than Number One. This was always a happy ship but tonight the air of ecstasy frightens me. Wish I were on the Beira Patrol.

Wednesday: Theatricals went ashore at Lyme Regis to lay hands on populace, but police laid hands on them, thank heaven.

Skipper nearly normal again.

On Ministry of Defence instructions took on board scratch lot of unemployed fairground folk from Employment Exchange, including dwarfs, fat lady and human cannonball.

Thursday: Chichester sighted. Fired human cannonball at him from No. 1 Torpedo Tube. Missed.

Edward Heath sighted, in *Morning Cloud.* No dwarfs or clowns aboard. All right for some.

Friday: Force Eight gale. Signalled our sister sub *Epicene* with André Previn and the London Symphony Orchestra aboard, wallowing horribly. *Epicene* can be smelled two miles downwind. She's to take part in a British Week at Rio. Sir Thomas Beecham would have known better.

Saturday: A Whitehall Public Relations Officer called Titching, chap with ginger moustache, is touring *Egregious* interviewing crew for stories for home town newspapers. Just my luck to have to vet his copy. Wonder how Mrs. McGrath of Butt of Lewis will feel when she reads in the *Stornoway Gazette* that her sailor son Hamish won the South Coast belly-dancing semi-finals submerged off Portland Bill. Or how Lt.-Cdr. Ralston-Drake, retd.,

of Plymouth will relish the news that his son Cyprian sleeps head-to-tail in a hammock with Dolores O'Cassidy, who earns her living being tipped out of bed at fairgrounds. Last night his mates tipped them out twenty times for laughs. For further details see *Plymouth Evening Chronicle* any day now. Have volunteered for the next cod war.

Sunday: Crew and passengers rushed ashore in Viking gear at Bournemouth to spread sweetness and light, pick up litter, rape the women, etc. They returned drunk lugging with them the entire company of the Alamo Hysterical Theatre Workshop who had gone ashore from *Erotic* with similar intentions. Scenes aboard indescribable. All clamoured for rum, unaware that issue is discontinued. Bring back the lash! Bring back keel-hauling!

Monday: The Mayor of Southsea thanked us for raising the morale of the town and presented a bill for £15,678.50 damages. He took his debagging in good part, but asked for his chain back at our convenience. Before sailing Egregious fired half-million psychedelic leaflets over town from forward gun and then left a working party of dwarfs to sweep them up. Our newly acquired Hystericals were still staging happenings all over town at midnight and not a citizen escaped participation. Hundreds of old-age pensioners were touched up with electric prods in an effort to end the war in Vietnam.

Tuesday: Report received that *Stars on Sunday* is being broadcast from a Polaris submarine under the ice-cap. Russian delegate to United Nations has lodged a strong protest against "this unspeakable atrocity."

Lord Mountbatten and Sir Noel Coward, those grand old men of the sea, came aboard today at Portsmouth and spent half a minute below before being carried off on stretchers.

Wednesday: This morning Skipper consigned vessel's only copy of Queen's Regulations to the deep, heavily weighted. It has no longer any relevance to life in the Senior Service. Not a moment passes without an outbreak of conduct prejudicial to good order and naval discipline.

Admiral Lord Plunkett-Raleigh-Hawkins of the Ministry of Defence News Room piped aboard with leading members of cast of *Jesus Christ Superstar*. To think my sailor grandfather had to send in his papers for marrying an actress!

Thursday: Crew and Hysterical Workshop waded ashore on exposed sandbank to play friendly game of cricket. Tide rose rapidly and crew regained vessel only in nick of time. Workshop Eleven left to their fate, having scored 35 for six. Ship's morale suffered only briefly. All hands are looking forward to next weekend when we put in to Hastings to pick up Billy Smart's Circus, the Burtons and a bunch of unemployed programme-sellers from the Adeline Genée Theatre at East Grinstead. We are to raise the morale of our NATO allies, starting in Brest.

Tonight Skipper revealed in confidence that French naval authorities are preparing a big welcome for us, probably with depth charges. Pray for us poor mariners—

(At this point the writer dropped dead, from a severe attack of foreboding).

By Command Of
BERNARD DELFONT
They Killed You At Cowes! They Slew You at Caernarvon!

And Now, Following An Enormous Public Apathy, We Proudly Present THE ROYAL VARIETY PERFORMANCE
★ ★ ★ ★

OVERTURE
Medley: One Of The Ruins That Cromwell Knocked About A Bit, Only A Bird In A Gilded Cage, These Foolish Things, I Want A Girl Just Like The Girl Who Married Dear Old Dad, Hey Big Spender! I've Grown Accustomed To Her Face, All The Nice Girls Love A Sailor.

Just Back From A Triumphant World Tour!
For A Limited Engagement Only!
TED WINDSOR AND WALLIS
Telling Their Own Stories!

Amazing! Almost Canine!
THE BALMORAL CORGI TROUPE
See Them Eat! Watch Them Doze!

Fantastically Forgettable! Uncannily Ordinary!
TONY
With His Hilarious Impressions Of Small Royalty!

First Time In Civilisation!
**GLOUCESTER'S HARMONICA FOOLS
With Beryl**

Never Before Under One Roof
THE GREEK IN-LAWS
Bouzouki and Cooking

A Triumph Of Incompetence! Every One A Loser!
ANNE'S FALLING HORSE ENSEMBLE
They Trip! They Roll! They Cough!

As Seen On TV!
THE DUKE OF EDINBURGH
In A Programme Of Insults And Oaths!

Your Favourite Dialect Songster!
**NORFOLK
With Dennis The Wonder Pig**

He Smiles! He Waves! He Nods! He Quips!
CHARLIE WALES
With An Inexhaustible Fund Of Hindi Speeches!

Grand Finale!
MY HUSBAND AND I
Ventriloquist

N.B. Patrons are kindly requested not to grab their coats and rush for the exits when the last item begins.

DOCTOR ON THE BOARDS
Richard Gordon

Like many medical people, I am incurably stage-struck. I love to be the focal point of admiring eyes, mostly female, to bait the breath with my every movement, to sense the applause which is unheard and sweeter. To behave, in fact, like any surgeon any day in his operating theatre.

My appearances on the medical stage are now safely restricted to race meetings and cricket matches, my cue a plea over the Tannoy for a doctor. I respond like a pantomime demon popping through his trap-door. If anyone in sight falls over in the street, and does not scramble up again instantly, I am on the patient in a flash, administering the kiss of life.

This is a most unpleasant form of therapy at the operator's end. The number of beautiful young women to be kissed back to life is, statistically obviously, negligible compared with the fat old men whose smell is improved once they actually stop breathing. As most of the subjects are incorrigibly dead, deep-throated embraces with a corpse have chilly overtones of Poe, and would very much upset Freud, I now delegate the kiss bit to the nearest policeman, while performing the cardiac massage. This is repeated flat-palmed pressure, rather like a hand-off at rugby, which is less spectacular but you don't have to clean your teeth afterwards.

As a lad, I was determined to be an actor ever since Noel Coward sent me his autograph. My big break was the speech-day production, as Lady Macbeth. At the last minute, I decided to play it for laughs. Today, this might have landed me rave notices for Ortonesque grotesquery. It got me only the cane, instant expulsion from the cast, and I think from the school.

At medical school there was naturally an enthusiastic and enormous dramatic society. I fancy they found my style too vulgar for the Chekhov and Barrie. My chance came only at Christmas, when the students organized an itinerant revue. This was performed for the bedridden sufferers from

"He doesn't like theatre-in-the-round."

ward to ward on Boxing Day, all patients likely to spoil the fun by snuffing it between scenes being tidied away into side-rooms.

These shows had a structure as rigidly formalized as the Noh Theatre of Japan. The audience was unsatisfied, and even mystified, if the students failed to don Sisters' drag, with a dozen pairs of rugger socks down the bosom. Or if bedpans, bottles, vomit bowls and similar fundamental pieces of hospital furniture did not appear among the props. The script was mostly satire on the little professional and personal quirks of the consultants, who sat through it all with grins as steely as their scalpels. An operation scene was as obligatory as the barrel of beer backstage. Anaesthesia was always induced with a mallet, the surgeons shared a two-handed tree saw, and the patient's innards expelled any number of amusing articles, like bright red inner tubes, alarm clocks, hospital cutlery and (male wards only) a string of inflated contraceptives. It would have made Mrs. Mary Whitehouse blush all over. But there is nothing like a stay in hospital to induce an earthy sense of humour.

I had a conjuring act, turning water into wine. After lunch on Boxing Day my aim was not at its steadiest, most of the fluid which was supposed to change colour from one jug to another hitting the mirror-like ward parquet. "Nurse," I heard the sister hiss, "Fetch a mop and clear up that young man's mess instantly." I continued jauntily with my patter, pretending that the earnest probationer swabbing round my feet was part of the turn. The following artiste did better. He started vomiting half way through *Tit Willow*, and won wild applause by singing it as a patient recovering from his anaesthetic. The next sketch was set in Out-patients', and when one of the actors passed out cold half way through, we carried on nonchalantly as though he had died suddenly in accordance with the plot. Thus I learned the most elusive of actors' arts, how to ad lib.

I was wildly excited when the director of the *Doctor* films offered me a small part. I played the anaesthetist, which was type-casting, as I had at the time just

"Anyone for tennis?"

stopped being one. It also enabled him to muffle me from the gaze of the public in operating kit, showing only my eyes. (One of the actors told me they were quite beautiful, like a sick spaniel's.) As I sat at a hired anaesthetic trolley beside a hired operating table in a cardboard-walled operating theatre, amid gowned and masked figures curiously fingering the property instruments, another actor asked if I was a member of Equity. I asked him if he was a member of the British Medical Association. That seemed to resolve the problem. Today, I don't know what Vanessa Redgrave would have done to me. But my career as a film star never flourished. In the next *Doctor* picture I was reduced to Man Walking Down Corridor, and in the one after to Man Walking Down Corridor Seen Through Glass. That's showbusiness, I suppose.

Two of my novels have been adapted for the stage by Ted Willis, though he turned down my suggested title, *Doc of Dixon Green*. The play of *Doctor in the House* opened in London with one of the students played by the unknown Edward Woodward, just as one of the passengers in the film of *Doctor at Sea* was played by an unknown titty French girl called Brigitte Bardot. The *Doctor at Sea* play opened later in London, and a very, very little later it closed in London. By then, I had discovered a fundamental principle of the British stage. It is not necessary for

a piece to sniff the sweet smell of success in the sickly West End. Far more invigoratingly for the box-office blow the salty breezes of our seaside resorts.

I am indebted to the theatre for some delightful early season weeks in a variety of coastal towns from Lytham St Anne's to Lyme Regis, whose pleasures would otherwise have escaped me. I have been to Morecambe-on-Sea when it was so bitter they were catching the famous prawns already deep-frozen. I have visited Jersey, which was a mistake. The management overlooked the fact that in the Channel Isles the good things of life are duty-free, holidaymakers arriving not for artistic refreshment but a fortnight's sunny boozing. This summer we're at Great Yarmouth.

As I sat in the stalls on the opening night, digesting my bloater supeer and wondering if I shouted "Author!" afterwards anyone would take up the cry, I played my greatest role. The lady in the row behind me went into labour. I upstaged our entire splendid cast. I carried her out, laid her down, demanded ambulances, gave the impression that the happy event would coincide with the curtain calls. Everyone in the foyer was running about and calling me "Doctor". I admit, I hammed it up. But had it reached its finale, I could modestly claim in this particular drama to have achieved a better delivery than Laurence Olivier.

THEATRE
David Frost

Attending the theatre as a representative of *Punch* is a responsibility. An undoubted responsibility. What does one wear, for a start? I mean, they've been going for an awfully long time—one doesn't want to let them down. To what image of *Punch* is one expected to conform? To the fustian pre-war approach still attributed to the magazine by Greek Street? Or to the anarchic progressivism of the Hollowood dynasty?

It is probably significant that in the event I turned up in a dinner jacket, and the Art Director of *Punch* arrived in casuals. Still, give them time and no doubt they can purge me of my conservative habits.

The first production which I attended in my official capacity was **Make Me A Widow** *(Comedy Theatre)*, one of those comedy-thrillers that turns out to be neither; one of those plays in which someone switches on the gramophone and someone else says "For heaven's sake, Mary, turn that thing *off!*" because it's so deafening, only in fact it isn't, and the audience has to strain its ears to hear it at all.

Paul, our hero, wears a pair of sturdy Daks-type trousers, and a good strong check coat, and would probably cut himself a stout stick of hickory if he had half a chance.

Women drivers come in for a drubbing, wives' birthdays are roguishly forgotten, and pregnant pauses are well to the fore, "What about......*us?*" asks one character and not content with that, when someone else is talking about sex, she wonders "But is that......*love?*"

No, darling, he just told you. It's sex.

Paul's wife—called "Vicky" as you'd probably guessed—rounds on him.

"I wish you'd stop making jokes out of everything I say."

The audience rises as one man.

"I wish he'd start..."

At the *Mermaid,* another comedy has just opened, but the jokes are newer.

Something of a poor relation at the moment, the Mermaid. It is dwarfed for prestige by our four National Theatres at Stratford, Chichester, Aldwych and the Old Vic. It is dwarfed for experimental fervour by the reputations of Joan Littlewood and the Royal Court.

Nevertheless down in the City something has stirred. There was an extraordinary family atmosphere at the opening of **The Shoemaker's Holiday** a splendid simple enjoyment of the play and the almost obligatory Mermaid references to farts and bums, and above all a rollicking appreciation of theatre itself. Mr. Miles is really on the way to creating a new audience.

There were faults too, of course. Early on, two or three of the cast seemed to be concentrating on colliding with as many pillars round the stage as they could find, and the attempt to burlesque much of the play failed some of the time because the performers had neither the self-confidence nor the instant audience recognition necessary. Burlesque always inclines to be an "in" joke, and it is at its best when you know the people involved, however obscurely.

The play itself is far above average for the knockabout comedy of the Elizabethan and Jacobean periods, though it is not without its wretched songs about Fol-de-riddle-i-do and Fol-de-riddle-dey, its pale heroines and its unspeakable lines.

"How far the churl's tongue wanders from his heart."

Say that and sound natural at the same time, if you can.

The minor highlights of the production are two walks across the stage by Mr. Jerry Verno, and the performance of Mr. Robert Gillespie, who has laid aside his acid pen to deliver about ten lines as Dodger the Spy which each bring the house down as he leaps and creeps about the stage, delivering good news with immense gloom, and disastrous tidings with utter delight.

John Woodvine as Simon Eyre, the Shoemaker, holds the production together well, coming into his own in the last half-hour.

Most members of the audience have found Sir Laurence Olivier's **Othello** at the Old Vic (and *Chichester*) a towering performance, a tremendous achievement.

Some have found themselves unmoved, conscious all the while of the technique, of Olivier himself.

They are both right.

The National Theatre production turns out in two different styles. Most of the company play it in worthy repertory fashion—a solemn attention to the verse, the ritual transmission even of nonsensical couplets.

Sir Laurence's performance is in the tradition of the great movies. One does not go to the cinema to see two parts X and Y played—though you'd scarcely know it—by Marlon Brando and George C. Scott, but rather to see Marlon Brando (this time giving his X) and George C. Scott (this time giving his Y). It is like that at Chichester. This is not Othello—played by Sir Laurence Olivier. This is Olivier—this time giving his Othello.

And with a play like *Othello*, this is not really a criticism. It is in any case, with Olivier, his personality, and his personal magnetism on a stage, that we admire as much as his ability to assume various characters.

Here those personal qualities triumph, though inevitably the result is a rupture in the production. Only one other character in the play has the ability to go with him, Maggie Smith as

A Visit to Stratford·on·Avon
for a Matinee Performance

Desdemona. In their scenes together she more than holds her own. When she is back with the repertory company, she can sink back into ensemble playing, and lose herself once again in impersonal recital.

Olivier—and Miss Smith—succeed in doing something that straight, faithful playing could never do—disguise the fact that *Othello* is in fact a bad, boring play, a succession of tiresome *non sequiturs*.

I don't blame Sir Laurence waiting this long to play it. The wonder is that he chose to do it now. But having chosen, he succeeds. Not so much as an actor. As a technician. And as a star.

27 January 1866

LITTLE PLAYS AND LARGE POSTERS.

WE wonder where the mania for big posters will stop. Really they seem to grow bigger every day, and there is scarce a street in London which is not defaced by these hideous monstrosities. The theatres are perhaps the greatest of offenders. No matter how little is the new piece they produce, the largest of large letters are employed to give us notice of it.

Now, are there really many playgoers whom placards can attract? Are plays so unattractive that a good house cannot be got without this broadcast use of paper? The work of advertising a new play is best done by the public. Let your piece be really bad, and it cannot much be helped by puffery and posters. Let your play be really good, and every audience will advertise its merit and attractions. Depend upon it, gentlemen, what you spend upon bad ink might be far more profitably spent upon good writing. If what is wasted on dead walls were paid to living writers, a great eyesore in our streets would be happily removed, and great good would be done to the condition of the drama.

"*Great little scene-stealer, Marchbanks.*"

DON'T CALL US
Tina Brown

New York's "Catch a Rising Star" is not so much a nightclub as a comic's gymnasium. On Monday nights any reckless tryer can "work out" in front of a sophisticated audience if he joins the afternoon queue for an audition card in time. His number might not be called until four a.m. but at least by the morning he'll know whether or not to drop the one about the glue sniffer and the budgie from his repertoire. "I never ban anyone from coming back," the owner, Rick Newman told me. "If a guy wants to put his ass on the line and die in front of strangers, who am I to be judgmental?"

The "Catch", as it is affectionately known by the regulars, is located under a karate school on the upper East Side of Manhattan. Chairs and tables leave a clearing for a small stage, furnished with bashed piano and chipped chair and warmed into seedy magic by a spotlight. Outside in the bar the night's thirty auditioners milled behind a rope, buoyed up by the flashing molars of the "Catch" success stories whose photos line the walls. If the newcomer makes an impression, Newman will call him back and perhaps offer him a weekday spot as house professional. Most are not called back, but keep trying. The "Catch's" one proviso is that two weeks must elapse before re-auditioning.

The previous night's Tony awards infused extra enthusiasm

OTHERWISE ENGAGED

ALAN BATES as Simon
JULIAN GLOVER as Jeff

into the queue behind the rope. At ten-fifteen they included a Times Square patrol cop who normally practices his routine on suspects in the jail ("if I can make a guy I just booked laugh, I figure I'm funny,") a telephonist, an A.B.C. receptionist, a tout for a massage parlour, four recipients of welfare and a London tourist who complained that it was a bloody disgrace to have to wait so long for his turn. Some, like the startled looking brunette from San Francisco, are regulars on the club circuit. "I bluffed my way into getting bookings," she told me. "I got my room-mate to ring up and pretend she was my manager." Those on welfare took a more defensive stance. "Why do I come here?" shrugged a fat Italian in dark glasses. "Low income urban ethnics are supposed to have a sense of humour, aren't they?"

About ten-fifteen the room began to fill and the voice of the first number performing to sparse titters filtered through. Two of the house professionals, a black comic and a singer with a bouffant hair-do, lolled in the doorway.

"I do a Las Vegas type of act," the singer, Aaron Jack, told me, staring hopefully at my notebook. "I guess you could say I model myself on Tom Jones."

"That's weird," marvelled the black. "I never had a model. I always tried to cultivate an absolute uniqueness of performance."

"Shall we just give the lady personal details one at a time?" snapped Aaron.

Number four on stage was a plump Pole who remorselessly cracked joke after joke about dildoes. When his prize anecdote, the one about the homosexual and the king size pepperoni, bellyflopped as well he produced a sheaf of index cards and began to search wildly for fresh material. He resorted to abuse, "You've got no taste," he stormed, readjusting the spectacles that had skidded down his nose. The audience talked among themselves. Ennui was relieved at last by Aaron Jack who offered a mean rendition of *You Lost That Lovin' Feeling*.

The auditioner's dream, of course, is that he'll be spotted by a talent scout. At midnight a spasm

of excitement went through the waiting group, when two of the big boys from the largest New York management company arrived. They seated themselves at our table and laser-beamed the stage. The little comic under the lights was working his brains out and winning a certain response.

"I heard that line before," sidemouthed one of the big boys suddenly. "Who cracked that joke first?"

"I think it belonged to the tall boy who was in last week," said Newman.

"Before that it was Woody Allen's." He accosted the comic as he swaggered, jubilant, past our table and advised him to get some fresh material. "It was my joke," yelped the comic. "I wrote it myself."

"I'm always hearing that joke," said the big boy stonily.

Newman, a big man with a dashing black moustacho, said he feels lucky if he gets as many as two potential pros out of an evening's audition. He managed a singles bar, before founding the "Catch" five years ago and it's a gimmick that has turned into his obsession. He admires the courage of the auditioners, even if they're as dire as Nancy Lavalle, a singer who returns week after week despite the

hoots of derision that greet her false blond plaits, stetson and glitter pants. "I want to be the female Elvis Presley," she told me sullenly. Sometimes, however, what looks like a desperate case behind the rope goes down a treat under the lights. The audience corpsed at the startled brunette, Shelley Warwick, who pulled a cardboard Statue of Liberty headpiece over her wig and tap-danced furiously.

"They say my headpiece looks like a sado-masochist's toilet seat," she twittered. "No shit."

The plump Pole who flopped at 11.30 watched her success with an air of baffled injury. In the early hours of the morning he approached Newman for a candid assessment of his own performance. Newman paused, "You need more work on your timing," he said.

The Pole sloped home, looking more thoughtful than depressed. No auditioner leaves "Catch a Rising Star" feeling he's no good, just undiscovered, unappreciated or simply not ready.

"See you Monday week," Newman called. He settled back to watch the London tourist who surprised us all with a truly staggering impersonation of a trumpet.

"Oh, I was on tour with this company doing 'Godot'
and we flopped. How about you?"

ADELAIDE RISTORI.

Madame Ristori, the greatest of living actresses, is now to be beheld at Her Majesty's Theatre. That bright southern star will be visible for a few nights only. In the interest of real and noble art, *Mr. Punch* begs to say, that in no English or American dictionary will be found words of sufficient strength to express his admiration of ADELAIDE RISTORI, or his compassion for the unhappy person who does not go and behold one or two of her performances. This is a debilitated understatement of the case, but the fact is that he is at present so absorbed in a retrospective vision of an awful old moribund Queen, haughty in her decrepitude, and fiercely clutching the crown of England (a vision which the subsequent sight of one of the loveliest of faces, flushed and smiling at a shouting audience, could not dispel) that he is conscious of not writing with his accustomed earthquake strength and lightning brilliancy, but he means to say that if he were not *Punch* he would be RISTORI. What a magnificent voice that is, and how artistically managed. The *vox humana* is the finest musical instrument in the world, but then so few can perform upon it. Our ADELAIDE is one of the few. Clapham—and we don't use the word disrespectfully—may go and see RISTORI. It will see and hear nothing to offend, or even suggest offence, and will comprehend what is meant by lofty tragedy. Hers are sensation dramas, with a sensation of which no decent person need be ashamed, and if anybody thinks that he knows what acting means, and has not seen RISTORI, let him to Her Majesty's Theatre, and afterwards write us his thanks for having educated him. He need not cross the cheque he will of course enclose.

"No, we're in the queue for 'Evita' - you're in the queue for Wimbledon."

27 June 1863

"Is there anything in this rumour that the caretaker from the National Theatre will be here tonight?"

AT THE PLAY

© Ronald Searle

TWELFTH NIGHT
(Stratford-upon-Avon)

It seemed fair to expect a great deal of a *Twelfth Night* produced by JOHN GIELGUD and containing a Malvolio by LAURENCE OLIVIER, a Viola by VIVIEN LEIGH. This opening production at Stratford is, of course, an improvement on anything we saw there in last year's meagre season, but considering the talents now assembled it remains strangely disappointing. SIR LAURENCE has chosen to give Malvolio a rather tortured lisp, as of an aspiring barrow-boy earnestly improving his English at night-school; and though the trick of speech is mastered with the utmost skill, it is difficult to see how it helps. Again, his Malvolio is subdued in the early scenes to nothing more than a reasonable disciplinarian, and is therefore not a man whose pretensions in any way justify the hatred of his fellows. He is very funny in the letter scene, and in his final interview with Olivia pathetic with a most touching dignity; but it is only intermittently the full Malvolio.

"Let's do 'Look Back in Anger' in modern dress."

Punkerella
by Larry

"Macbeth does murder sleep..."

MEANWHILE, BACKSTAGE... Jeremy Kingston

It's often maintained that theatre critics should hold themselves aloof from events behind the theatre scenery. It's no concern of theirs if the leading actor has stopped sleeping with the leading actress, or won't start sleeping with her, or swallowed his contact lenses that morning, or hates the director, or loves the director or any of that. If the stage management have been breaking ankles throughout the pre-London tour—too bad. A maniac understudy slashed the scenery one hour before the opening? It'll make an intriguing story in the gossip

page but hasn't anything to do with the critic's prime and immediate function which is to think about what is being shown to him by the actors and write about what he thinks.

If I ever maintained that, I don't any longer. Writing *Signs of the Times* and then getting it accepted and cast and set and costumed and cut and rehearsed and toured and premiered has substantially upped my contribution to the profits of the makers of Valium. It has also upped my appreciation of what is done to bring a play to the point at which I

and my colleagues can scrawl our comments across First Night programmes in the dim light of an aisle seat.

I don't know to what degree it's going to affect my reviews from now on. One always has, of course, made allowances for backstage calamity. If in the final week of rehearsal a production of *As You Like It* first loses its Orlando with a skewiff disc and on the eve of opening has its Rosalind and its Audrey pull ligaments in their feet, then naturally the final nuptial dancing is not going to be so spirited as the director planned; one makes an allowance and an imaginative leap to envisage what the director did plan. My newfound knowledge of how a performer sets about building a character isn't likely to make me praise (because I know the creative effort involved) some unachieved performance in the future. What it is likely to do is clarify my appreciation of what makes a performance good. And I might, though I'm not sure about this, be better equipped to detect the contributions separately made by the director and author.

The idea of *The Times* starting a daily horoscope seemed a fruitful idea for a comedy. The funniest way of doing it looked like having a sceptical journalist forced into writing the horoscope by his editor. The most effective, if traditional, spur to make him accept the job would be the opportunity it offered to re-organise his love-life. And the logical development was to have his unconsidered forecasts start coming true.

It would be a gross distortion of the truth to say these ideas and the necessary dialogue sprang immediately to mind as I stood that evening on Hammer-smith Station waiting for the District train. But eventually, months later, the first draft was finished, the European magic of the retired Anglican missionary and the tribal magic of the African prime minister had come together to sort out the hero's love-life, and the script was sent out to find itself a director, a manager, a cast.

Something very peculiar occurs when actors begin to take possession of characters that have hitherto talked to each other only in the author's head. During the first reading of the play, the occasion at which the whole company meet for the first time, they are already staking out their claims. But the rhythms are all to cock. Quick exchanges build to nothing. I remember fixing a glassy smile on my face and taking notes. Casually it was suggested that I would probably prefer to stay away from the first few rehearsals. Since I can spot an implicit instruction as well as the next man, the cast were left to make their early, bold, wild stabs at the characters, without the astonished author sending out thought-rays of "No, that's not it," in their direction.

Because bold, wild stabs is how some actors establish themselves in their characters. Others prefer to stalk them gradually, adding shade to shade. In both cases the early roughs are rough. But as time passes the performances acquire their own consistency. They differed from my first conception in as much as I had no particular actor in mind, no special actress, and the cast drew on private experiences of their own. But I can't think of any line that was cut because their growing notions differed from mine.

Another curious change occurred as rehearsals progressed. When certain lines were spoken on the stage, I found they prompted, inside my head, a vivid recollection of the place where I had dreamed them up. There would come a nonsensical line about burglar alarms sounding like telephones so as not to alarm the burglars or a remark about bean feasts or nuns on the roof, sometimes quite ordinary lines, not funny at all, but there I would be again walking down the Goldhawk Road or Brighton Front or the Temple or wherever. These irrelevant shadows persisted until the first public performance whereupon they disappeared and never returned. Once the lines had been greeted with laughter or chuckles or even the silent attention of a theatre full of people my personal association with them was reduced to vanishing point. The cast had made the characters into something of their own.

COMEDIANS

JONATHAN PRYCE as Gethin Price
JIMMY JEWEL as Eddie Waters

A Critical Guide to the Critics 1977

B. A. YOUNG (Financial Times)

Young was one of the best arts editors the FT ever had and is still a fine drama critic, enjoying among other things a good late deadline. (He, Levin, Kretzmer and one or two others used to share a cab after the theatre, dropping each one at their respective papers with Young getting off last and paying the driver at the distant *Financial Times*. He is said to have made a nice small profit from the silver collection from the other fares.) In one sense he is the last of the old school of reviewers, admiring the elegance of Rattigan and Coward, yet he also makes more effort than most to get out into the regions and discover budding talent. Hard to fool. Is said not to like musicals; in fact, likes them so much that he is hypercritical about them.

JACK TINKER (Daily Mail)

A good, bright reporter/critic, restricted by his paper to about 400 words + big photo of actors + big headline. He used to review for the *Brighton Evening Argus*, where his notices of the big pre-London productions often carried great weight, more perhaps than he does now in the *Mail*, where his space doesn't let him do more than a swift journalistic summary. Unlike other critics, he doesn't return to his paper to write his piece; he goes to Victoria Station en route to home and phones it in from there.

ROBERT CUSHMAN (Observer)

Cushman is a good reviewer who suffers from being on the *Observer*. The *Observer* has not given any drama critic lately a long time to settle in, nor does it believe in boosting or building up its critics, except for Clive James who has built-in boost anyway. Perhaps because of this, Cushman's personality hasn't really come through his writing yet, leaving one uneasily unaware of an identity against which to measure his opinions.

FRANK MARCUS (Sunday Telegraph)

An unusual example of a dramatist turned critic (the only other current example is E. A. Whitehead on the *Spectator*). As a result he has an insight into the practical side of theatre denied to most critics, but also a tendency to draw introspective conclusions from the best and worst of what he sees. His stint as a critic does not, unfortunately, seem to have helped his progress as a dramatist; probably the reverse. Ominously, he, Levin and Cushman are now the only three drama critics regularly featured by Sunday papers.

HERBERT KRETZMER (Daily Express)

Even more ominously, Kretzmer has been withdrawn from the first night review race and is now allowed only to produce a Saturday round-up. (Are we in at the start of the withering away of the drama critic? Do editors, caught in the office till after curtain-up, consider the theatre less than essential?) A pity, because Kretzmer is an intelligent writer. He is also a talented lyricist (he wrote the words for Aznavour's *She*) and is very good on musicals, even when they are not quite as good as he says.

BENEDICT NIGHTINGALE (New Statesman)

Bright young man who has already done ten years as the *Statesman* critic (and become one of the magazine's directors). Nightingale makes his long wordage work in a way that Levin doesn't. Though some would say that he has acquired lazy habits, his generally thoughtful approach has given him a reputation out of proportion to the circulation of the magazine. There were even some who were surprised that he did not get the *Sunday Times* job.

IRVING WARDLE *(The Times)*

Probably the best theatre critic operating in London. He has been right more often about new playwrights than anyone else, and is the nearest thing to a father figure that the younger critics have. Although Tynan was the first post-war critic to break away from the simple reporting stance and provide personal, emotional reactions, there was still something of the elegant Edwardian about him; Wardle was the first tough, modern, no-nonsense reviewer. He seems to be becoming increasingly impatient with the West End commercial theatre and its familiar ingredients; his very audible groan can sometimes be heard on first nights after only five minutes. He will even send his second string, Ned Chaillet, to West End openings while he goes himself to fringe events. Leftish, in a slightly old-fashioned way, like Callaghan. Eminently trustable.

BERNARD LEVIN *(Sunday Times)*

Not the most reliable of critics, but one of the most entertainment and controversial, which is just what the *Sunday Times* wanted to fill Harold Hobson's footsteps. He loves the theatre and went there assiduously in all the years he wasn't employed as a critic, but having his heart in the right place does not prevent him from having rushes of blood to the head and extravagantly praising or damning unexceptional plays.

"For a Rep Company they certainly put on a good cup of tea."

JOHN BARBER *(Daily Telegraph)*

Because the *Telegraph's* readership coincides so much with the theatre-going public, it has been said that even if a giant panda did the *Telegraph's* reviews it would still be the most influential daily reviewer. Barber is a great deal better than the average panda as a drama critic, but he does still tend to be reliable, steady and safe rather than inspired.

MICHAEL BILLINGTON *(Guardian)*

One of the bright younger reviewers, Billington used to be second string to Wardle on *The Times* but is less seriously academic than Wardle. He sees his job as being, among other things, to entertain, and will unashamedly go for the good phrase or good laugh. As befits a slightly showbiz attitude to drama, he has a great taste for music hall, Broadway razzle dazzle etc., and has a book forthcoming on Ken Dodd. He certainly knows his stuff, though he is perhaps better on the newer playwrights than the old; it is darkly hinted that he hasn't a great ear for poetry. Pretty readable, pretty reliable.

SHERIDAN MORLEY *(Punch)*

An excellent reporter of the theatrical scene (though not the author of this page), Morley believes, like his contemporary Billington, in combining a faithful verdict with considerable readability. If he has a blind spot, it is that he tends to go overboard for anything with a Broadway accent; he raved over Sondheim and went to see *A Chorus Line* three times *after* he had reviewed it. Is on first name terms with many great theatre names, such as Robert Morley. Like all theatre critics he gets two free tickets, but unusually takes along an artist with him instead of a wife.

"What's happened so far?"

WHAT IS AN AUDIENCE?
Ralph Richardson

PRIVATE VIEW

The audience is strange, ever changing, wilful, yet it obeys various pulls and forces, like the sea; sometimes it comes rolling in with splendid sparkle and splash of invigorating ozone, other times it drags out, exhausted, or sits quite strangely still without a ripple.

What mysterious call have the audience answered that brings them, night after night, to assemble in so precise a number? The migration of birds is mysterious, but conceivable. As understood, at a certain time all available starlings, for instance, obey an instinct to gather together to make a combined flight to a certain place; they go together as fish go in shoals, for the safety of numbers. But the number of people who wish to go to a certain play divide themselves into small, precise numerical groups; that is to say in a theatre where there is an attraction, there may be one thousand seats but that theatre will very seldom have to turn anyone away because it is full, and it will seldom sell less than nine hundred seats. Every night just about nine hundred have obeyed an instinct; and there they sit in rows not unlike starlings perched on telegraph wires, twittering and chirping, trying to gauge its note, hoping that it is gleeful and harmonious; and then before the house lights go

44

down an actor may steal a peep, wondering what they look like.

An actor is something of a bird watcher and only the other night a rare species was spotted in the stalls; it was the white-throated, long-black-tailed, night bird. These are not seen in such places in any numbers now. There is a work in three volumes by the ornithologist W.T. Green, *Birds in Captivity* which players can study with profit. It starts with notes on "The care and happiness of those who have happened to pass into your custody." Green insists on "The use of patience and perseverance" and there is a reminder that, "Many become very tame and gentle, full of life and spirits brimming over with fun and happiness." Few actors need reminding that "some birds never learn anything." The author can be left alone to play with his feathered friends when he comes to "Bronchitis and Croup." Players are familiar with every croup, cough, gasp and sneeze, whoopsnort and snizzle and all the drips and wheezes that flesh is heir to. These are baneful interruptions but here some patience must be exercised for the flesh is weak. Some arrive bringing with them a large, mongrel-barking, pet cough and are so careless and callous as to constantly give it an airing. There is only one cure, shoot with silencer on. Actors cannot see the audience, so develop sense for the slightest sound and sometimes there are odd ones. There are things that go bump in the night; mostly explained by people coming in late and bumping the seats down, or by others stomping out and banging them up. Then there are sounds that those not in the know might find hard to explain; there are mostly heard at matinees.

There is a snap and a click, then a clink and a clonk, then snap, snap, snap. These sounds are made by elderly ladies with second sight who have divined that the final curtain is about eight minutes off and who snap shut their handbags, ready to be off. In some plays this does not much matter, but in others it is disconcerting; sometimes the denouement is planned as a surprise and such clairvoyance is hurtful, like being discovered in hide-and-seek. A rich collection of curious sounds and noises made by the audience could be assembled and John Gielgud possesses a museum piece. He says, "I was playing Hamlet, and thought we had got through the performance rather smoothly, until near the end I came to the line 'The readiness is all.' Then a man in the stalls took out of his pocket a large nickel watch and wound it up, shatteringly."

The audience is strange. When the curtain goes up the single units sitting together, without being conscious of it, slide, merge and melt until they form a single entity; losing a little of their single selves they create a new dimension, they become a *one*; this one, compact as it is of humans, is not quite like a human being, it is more like a gas or a ghost. It can flow right up upon the stage, can change the temperature in the house from chill to very warm. It can enter into a play and occupy and take possession there, increase its dimension, light it, sharpen its wit, as good company can. It can solidify, build a tension that is tangible; it can be cut with a knife, bottled, canned, could be stuffed into sausages.

All who go to the theatre take part in the performance; they have joined a community and whatever they do is communicated. If they go to sleep it will have an effect, and if they should snore they could steal a scene. In the theatre there is a trinity; it has three 'A's: Author, Actor, Audience. The actors look back to their author for the first inspiration and guidance, then look forward to the audience for its continuance; they are the ultimate teachers.

Sometimes when the curtain falls and the three-handed game is over, the actors are sorry that the partnership is broken because that performance can never be repeated; the audience is ever changing.

THE BEST SEAT IN THE HOUSE

Those two weeny little women
        do not know
        where to go,
but I have no doubt the usherette will
        show
them into *this* row.

        And that tiny little man in
        grey
coming this way,
I bet you all my pay
he is going into Row K.

        As for those minute Siamese
who only come up to my knees,
they are settling like homing bees
into the D's.

But there, ah, there, standing six
        foot three
in his socks, and broad as a tree,
is, as you will shortly see,
the man who is going to sit in front
        of *me!*   V.G.

"Well, if it has got a message it's not getting through to me."

CIGARETTES BY ABDULLAH, STOCKINGS BY KAYSOR BONDOR, MATCHES BY BRYANT & MAY, Programmes by Benny Green

The first theatre programme to crucify me personally, as distinct from crucifying the arts generally, was for a dramatic-cum-musical performance in which I was appearing in what might laughingly be called an instrumental capacity. As it happens, my instrumental capacity was very low indeed in those far-off days, but being a desperado willing to commit the grossest outrages in an attempt to avoid going to work, I had fallen in the habit of sucking and blowing a hideous blunderbuss of a contrivance called a baritone saxophone. Now there was a universally accepted abbreviation for the name of this instrument, so that the customary entry usually read:

BENNY GREEN—BAR SAX.
Or, if the printers were feeling unusually generous, as once happened:

BENNY GREEN—BARI SAX.
Or, if the printers were feeling

THEATRE ROYAL, WINDSOR CASTLE.

THE QUEEN'S loving subjects will rejoice to hear that HER MAJESTY intends to establish a theatre at Windsor Castle; a house which will be pre-eminently a Theatre Royal, entitled to be called Her Majesty's Own Theatre.

There is something that raises the spirits of the nation in the effort thus made by the QUEEN to sustain her own. It is plain that HER MAJESTY has resolutely determined from a sense of duty to resort to amusement as an alleviation of a grief that may be incurable, though due consideration might change it into hope, capable even of rising into joy. For such a grief, the theatre affords one of the most effectual of earthly remedies. The suggestion, naturally raised by dramatised human life, that "all the world's a stage, and all the men and women merely players," tends to elevate the beholder above all the world. When the curtain has fallen on a noble tragedy, and whilst the grand words of SHAKESPEARE are still ringing in the ears, the mind looks above and beyond mortal ills; and the spectacle of a well-acted part must hint a particular consolation for a sorrow such as the QUEEN'S.

It was a happy and queenly thought to instal the Drama at Windsor Castle; the thought of a mind friendly to ennobling art. The question, by what Intelligence may this thought have been inspired, is one which, well weighed, may also afford some comfort to the Royal Widow.

May the successor of ELIZABETH be rewarded for her patronage of the English Stage with a Victorian Drama, and live to be the Sovereign, of, if possible, another SHAKESPEARE

unusually drunk, as also once happened:

SACK BENNY GREENBERRY. But on this occasion, the printers, being more aware than was usual, at this embryonic stage in my career, of the extreme nobility of my musical style, decided to elevate me, if not quite to the peerage, then at least halfway. This charitable leg-up took the following form:

BENNY GREEN, BART.

Having made desperate and on the whole fairly availing attempts to disown my knighthood ever since, nothing will shake my conviction that theatre programmes are an excellent thing provided you hold shares in the organisation marketing them. Presumably they are also of some marginal usefulness to the assorted hairdressers, cooks, musical hustlers and other sub-species which care to advertise their tariffs there. But so far as that sad, put-upon creature, the average theatregoer, is

concerned, they are very nearly of no use at all.

I am often asked, once a day and twice on Thursdays and Saturdays as a matter of fact, why it is that the theatregoer acquiesces in an extortion racket which not only expects him to pay for an amenity which ought to be included in the price of admission, but which, once he has paid for it, leaves him emptier-headed than he was before about the implications of the drama he has come to see, and then rubs salt in the wound by haranguing him with all the latest news about hotel life, where to get stoned, how to buy a pair of tartan underpants, about practically everything, in fact, except the theatre.

The answer is that your average theatregoer is a chicken-hearted, lily-livered born victim, who, if he had any gumption, would make a pile of all his old programmes, set light to them and post the whole conflagration to the

Director of Public Prosecutions, instead of which he sits there in the dark reducing his own life expectancy by munching soft-centred chocolates.

The reader will have realised by now that, fortunately for pedlars of theatre programmes, I am not jaundiced against their product, and am able to take a calm, even amiable view of the situation. But I must admit that even my marmoreal placidity is in danger of cracking up. The other day I attended a theatre to watch the enactment of a neglected classic about whose background I was quite as knowledgeable as all the other well-informed people in the audience, that is to say, I knew absolutely nothing about it at all. And so, poor gullible fool that I am, I turned for help to the programme, to be enlightened by many priceless gems of knowledge, for instance that there was to be a water carnival in Westminster, that good girls go to heaven, that Scotland is famous for its heritage, that Notting Hill is losing its Victorian personality (which is more than you can say for theatre programmes), that you haven't seen London till you have seen Selfridges, that Madame Tussauds is a very popular all-round attraction for visitors to London, and that a certain eating house, not more than fourteen miles from the stage door, is "an intimate restaurant frequented by most of the leading personalities in theatre and opera."

Apart from the fact that a restaurant frequented by most of the leading personalities in theatre and opera is not a restaurant but a menagerie, that wild horses could not induce me to eat in such an establishment, that I would rather fade quietly away of malnutrition than be seen dead inside its precincts, I felt deprived of the information after which I lusted. And when you remember that all these glittering gobbets of intellectual wisdom had cost me two-thirds of the price of a copy of *Punch*, you begin to understand why I spent most of the first act kicking my toes against the seat in front of me, in the faint hope that its occupant might be connected in some way with the compilation of the programme.

But I realise that it is unfair

Don't put your mother on the stage, Mrs Worthington!

"You're on in five hours, Mavis."

"Mrs Fisher was very kind. She bequeathed her body to science and her head to us."

to be destructive like this without offering some practical alternatives. Very well, here are two. First why not print our theatre programmes on rice paper, so that even if its contents offend the eye, they may at least gratify the stomach? Most of the people I know who go to theatres, being of an excessively nervous disposition, nibble the programme anyway, so the least the managements can do is to make this occupation a little more interesting. Obviously the calorific content of a Shaw or Chekhov programme would be higher than that of one for, say Agatha Christie

or Harold Pinter, but the principle would be the same. Also I see no reason why each sheet of each programme could not be treated with some kind of hot beverage, so that patrons could spend the interval sucking the individual pages instead of climbing over each other and very nearly scalding themselves with lukewarm coffee.

My second suggestion is altogether more radical. It is to enclose in each programme a luminous biscuit or wafer, which could later be devoured while sucking the programme itself. This luminous biscuit could be held over

the print, enabling the customer to get his information right, and thus bringing to an end at last the era in which we exist at present, where the following dialogue is heard nightly:
SHE: What's his name? The one playing Othello?
HE:(Peering at programme). Er, Othello is Harold Maestro Mazzini who is always ready to welcome you with a smile and an Escalope Holstein.
SHE: And how much time has passed since the end of the first act?
HE: (Still peering). This scene takes

48

Age Concern
has published a leaflet
urging over-sixties to
take up amateur dramatics.
HONEYSETT
waits in the wings...

"You'll have to shout, he's a bit deaf."

"It took us ages to knit the costumes."

place three hundred years later, when the Bard's four hundredth birthday was approaching.
SHE: Are you sure? How old is this play anyway?
HE: *(Turning over programme pages and still peering).* Let's see. Shakespeare is said to have completed the play *(turns over page)* in 1951 for the Festival of Britain.
SHE: But that's impossible. Shakespeare died years before the Festival of Britain. Do we get another interval? I'm thirsty.
HE: Well, it says here in black and white that the second interval will

be followed by *(turns over two pages at once by mistake)* an air raid destroying the roof of the building.
SHE: What?
HE: And that in Princes Street, Edinburgh, there's a Hopscotch Shop for the children.

And so it goes on, until the lights go up and the poor fool realises he's been trying to read the thing upside down, and that the cherry nougat he tried to slip himself during the strangulation scene gummed up all the pages. Still, his fate is better than that of the customers who watched Marcel

Marceau recently and were informed that the noble Nave of the Abbey is one of the greater glories of London, a new Kensington emporium sells oven mitts decorated with astrological signs, that every packet carried a government health warning, that Harry Smith adds a delicious piano accompaniment to your French dinner or supper, that Burberry's is the home of the finest weather-proofs, and that you can now buy an album of Dorothy Squires singing the original recordings of *A Tree in the Meadow* and *The Gypsy*.

THE RAKE'S PROGRESS:
THE DRAMATIC CRITIC
Ronald Searle

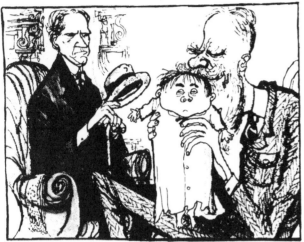

1. PROLOGUE   Kissed by Bernard Shaw when young in the presence of Granville Barker. Inspired

2. EMERGENCE Produces Othello in bathing costumes for OUDS. Praised by Isis. Bad notice in The T*mes

3. RECOGNITION Writes to The T*mes suggesting their critic's retirement in favour of a more contemporary approach. Offer declined. Piqued

4. SUCCESS Joins R*veille. Writes slashing attack on Dramatic Criticism Today. Immediately signed up by popular Daily. Thrilled

5. TRIUMPH Meteoric Success. Banned by West End Theatres for kindness to H*nnen Sw*ffer. Expelled from The Caprice. Nervous Breakdown

6. DOWNFALL Brilliantly restrained comeback on BBC Critics Drama Adjudicator Arts Council. Treasurer Critics Circle. Respected

COMING OBITUARIES

Kenneth Tynan O.M.
CRITIC AND CENSOR

We record with deep regret the death of Mr Kenneth Tynan. The Grand Old Man of the British Theatre was attending the controversial performance of the fully-clothed *Peter Pan* at the Cruelty Theatre, when, rising to protest at the production, he was struck on the forehead by a flying Darling and instantly expired.

Kenneth Peacock Tynan was born in 1927, educated in Birmingham and Oxford, and served his theatrical apprenticeship as the Drama Critic of a number of forgotten newspapers and magazines. It is a mark of his peculiar talents that very rapidly he insinuated himself, despite his rickety foundation, at the very centre of the British intellectual Establishment. He was appointed Literary Manager of the National Theatre in 1963, and thanks to the debility of the rest of the British Theatre managed to make this a post of some prestige.

But the narrow world of the arts in a philistine age soon proved insufficient for his genius. In the mid-Sixties he struck up a lucky mutual admiration with an American magazine proprietor called Hefner, who offered Tynan a platform from which to pronounce on the moral problems of the world. It seems curious to us that the magazine from which this high and dedicated task was undertaken

should have been named *Playboy*. But we live in a degenerate age.

All Tynan's theories have of course long become unfashionable; most of his arguments were demonstrably irrelevant; his few practical proposals (such as the introduction of compulsory bull-fighting in fee-paying schools) failed; and his central tenet—the practice and subsequent discussion of every variety of sexual experience as the answer to all moral problems—soon was proved by its adherents to be both physically and socially unrewarding.

Tynan's standards, in fact, were too high, his moral judgments too severe, for the frail run of mankind. Soon the British people relapsed into an apathetic acceptance of marital fidelity, of restrained language, and of unthinking good manners. Life may have proved for them to be easier that way, but Tynan lived on in their midst, shouting between murmurs and murmuring between shouts, to remind them of the people they might have been. He was a giant from a vanished age.

Only in the world of the Theatre was his effect more lasting. Ceaseless experiment continued. The riches of British history were ransacked for heroes to denigrate (it was a constant source of sadness to Tynan that our recent leaders have

lacked the stature for this treatment), and in the intervals foreign plays of unique banality were staged.

No one who was there will ever forget the night when the entire audience of thirteen sleep-walked out of Act Nine of the Icelandic monologue *Refrigerator*.

The de-bowdlerisation of English classics such as *East Lynne* and *Pride and Prejudice*, on the grounds that their authors would have written more freely had they lived in a more "permissive" age, was steadfastly pursued, despite the growth of the so-called "Deep Underground" theatre in which the originals were performed as written. Many Home Secretaries promised Tynan that they would legislate to stop this trend, but none was sufficiently brave to offend the voters. The restoration of the Lord Chamberlain to pass stage productions for performance was soon proved an inadequate measure when thousands of "private" clubs sprang up in Soho cellars for the performance of "decent" plays.

Public opinion continued to set against Tynan's Theatre. The open defiance of the production at the Cruelty was delayed, but inevitable. The tragic denouement was symbolic, but might well have pleased Tynan as the ultimate step in audience-involvement.

DOMESTIC DRAMA

Alan Coren

The court case involving John Osborne and the domestic couple he sacked for inefficiency has of course had immense repercussions throughout the sensitive world of the theatre.

Dramatis Personae

SNOUT	*Ex-caretaker to Mr Harold Pinter*
ANTONIO)	*Ex-couple to Mr Tom Stoppard*
IGNACIA)	
SADIE	*Ex-cook to Mr Arnold Wesker*
FIFI	*Ex-au pair to Mr Brian Rix*
HODGE	*Ex-butler to Mr Alan Ayckbourn*
MRS GLAND	*Ex-governess to Mr Paul Raymond*
SPOT DOUGLAS-HOME	*A dog*

The action takes place in the waiting-room of Madame Parvenu's Domestic Agency, South Kensington.

(The curtain rises to reveal Snout sitting in one of a dozen armchairs, examining his boot. To him, enter Antonio and Ignacia.)

ANTONIO	Buenos dias!
SNOUT	I come here by boot.

There is a long pause.

IGNACIA	Woddy say?
ANTONIO	E say e gum ere by boot.
IGNACIA	O! Wi gum ere by boot, also! Wi gum ere wid. S.S.Malateste in 1972 !

They perform hand springs. Snout feels inside his boot.

SNOUT	I picked up a stone in Osbaldeston Road. Probably at the junction with Pondicherry Crescent.
IGNACIA	I PICK UP A STONE IN IVER HEATH! I gum to bloody Stoppard ouse, I weigh one hundred pounds, pretty soon I fat like pig.
ANTONIO	She never see bourbon biscuits before. Is ole new world. Is one reason we get bullet. One day, she eat ten packs penguins.
SNOUT	Or possibly at the point where Mafeking Villas runs parallel with the North Circular. You would not believe the amount of gravel they have put down there. Gravel and loose shale. Loose shale and chippings.

ANTONIO	One day, she eat ten pounds chippings.
SNOUT	Had I come by bus this situation would not have arisen. It would not have come about. Had I taken a Number Fourteen, I could have transferred to a Number Twenty-nine as far as Turnpike Lane. I could then have taken the underground. I could have gone down into the underground. I could have hopped aboard the underground, as it were. My boots would have been completely safe against shale on the underground. Manor House, Finsbury Park, Arsenal. I might have come up at any point.
ANTONIO	Mr Stoppard gives us heave-ho.
IGNACIA	E say we no good. E say we bad.
ANTONIO	So I say to im: wod you min, good, wod you min, bad? You min good/bad in metaphysical sense, you blidding ponce? You min good/bad in empirical sense? You min good/bad in comparative descriptive sense?
IGNACIA	You tole im all right! You say: Wod about them situations where it is better to be bad than good? You say: Wod about definin your terms, you iggerant sod?
ANTONIO	E look at me a long time after that. Then e it me wid a double-boiler.
IGNACIA	Then we give notice.

They perform double back-somersaults, with half-gainers.

SNOUT	Alternatively, I could have called a cab. I could have hailed a cab. It might have set me down on the wrong side of Pontings, of course, if it had come down Kensington Church Street, and I would have been compelled to have crossed the road by the Kentucky Pancake House, walked up as far as the Alpine Restaurant at the bottom of Campden Hill Road, and then taken a Number Nine to Hyde Park Corner. If he wasn't so mean. If Pinter wasn't so bleeding tight. If he wasn't so sodding stingy. *(He begins to rub his lapel, vigorously)* I had no severance pay. I was given no notice. I was offered no compensation in the way of, in lieu of, as an alternative to, I WAS NOT GIVEN TWO HALFPENNIES TO RUB TOGETHER, CONTRARY TO WHAT IS CLEARLY SPECIFIED BY THE LAWS OF THE LAND NOW OBTAINING!

Enter Sadie.

SADIE	You bring up playwrights, what do you get? Heartaches you get. Ulcers you get. Possibly a malignant disease. You feed him, he shouldn't get God forbid a chill on the liver, all weathers he goes out in to meet his arty friends, I wouldn't give you a thank you for them, you lay out Sea Island cotton underwear for him. Comfort you already washed it in, it should be nice and soft, it shouldn't give him God forbid a rash on his little pippick. Also it should be nice and clean and a credit to his dear parents, may they rest in peace, they worked, they slaved, in case God forbid he should get knocked down and taken to hospital, you hang garlic flowers round his windows in case God forbid a vampire should get in one night he's not looking, he's lying there, he's drunk from his lousy friends, he's worn out from whatever it is he does all day, such as nothing, which is what he does all day, his poor father should only see him, years he stood in that shop, varicose veins, an enlarged prostate, when they took it out they

"The Equal Opportunities Commission have ruined it."

53

needed three surgeons, three qualified men, just to carry it out of the operating theatre, but does *he* care? He used his flat like it was a hotel, you use this flat like it was a hotel, I used to tell him, it's *my* flat, he used to say. You're answering back already? I used to enquire, you're already too big to take criticism, Mr Playwright, Mr Big Shot, you're too old to listen to people, Mr Show Business?

SNOUT   Or I could have crossed over when I got to the Alpine Restaurant and gone down the underground next to Derry and Toms.

ANTONIO   I miss Tom and Derry. I say to Mr Stoppard, why wi no got colour tee vee, you bum, as per Ome Office regulations? E reply television is a bastard word, it not exist, philologically spikkin, as it do not exist, wi do not ave it. I tell im, if it do not exist, wod is all that flickerin across the road?

HAMLET

MARIANNE FAITHFULL as Ophelia
MARK DIGNAM as Polonius
NICOL WILLIAMSON as Hamlet

IGANCIA   I say, ow you define exist, wod terms wi dealing wid ere? Then e it me wid a liquidiser.

ANTONIO   Then wi give notice again.

SADIE   Also, Mr Shakespeare, Mr Impresario, while we're on the subject, I said, when was the last time you had a play on in the West End, all of a sudden you're complaining about my work, I haven't got also the right to complain about the work of some people I could mention, they're not standing a million miles away from me, as it happens, God forbid I should mention any names, you think it's nice for *me*, I said, I'm standing in the butcher's you should have a nice piece calf's liver, a chop, a fresh portion sidebowler, and people say: Well, Sadie, did he write anything new yet, a classic, possibly, a musical, maybe, tunes you can whistle?

SNOUT   I am also prepared to blame *her*. I am also prepared to blame his leman. I am also prepared to lay certain charges at the foot of his paramour.

SADIE   So he sacked me.

SNOUT   Now he is living with me, she said, now he is living with me, she remarked, I should be grateful if you would take yourself in hand. I do not require a caretaker, she expatiated. I require a butler. *(He begins to pick furiously at a shredding buttonhole)* I WAS ENGAGED AS A CARETAKER, I told her, I WAS ENGAGED TO BRING IN THE COKE, TO POLISH FRONT STEP TO REQUIRED STANDARD, TO ENSURE TRADES-PEOPLE CAME ROUND TO SIDE DOOR! I AGREED UNDER THE TERMS OF SAID EMPLOYMENT TO WEAR A KHAKI WAREHOUSE COAT, BUT TO PROVIDE OWN STRING FOR KNEEPADS, I informed her, THERE WAS NEVER ANY QUESTION OF BUTTLING, THERE WAS NEVER ANY QUESTION OF THAT AT ALL!

Enter Fifi.

FIFI   Ooh-la-la! Ma knickers ave disappear! Ah ad zem when ah lef zer ouse! Where can zey bi? Can eet bi e av stuff zem bah mistek in is brifcase for zer umpteence time? Sank God ah ave lef is employ at last! Ah do not ask for much in zis life, only an employer oo does not expeck mi to spen alf zer day in zer wardrobe. *(Faints. Bra falls off.)*

SNOUT   I WAS NOT ENGAGED TO MINCE ABOUT WITH A SILVER BLEEDING TRAY, I explained to her. IT WAS NOT AN UNDERTAKING WHICH APPEARED ON MY CARDS!

Enter Hodge, backwards

HODGE   Thank you very much, sir. Will there be anything else?

IGNACIA   Woddy say?

HODGE   I do beg your pardon, madame. I have grown somewhat used to backing into rooms. At Mr Ayckbourn's, do you see, all the rooms were always filled with people, invariably called Ron, Reg, Alf, Sid, Ned, Norman, or Don. There were usually two or three Maureens on the premises, and on one occasion, five Beryls. They were all related to one another, though not always in immediately apparent ways. They tended to drift from one part of the house to the other and carry on extraordinarily confusing conversations under the mistaken assumption that one knew what they were talking about. It was very convenient for Mr Ayckbourn, who used to walk about with two typewriters and a running tape-recorder, thus enabling himself to knock off several tetralogies a week by the simple expedient of overhearing, but it was most confusing for, ahem, a gentleman's gentleman. It has been said, though not, I hasten to add by me, that these people were not Mr Ayckbourn's acquaintances at all, but retained by his several agents on a salaried, if tiny, basis. In any event, I have left his service to seek employment elsewhere, despite the fact that I have no references: when I asked for them, my employer began to type on both machines simultaneously, and by lunchtime they had turned into an eighteen-part sit-com series for ATV.

SNOUT   BUTTLING, I riposted, *BUTTLING?* I should rather, I should prefer, I should be more willing to take my chances as a conductor on a 737 Green Line bus, commencing at Marble Arch, continuing down Edgware Road, along Maida Vale, up Kilburn High Road as far as the point where Cricklewood Lane crosses Cricklewood Broadway, bearing right past the point at which the old Handley Page aeroplane factory used to...

The light begins to fade. Snout's monologue drones on, counterpointed, after an hour or so, by the sound, from the corridor, of Mrs Gland beating Spot Douglas-Home with a rhinestone-studded riding crop as

THE CURTAIN FALLS

"I expected nothing and got nothing - that's what I call a good show."

"Amazing, Mr Springlow, but, alas, impersonations are no longer box-office."

15 October 1913

THE NEW WAY OF ADVERTISING PLAYS.

THE observer of contemporary journalism can hardly fail to have been struck with the change that is coming over theatrical advertising. Should the present tendency continue, this is what we are coming to:-

Why suffer from Autumnal Depression when for a price within the reach of all you can forget your woes by witnessing the enormously successful farcical comedy

"WELL, REALLY, I MEAN—"

Every evening at 9.   DRYTEARIAN THEATRE.
Just the thing for the chilly weather.
Try it before you go to bed to-night."

THE DESCRIPTIVE TOUCH.

"How glorious is the crisp morning air up on this mountain side! How the waters of the burn sing with gladness as they go splashing and flashing towards the tarn in the valley below. The cottagers sing also, for blitheness of heart, as they stand at their doors to match the passing of the Duke of Shaftesbury-Avenue and his high-born house-party on their way to stalk the stag. See! There goes a golden eagle; it has carried off a little child to its eyrie amongst the mountains, but no one seems to mind. The day is too sparkling and fresh for repining. Now the stag runs away, and all the house-party follow. "Tally-ho! Tally-ho!" they cry, tumbling over one another in their light-hearted eagerness to secure the quarry. But, swift as they are, there is one amongst them, a tall and beautiful English maid, who is faster than any. Her name is—

Ah! For that you must witness Act I, of

"THE TWIRL GIRL."
ARCADIAN THEATRE. Every evening at 8.30"

MORE TESTIMONY FROM THE MIDLANDS.

"Perhaps you remember what the critics said about *The Powder Puff?* (Anyhow, we are not going to repeat it.) Now let us hear what the Public, those who really know, think:

Mrs. Harris, Charwoman, of 225, Bath Brick Cottages, Rugby, writes:—

"In the summer of this year my health had become very low. My husband and all my friends noticed it. I was unable to rouse myself, and even the exertion of attending a picture-palace was frequently too much for me. One day a friend, who had seen your advertisement, advised me to try a visit to the World Theatre. At first I resisted the suggestion, but ultimately allowed myself to be persuaded to take advantage of a cheap excursion to attend your Saturday *matinée*. The result was *well-nigh incredible.* After the First Act I was able to sit up and take nourishment. Before the end of the Second my lassitude and general apathy had entirely disappeared; and I left the theatre a different woman. I consider your piece is nothing short of marvellous, and I am directing all similar sufferers to at once visit

'THE POWDER PUFF'
WORLD THEATRE. Evenings 9.
Wednesday and Saturday, 2.30."

AT THE PLAY

July
1929

BITTER SWEET
(His Majesty's)

Let a lot of paper-roses,
Paeonies and old-world posies
Be immediately showered
On the head of Mr. COWARD
And be cast about his feet
For creating *Bitter-Sweet,*
Musical phantasmagoria
Of the midday of VICTORIA.
Here are fairly lively ditties,
Fallen loves and faded pities;
Here in neat and tuny numbers,
Roused from their forgotten slumbers

(Out of Heaven or out of Hades)—
Here are gallants, here are ladies
Moving in the Might-have-beens
Of absurd Victorian scenes.
Did you ever see, ma honey,
Any kind of dress so funny
As the mid-Victorian bustle
For the girl who wants to hustle?
Or the clash of comic songs

Sarah Millick .... MISS PEGGY WOOD
Carl Linden .... MR. GEORGE METAXA

Sung by mid-Victorian throngs,
With the "green carnationed" beaux
Of the dear dead long-ago?

One there was, a tender maiden,
In those hours convention-laden
Who could risk her fame's disaster
With an Austrian music-master,
Follow him and be his wife
In the Austrian café life,
Mixing up with lots and lots

Of bonneted and flounced cocottes.
(Impropriety's improperer
In a mid-Victorian operer
When a bad Victorian swell
Meets a frail Victorian belle—
Mr. COWARD knows this well.)

Now, then, that she's lost her lover
How shall our fair maid recover,
What without him is she gonna
Do? Become a *prima donna?*
Yes, she does, and wins a peer;
Such is *Lady Shayne,* my dear,
Lovely, though her heart is sere,
Lovely now as in the day
Of "Ta-ra-ra-boom-de-ay,"
When for love she ran away,
Facing ruin and disaster
With her Austrian music-master.
Was she wiser, that fair rose,
Than the modern girl? Lord knows.

For his songs and for his dances,
For the dress which gives him chances,
For his bitter-sweet delight
In the ladies of the night,
For his pathos and his jazz,
Nay, for everything he has,
With forget-me-nots embowered
Shall, I say, be Mr. COWARD;
And his piece will be, I guess,
An unparalleled success
And most likely run for ages
On the Anglo-Saxon stages,
Being by such skill begotten.
Nor with him shall be forgotten
Anyone so sweet and good
As appeared Miss PEGGY WOOD.
Praise for songs and praises due
Fall to Miss ST. HELIER too.

EVOE.

" A PAIR OF SPECTACLES."

THE first spectacle classic and Shaksperian : t'other burlesquian, and PETTIT-cum-SIMS. The one at the Princess's, the other at the Gaiety. *Place au* "Divine WILLIAMS"! *Antony and Cleopatra* is magnificently put on the stage. The costumes are probably O. K.— "all correct"—seeing that Mr. LEWIS WINGFIELD pledges his

honourable name for the fact. We might have done with a few less, perhaps, but, as in the celebrated case of the war-song of the Jingoes, if we've got the men, and the money too, then there was every reason why the redoubtable LEWIS (whose name, as brotherly Masons will call to mind, means "Strength") should have put a whole army of Romans on the stage, if it so pleased him.

For its *mise-en-scène* alone the revival should attract all London. But there is more than this—there is the clever and careful impersonation of *Enobarbus* by His Gracious Heaviness, Mr. ARTHUR STIRLING ; then there is a lighter-comedy touch in the courteous and gentlemanly rendering of *Octavius Cæsar* by Mr. F. KEMBLE COOPER —one of the best things in the piece, but from the inheritor of two such good old theatrical names, much is expected. And then there is the *Mark Antony* of Mr. CHARLES COGHLAN, a rantin', roarin' boy, this *Antony,* whom no one, I believe, could ever have made really effective ; and finally, Her Graceful Majesty, Mrs. LANGTRY, Queen of Egyptian

The Last Scene of Autony and Cleopatra.

Witchery. Now honestly I do not consider *Cleopatra* a good part, nor is the play a good play for the matter of that. I believe it never has been a success, but if, apart from the really great attraction of gorgeous spectacular effects, there is any one scene above another which might well draw all London, it is the death of *Cleopatra,* which to my mind is—after the fall of WOLSEY, and a long way after, too,—one of the most pathetic pictures ever presented on the stage. So lonely in her grandeur, so grand, and yet so pitiable in her loneliness is this poor Queen of Beauty, this Empress-Butterfly, who can conquer conquerors, and for whose sake not only her noble lovers, but her poor humble serving-maids, are willing to die.

Her last scene is beyond all compare her best, and to those who are inclined to be disappointed with the play after the First Act is over I say, "Wait for the end," and don't leave until the Curtain has descended on that gracious figure of the Queen of Egypt, attired in her regal robes, crowned with her diadem, holding her sceptre, but dead in her chair of state. *Ça donne à penser.*

The Run of Cleopatra.

The Gaiety.—In calling their burlesque *Carmen up to Data,* possibly the two dear clever boys who wrote it intended some crypto-jocosity of which the hidden meaning is known only to the initiated in these sublime mysteries. Why " *Data* "? On the other hand, " Why not ? "

However attractive or not as a heading in a bill of the play, the Gaiety *Carmen* is, on the whole, a merry, bright, and light burlesqueish piece, though, except in the costume and make-up of Mr. ARTHUR WILLIAMS as *Captain Zuniga,* there is nothing extraordinarily "burlesque" in the appearance of any of the characters, as the appearance of Mr. HORACE MILLS as *Remendado* belongs more to Christmas pantomime than to the sly suggestiveness of real burlesque.

As Miss ST. JOHN simply looks, acts, and sings as a genuine *Carmen,* I can only suppose that her voice is not strong enough for the real Opera ; otherwise I doubt whether any better operatic impersonator of the real character could be found.

Scene from the Cigarette History of *Carmen.*

She is not the least bit burlesque, and though the songs she has to sing are nothing like so telling as those she has had given her in former pieces, yet, through her rendering, most are encored, and all thoroughly appreciated.

Mr. ARTHUR WILLIAMS as *Zuniga* is very droll, reminding some of us, by his make-up and jerky style, of MILHER as the comic *Valentine* in *Le Petit Faust.* Mr. LONNEN is also uncommonly good as the spoony soldier, and in the telling song of " *The Bogie Man ;*" and in the still more telling dance with which he finishes it and makes his exit, he makes *the* hit of the evening.— in fact the hit by which the piece will be remembered, and to which it owes the greater part of its success.

In the authors' latest adaptation of the very ancient "business" of "the statues"—consisting of a verse, and then an attitude, I was disappointed, as I had been led to believe that here we should see what Mr. LONNEN could do in the Robsonian or burlesquetragedy style. The brilliancy of the costumes, of the scenery, the grace of the four dancers, and the excellence of band and chorus, under the direction of that ancient mariner MEYER LUTZ, are such as are rarely met with elsewhere.

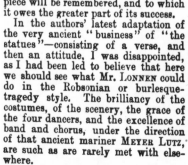

In for a good Run on the " Bogie " System.

Mr. GEORGE EDWARDES may now attend to the building of his new theatre, as *Carmen up to Data* will not give him any trouble for some time to come.

6 December 1890

A CHORUS LINE

"You're a disgrace to your uniform!"

"I'm warning you — either there's a hell of an improvement or we put the whole show on ice!"

IT JUST ISN'T CRITIC!
Sheridan Morley joins battle across the footlights

"Michele Molese, a leading artist of the New York City Opera, struck a blow for liberty that must have been cheered by singers throughout the world. Through the years he has been criticised by Harold C. Schonberg for his 'pinched' vocal production. Molese suffered in silence, but something colossal had been building up inside him and about two weeks ago the dam broke. He did something that other singers have muttered about but that nobody has had the nerve to do. After a fortissimo high C in 'The Masked Ball' he suddenly advanced to the footlights. 'That pinched high C,' he loudly announced, 'was for Harold C. Schonberg'."

International Herald Tribune.

"Right lads, this is it—full frontal war at last." Brother Shulman put down his *Herald Tribune* and leant across to where Brother Kretzmer and Senior Circler Darlington (so called because he is the only paid-up member of the Critics' Circle to have had a permanent press pass to the Globe Theatre … Shakespeare's Globe Theatre) were dozing fitfully in their armchairs. It had been a rough night: *King Lear* at the Roundhouse, performed in silence by a group of midget Hungarian mime artists—four and a half hours and by the time the critics had to meet their deadlines the Hungarians were only just starting to form their human pyramid for the blinding of Gloucester.

"For too long," continued Brother Shulman, "we have allowed ourselves to be attacked, vilified, abused and even criticised by actors and singers alike. Demarcation Day is here: it's time to decide who is allowed to attack who, or rather whom. Only the other day there was that chilling story of Brother de Jongh, one of our younger and braver members, who in the course of his duties for *The Guardian* ventured without armed guard as far as The Place, an apparently disused helicopter hangar behind Euston Station, only there to find himself physically restrained by RSC actors from leaving to file his notice. Then at that very same theatre our revered Brother Lambert of the *Sunday Times* had his glasses smashed and found himself in close proximity to, viz. sat on by, an actor of uncertain intentions. And now this account from our music section of Brother Schonberg's troubles in New York. It really will not do…"

At that moment the door burst open and there stood Brother Billington, gasping and visibly bruised, just back from the first-ever underwater Anouilh Festival outside Dijon.

"It's hell over there—critics being hauled into the water, others being told unless they write favourable reviews they risk unilateral drowning. Harold Hobson being asked to explain himself—I've never seen anything like it."

A voice spoke up from the back of the room:

"Sanctions," said Brother Marcus of the *Sunday Telegraph* (for it was he) "unless we are guaranteed absolute safety from physical or verbal assault by actors and singers alike we shall withdraw our labour. No more coverage of open-air productions of *Peer Gynt* in the nude, and an absolute refusal to stand on our hands while Peter Brook shows us the true Australian meaning of *Macbeth*. No more reviews of shows lasting more than four hours without an interval, and an absolute refusal to pay more for our own ice-creams."

There was another long pause; eventually Brother Nightingale, who'd been converting some long-unwanted CND badges into Campaign for Niceness to Drama critics, spoke up:

"Courage, brothers, we have survived worse in our time: remember the letter from John Osborne? The one about how we should be regularly exposed, like corrupt constabularies or faulty sewage systems? That was ten years ago now and here we all are, not visibly worse for wear (except for Brother Billington, of course, and that's what you get for going abroad).

" 'Seekers after the bare approximate' Osborne called us, one of his better phrases, but we managed to struggle on. Mind you, we had a few phrasemakers of our own in those days. Remember Tynan on Anna Neagle? Or his review of *The Importance of Being Earnest* in which he said the cast were dressed to kill and what they were dressed to kill was the play? Courage, brothers, we can fight them in the stalls, we can fight them in the circle, we shall never surrender."

"I don't like it," Brother Barber of the *Telegraph* spoke up at last, "it's not like the old days. James Agate never had to suffer anything like this: he went along to the theatre, 7.30 sharp, curtain up, drawing-room, French windows, butler on the telephone, 'Master's expected any moment now, Sir—he'll be worried about the Lustgarten murders of course, him being a lawyer and Mrs. Lustgarten's first husband, but he'll take it in his stride'. 8.15 interval, brandy and soda, back for the police inspector and home by 10. Straight notice, 800 words, 'impressive playing by Miss Fortescue in elegant settings' and that was your lot. Nowadays it's all so unpredictable, nude ladies in your lap, no plots,

"As an actor he was a great success in the early 60's, but he didn't seem to move with the times."

only one interval, how do you know when it's all over?"

"What I don't like," said Brother Tinker, one of the newer members of the Circle, "is the way the dispute is spreading. Brother Schonberg for instance belongs to our music section—if he's under attack are any of us safe in our stalls?"

All eyes turned toward the East and Brother Hope-Wallace:

"There are," he said, thoughtfully rubbing his glasses with a felt-tip pen, "certain problems with opera. I'd not care to review the Barber scene from *Figaro*, for instance, if I thought I'd offended the singer with the razor. Then again you want to be careful with ballet—those swans could turn very nasty."

"Right lads," Brother Wardle it was now, "the time has clearly come to call for help from our brethren in allied fields. Television critics, for instance, could be called out in sympathy: Elkan Allan should be instructed to preview the wrong week's viewing, thereby causing dismay and discontent throughout the land. This is no time for half-measures: if necessary we shall have to go as far as withdrawing Cyril Connolly's labour."

A hush fell over the room at this awesome prospect: then, ever so quietly, Brother Trewin of the *Illustrated London News* began recalling some of the great critical triumphs of the past.

"There was the Hilary Spurling campaign of 1969 when we boycotted the Court, then there was the Bernard Levin/Emile Littler dispute of 1962 (though admittedly that was one down for our side). Ah, memories, memories... what price a libel suit nowadays, and is old Swaffer dead?"

It was Brother Shulman who called the meeting to order for the last time:

"We are agreed, then, on a unanimous declaration of non-co-operation. Unless certain safeguards are forthcoming from actors and singers alike, we shall not give them the privilege of our opinions as to their worth. We are not to be abused, either physically or verbally, nor are we to be prevented from leaving the theatre at any moment we choose, nor from helping ourselves to the lower tray of a Cadbury's Assorted box. We are not to be invited on to the stage of the Palladium to join in Christmas songs, nor are we to be asked by Tinkerbell if we believe in fairies, a question which has always caused some distress. Above all, our reviews are in no way to be the subject of litigation or comment. We critics are not, in short, here to be criticised."

A POET'S DAY.

(*From an American Correspondent.*)

OSCAR AT BREAKFAST! OSCAR AT LUNCHEON!!
OSCAR AT DINNER!!! OSCAR AT SUPPER!!!!

"YOU see I am after all, but mortal," remarked the Poet with an ineffably affable smile, as he looked up from an elegant but substantial dish of ham - and - eggs. — Passing a long, willowy hand through his waving hair, he swept away a stray curl-paper with the *nonchalance* of a D'ORSAY.

After this effort, MR. WILDE expressed himself as feeling somewhat faint; and, with a half - apologetic smile, ordered another portion of

HAM AND EGGS,

in the evident enjoyment of which, after a brief interchange of international courtesies, I left the Poet.

Later in the day I again encountered the young patron of Culture at the business premises of the

CO-OPERATIVE DRESS ASSOCIATION.

On this occasion the Poet, by special request, appeared in the uniform of an English Officer of the Dragoon Guards, the dress, I understand, being supplied for the occasion from the elegant wardrobe of MR. D'OYLEY CARTE'S *Patience* Company.

Several Ladies expressed their disappointment at the "insufficient leanness" of the Poet's figure, whereupon his Business Manager explained that he belonged to the fleshly school.

To accommodate MR. WILDE, the ordinary lay - figures were removed from the show-room, and, after a sumptuous luncheon, to which the *élite* of Miss ****'s customers were invited, the distinguished guest posed with his fair hostess in an allegorical tableau, representing "*English Poetry extending the right hand to American Commerce.*"

"This is indeed Fair Trade," remarked MR. WILDE, lightly, and immediately improved a testimonial advertisement (in verse) in praise of Miss ****'s patent dress-improver.

At a dinner given by "JEMMY" CROWDER (as we familiarly call

him, the Apologist of Art had discarded his military garb for the ordinary dress of an

ENGLISH GENTLEMAN,

in which his now world-famed knee-breeches form a conspicuous item, suggesting indeed the Admiral's uniform in Mr. D'OYLEY CARTE'S *Pinafore* combination.

ARIADNE IN NAXOS; OR, VERY LIKE A WAIL.

DESIGN BY OUR OWN GREENERY-YALLERY-GROSVENOR-GALLERY YOUNG MAN, IN HUMBLE IMITATION OF THE PICTURE BY PROFESSOR W. B. RICHMOND, SYMBOLISING "THE GRIEF OF ÆSTHETICISM AT THE DEPARTURE OF HER OSCAR."

"I think," said the Poet, in a pause between courses, "one cannot dine too well,"—placing every one at his ease by his admirable tact in partaking of the thirty-six items of the *menu*.

It is not till after dinner that Mr. WILDE shows his wonderful power as a *raconteur* and observer of mankind. I noticed that he has a way of avoiding repartee by carrying on his conversation uninterruptedly. He has been intimate with GLADSTONE, and considers him a meritorious politician, though he finds fault with his views on HOMER. He prattled glibly of his friend Sir WILLIAM HARCOURT, and expressed himself generally in harmony with the leaders of Continental nations.

When asked, "Whom do you consider the *greatest living Poet?*" our illustrious guest deprecated so personal a question, but frankly avowed his conviction that his well-known predecessor, W. SHAKSPEARE, was in many respects quite valuable. Questioned as to Contemporary Poets, Mr. CARTE'S * latest novelty said

"ALFRED TENNYSON is a prolific, though somewhat old-fashioned writer, whose verses, I am given to understand, have an extensive sale, but who does not appear to advantage in a court suit.

"SWINBURNE, though in some respects in sympathy with myself, has, I fear, contracted a fatal taint of Bohemianism, perhaps from living in an unaristocratic neighbourhood. BROWNING is a conscientious, though somewhat uneven writer. As to MORRIS, his verses are prosy, but his wall-papers are eloquently poetical." The Poet spoke in terms

* From the constant mention of this well-known English *Entrepreneur's* name and his entertainments, we are almost induced to believe that the Gifted Æsthetic simply appears in America as a sort of Peripatetic Showman's Advertisement of Mr. CARTE'S numerous ventures.—ED.

SPRING ON THE BOARDS Barry Took

In *Oh What A Lovely War* there is a point in the action at which Earl Haig prays, "Oh God give me victory before the Americans arrive." In theatrical circles Spring is the time when, I suspect, impresarios make the plea—"Let my play survive *until* the Americans arrive."

The Spring is a testing time in the theatre. In the winter it's an act of faith to brave fuel crises, bomb hoaxes and the weather, not to mention the rubbish available, and the sturdy British playgoer feels a sense of duty well done to go to a show. In the Spring he has other things on his mind—laying in supplies of laxatives and sunburn remedies in preparation for the summer holidays, whether to change the car or not, the state of the garden, the budget, Easter—Passover. Only plays of great brilliance or of unfathomable fatuity survive—but when the Americans *do* start to arrive around the end of April, the London theatre generally starts to boom.

I soldiered through two West End Springs at the Apollo Theatre in a chirpy revue called *For Amusement Only*. Around the end of March when the curtain went up we noticed that the atmosphere became perceptibly different—the decibel level of crackling chocolate wrappings dropped, the smell of rained-on musquash became less pungent.

You could identify individual coughers in the sparsely populated stalls and the coughers outnumbered the laughers by about three to one. The conversations of the usherettes became easier to hear than the stage dialogue, and if there *were* people in the boxes, they were lying down.

Under these circumstances performances became a bit slapdash and matinees were often a riot of improvisation. Sometimes we played to no more than a dozen hardy matrons who must have been baffled by sketches that bore only a fleeting resemblance to the programme matter.

One matinee, every quip was greeted by a gargantuan laugh from somewhere in the stalls. At first it was stimulating but after an house or so it began to grate and we suspected that the "mystery laugher" had been planted as a gag by some joker in the company. The Manager was asked to investigate. He came backstage to tell us that it wasn't a plant but that in fact the laugher was Jack Benny, in town for a TV performance, genuinely convulsed by his first taste of intimate review.

If West End business tends to fall away in the Spring—in the provinces it all but vanishes. In Spring in the 1950s, Variety Theatres resembled Highgate Cemetery. Accrington in April can be very pleasant, I'm told, but I worked there once when in the whole week less than one hundred people came to the theatre. When you consider that this number included old age pensioners at specially reduced prices and shopkeepers who got in free in exchange for exhibiting posters in their windows, it's small wonder that the theatre closed soon after.

The W.C.Fields gag about the store "closed on account of molasses" was nothing to Accrington. Their football club, Accrington Stanley, packed up as well around that time. The good people of Accrington must have led deeply fulfilling home lives to feel so disinclined to venture out. Or perhaps it was as the Musical Director of the Accrington pit orchestra suggested:"Why should people come here—after all they can go to Burnley or Blackburn."

Ah Burnley! Ah Blackburn—!!

Burnley, where a fellow comedian said to me, "Whenever I hear them going to work in their clogs, I think the Dutch will never understand my material."

Blackburn, where my landlady, after seeing the show on Monday night, gave me coffee to drink for the rest of the week, saying, "When I saw you up on t'stage wearing a dinner suit I knew you were too sophisticated for tea."

My most Spring-like experience was at Lyme Regis. I was head cook and bottle washer of a tiny concert party booked to play two weeks as a pre-season attraction in what I seem to remember was a converted Lifeboat shed. In any event, it was on the extreme edge of Lyme Regis on the way to the lighthouse and a stiffish climb up from the promenade. We had the usual concert party set up—comedian, soubrette, a dancing act, straight man cum compere (me), the pianist, and a juggler whose speciality was to balance on one finger on a champagne bottle. (He didn't really, of course. He would palm one of those T-shaped keys they used to lock railway compartments with, insert it in the neck of the prop. bottle and hoist himself shakily up on that, but the illusion when he made it was of balancing on one finger).

It was a mixture that the London agent thought most appropriate for the good people of Lyme Regis and we started our short season full of hope.

The first night was a sell-out, or to be accurate, a give-out. Every local notable had been given a free ticket and complimentaries had been showered on the Lyme landladies in the hope that they would put in a good word with their guests. I took the tickets at the door, then as the overture started I sprinted round to the stage ready for the opening chorus. We opened with a medley of "Happy" songs. *I Want To Be Happy; Happy Days Are Here Again; It's A Hap-hap-happy Day; I'm Happy When I'm Hiking,* and for reasons that escape me now, *All The Nice Girls Love A Sailor.* That was greeted with mild enthusiasm and the audience began to warm to the show—the dancers were young and pretty and kept time, the pianist was encored for the *Sabre Dance*—the finger balancer not only got up but stayed up and twirled, what was for him, a record number of coloured rings on various parts of his anatomy. By the interval we felt we were onto a good thing.

The second half started as the first had finished, but alas, trouble was on the way in the shape of the comedian, a self styled "miracle of mirth" who was one of the "'ere missus" school of comics. His brief appearances so far in the programme had led him to believe that at last his talent was being recognised. His funny walk in the Napoleon and Josephine sketch had been applauded, the "sewing on a button" routine had gone down well and the mime of eating hot chips including the celebrated "drinking the vinegar out of the paper" business had never gone better.

There was a light of madness in his eyes when he went out to deliver the coup de grâce—the penultimate number in the show—his solo. He started with some quickfire patter about his girlfriend, "She's so thin—last week she swallowed a pickled onion and all the boys left town" etc. Not quite Lyme Regis, but the audience responded indulgently—then he turned to the subject of landladies.

"Now take my digs this week, please!"

"Two minutes from the sea—by rocket!"

"The landlady was out in the back garden beating a mattress. I said, "That won't kill 'em". She said, "No but it'll make 'em dizzy for the night".

"I said, 'What are your terms'. She said 'Thirty-five shillings a week and I don't want any children'."

"We're too far from the sea to get sea air, but every meal time she comes in and waves a kipper in front of the electric fan."

And so on. It was like watching a rat leap onto a sinking ship and bury its teeth in the Captain's leg. His act and the show ended in almost total silence as the audience of landladies trooped out, tight lipped, into the night.

For the rest of our short season, we played only to people who'd decided to walk to the lighthouse and wanted a sit down before returning to the town. It wasn't the fault of Lyme Regis or of the poor comedian—I blame the Spring—at least the Spring can't argue back.

THE NEW MAYHEW

In 1858 Henry Mayhew, a former joint-editor of PUNCH, wrote "London Labour and the London Poor." ALEX ATKINSON and RONALD SEARLE make a modern reassessment a century later.

RATHER less gusto and liveliness is apparent in the leisure occupations of the poor of the city, as more and more of their traditional entertainments tend to be displaced by fresh novelties of one

68

—AN EXHIBITOR OF TABLEAUX, VOCALISTS, ETC.

kind or another. The report which follows was obtained from an exhibitor of tableaux and living performers of all sorts, who, faced with a steadily declining business, was considering a return to the wholesale garment trade, in which he had made an adequate living until the age of twenty-five.

"Then I branched out into this lark, and why I done it, I can't rightly tell you. I oughter had my head examined, that I can see. Well, the lark is simple enough. What you have to do, you take out a licence as a manager in the theatrical line, and you think up some title as will be an attraction, and look well on a bill. Yes, something pleasing to the general public, as you say. Like, for instance, you might have *Nothing On To-night, Boys!*, or *Legs, Busts and Belly Laffs of 1958* ('laughs' being spelt with two F's—a very humorous touch, see). One time I done very well with *Look, Ma, I'm Naked!* Then another of my titles was *The Sexy Strip Show*, but I never reckoned much to that: it was dull, as you'll agree, and didn't have the same wittiness what the others had. Oh, yes, wittiness is half the battle in a title, without a doubt. That and being catchy, that's what you have to aim at. Why, sometimes a title of this kind might take you weeks before you get it perfect. No, the show itself isn't nearly so much trouble.

"What you need to make a show is, first, any bits of scenery you can pick up cheap, and gaudy if possible. Then you want a girl as will stand naked without busting out laughing, and a few others to be only *half* naked: they come cheaper, as is only fair. Three of these is a good number, unless you have the word 'lavish' on the bills; then you might run to four. Also you want seven or eight as can dance a bit, and roll their eyes; and a singer, or what we term a 'vocalist.' Then an opening act, like it might be an old man and his

daughter doing an *adagio* dance, glad of a few quid. Then what's called a comic. The rest you can make up with, such as an instrumentalist, a juggler, some comedy acrobats, or a girl in tights who can walk about and smile.

"Next, you must book a few touring 'dates,' and try to keep going as long as you can. But things being what they are to-day it's a hard life, and hardly ever a profit. The public is fickle, you see. Where at one time they'd queue up in their hundreds to see a good, spicy, family show like the one I have here this week, called *Harem-Scarem Strip*, nowadays you can't hardly hope to three-quarter fill the house on any night unless you've got a real good poster to entice them. Well, what I call a *good* poster is one that makes it seem like a show as would never be allowed by the police in Port Said. The public loves to see a show of that kind, being naturally curious; although of course when they get inside they might find some of the items not quite so pleasing as they appear on the bill. Now, take this item here in big red letters: 'The Barbaric Orgy of the Slaves and Virgins—They Dared Us to Show It!' Well, that's really three Leicestershire women in butter-muslin larking about behind a gauze in their bare feet, and the band playing 'The Blue Danube.' But what do they expect for four and a tanner in the front rows? I tell you, it's a tragedy that a famous English entertainment like this should be allowed to die out through apathy. There'll have to be a subsidy if I'm to carry on the work much longer."

He next assured me that as he now intended to "nip in and count the house" I would be welcome to accompany him, there being "several nice seats left" at very reasonable prices. Being anxious for a glimpse of this declining form of urban amusement I entered the hall, which was a graciously designed theatre in a side

street, now considerably decayed and smelling powerfully of carbolic mixed with lilies-of-the-valley. There was a meagre attendance, so that the voices of the performers echoed. Near the orchestra, however, three rows of seats were quite well filled. Here men of all ages lounged at ease, wearing their overcoats against the draught; one elderly man, indeed, had also kept his cap on. He read a newspaper until the boom of a gong announced the Barbaric Orgy, thus depriving himself of the pleasure of observing a boy, dressed as a bull-fighter, playing a selection of Irish airs upon the piano-accordian, his smile becoming less secure at each fumbled *arpeggio*. He also missed a gentleman of Chinese appearance who strenuously contorted himself to the strains of "In a Monastery Garden"; a tenor and a soprano whose repertoire proved too extensive for the patience of a patron in the gallery; a troupe of local young ladies, apparently disguised as *bedouin*, who performed a ballet of mystifying complexity entitled "Secrets of the Sphinx"; and a plump, north-country humorist in a frock coat and knicker-bockers, who delivered a number of unsavoury anecdotes before singing a song about the power of prayer. Next there came a series of ill-lit tableaux, in which ladies in various stages of undress represented the seasons, Hades, and the Botticelli "Venus"; the latter proved most amusing, since Venus herself bore the indentation of a suspender upon her leg.

The gong then sounding for the *pièce de résistance* the gentleman in the cap sat upright and began to devote a great deal of energy to breathing. I departed as quietly as I could.

I have described the proceedings as faithfully as possible, for I cannot believe that such entertainments will long survive. I wish I could find it in my heart to regret their passing.

Scene One:
THE ROYAL ACADEMY
OF DRAMATIC ART.
THE TIME IS 1926
Enter Robert Morley...

S. McMURTRY.

Over cocktails she bemoaned Milton Keynes. She had spent the afternoon there doing things for the County. Not that there was anything to be done for Milton Keynes itself; far too many houses too close together and an absence apparently of skilled labour. "All these planners," she lamented, "such a botch, it's difficult to forgive what they have done to the Whaddon Chase Country. I stay on but my son has given up completely, moved to the Quorn."

"I understand exactly how you must feel," I told her. "I myself have spent the afternoon revisiting happy hunting grounds to find them sadly changed."

"You still ride?" she asked incredulously.

I never rode, but what is even more surprising, at my age, I still act. I had spent the afternoon at the Royal Academy of Dramatic Art where fifty years ago an eager child of nineteen first showed his paces to an astonished selection committee, a member of which, as I have always affirmed, was the late Gerald du Maurier. Alas, the files, one has now to call them archives, do not support my claim. The examiners are listed as

Kate Rourke and the Principal himself in those days Kenneth, later to become Sir Kenneth Barnes.

Sir Kenneth was the brother of the Vanburgh girls, Irene and Violet, the equivalent in those days of our own Dame Wendy Hiller and Dame Peggy Ashcroft.

Father, who knew everyone slighly but no-one quite enough, provided a letter to Irene who seemed surprised to receive it at my hands. It dealt at some length, I gathered, with the difficulty of finding a suitable occupation for a young gentleman without private means or much expectation of inheriting any. It went on to beg her intercession with her brother that a place might be found at the opening of the autumn term.

"I don't think," she opined after having read the missive, "that there is likely to be a problem, just go round to R.A.D.A. and ask for the enrolment form. They'll tell you when you have to audition and I am sure they'll be delighted to have you as a student, dear boy." Irene was famous not only as a comedienne but also for her good manners. A study of the candidates' list on which my name appears proved her correct in her surmises. In those days few indeed were ever turned away, and they were invariably girls. Against a list of forty or so candidates the word "no" appears only three times. It was easier in those days, I opined to Mr. O'Donoghue, the present registrar, who had received me most warmly at tea-time, proffering chocolate biscuits and the relevant files for my consumption.

"It had to be," he replied. "In those days the Academy was not independently wealthy as it is today, thanks to the Shaw Bequests, and Kenneth had to see it paid its way. The number of students was roughly eight times what it is today. Of course the whole place was a great deal smaller. We rebuilt after the bomb." Crunching the biscuits I recalled for him the magic of Bernard Shaw's first lecture which I was privileged to attend.

I can see him now striding on the small stage, removing his hat and beginning to unbutton his overcoat. "I want you to watch carefully," he told us, "while Bernard Shaw, the great Bernard Shaw, takes off his coat." In point of fact, although I never knew it at the time, Shaw's participation in the life of the Academy had been constant since its foundation. An active member of the Council, there are many minutes of his suggestions as to how the school should be run in the early days. Once he opined students should be made to stand on the stage and read a page of the French telephone directory aloud so as to grasp of Gallic pronunciation. Another time he thought that the students should perform a play in a completely empty West End theatre, empty save for the Council who would watch from the top of the gallery. I have written elsewhere of my adoration of Saint Bernard who awoke me at the age of thirteen from the stupor and despair of adolescence and during a performance of *The Doctor's Dilemma* made me realise there was to be no life for me hereafter save in the theatre. Now here he was in the same room granting me a semi-private audience.

What astonished me most in those early days at the Academy was to discover that actors and actresses like Norman Page, Herbert Ross, Helen Haye, Rosina Phillipi, Dorothy Green were alive and well and visiting Gower Street. I don't know exactly how I expected people who acted would look like or behave, but I was unprepared to find them no different in appearance from men who pushed pens or flogged stocks and shares. They weren't even so very different from my own Uncles and Aunts, though none of the latter included a member of the "Profession" among their acquaintances and if they ever spoke of or visited the theatre took a certain pride in never being able to accurately record the impressions gained. Thus they would remark that the other night someone had taken them, they never ventured on their own, to that theatre in the Haymarket where there was quite an amusing piece written by that fellow with the double-barrelled name and acted by the chap who used to play Shakespeare. "I tell you who was in it as well, that short comedienne who used to be married to Cosmo Gordon Lennox, didn't she?" They would look round feigning ignorance and someone would helpfully change the subject. No one cared to state unequivocally that St John Ervine had written *The Second Mrs Fraser* and that Harry Ainley and Marie Tempest were its stars. Inexplicably the only name they never seemed to forget was Matheson Lang's.

My father was the exception; he actually played Auction Bridge with Charles Hawtrey and once took me behind the scenes to see Fred Neilson-Terry when he visited Folkestone and insisted on my actually perching on the chair he had recently vacated as the Scarlet Pimpernel himself. Neither Mr Neilson-Terry nor I thought it a good idea at the time. At the age of six I don't think it occurred to me that the star was anxious to be off home for his tea and that the costume he was wearing would soon be changed for something more casual. Of course I didn't expect the staff at the Academy to be in costume when I first set eyes on them, but then I don't think it occurred to me they would be in flannels and sports coats either. Norman Page, who was more or less second in

"I'm told he's also having trouble with the income-tax people."

command to Kenneth Barnes, was currently playing in *Marigold* at the Kingsway Theatre. The piece had already been performed for nearly a year which was something of a phenomenon in those days and Mr Page had the reputation of having been the best pantomime cat within living memory and had only recently shed his skin forever on being pushed by a young admirer off his perch on the dress circle rail and fallen heavily into the stalls beneath without causing much damage, except to himself and a number of tea trays. He was the kindest of men who seldom took acting seriously, his interest constantly caught and often sustained at least for a term by a more than usually pretty student.

At the first class he conducted with the new intake, he always enquired which of his charges had decided on a stage career against the express wishes and advice of their parents. Quite untruthfully my arm shot up. I was anxious to impress him of my single purpose and determination, but it was a girl child in the front who caught and held his attention and he closely questioned her as to whether she had actually run away from home or whether her parents were supporting her at the YWCA. It was surprising how many of the class seemed to have braved parental disapproval, but in those days to have a son or daughter on the stage was not as it is now an occasion for congratulations.

A couple of years ago on the Isle of Wight a proud father showed me a record sleeve featuring his nubile daughter completely nude, though admittedly photographed from behind. He was justly proud of the number of records which she had sold for the group of which she was not yet a member; such an attitude would have been unthinkable in my early days, even on the Isle of Wight, but then of course no one had thought of record sleeves.

But if we parents were different then so were we students. A great many of us were hell-bent not on dedication so much as fornication. Here I must make clear that I am speaking principally of my own sex who were happily outnumbered by the girls in the ratio of seven or eight to one. That meant not only that most of us young pashas were never again to have it so good on or off stage, but that we enjoyed inestimable benefit of being allowed to play Hamlet or even in my own case Shylock from start to finish supported by a constantly changing Juliet or Portia. There would come a moment during the performance when one Juliet would disentangle herself from Romeo's embrace, demurely leave the stage and be instantly replaced by another hopeful debutante. It made for a certain amount of confusion but must have often proved a relief to Sir Kenneth who made it a point of honour to watch every single performance given under his roof. It would be impossible to pay a sufficiently high tribute to his sense of dedication and his infinite compassion and patience and it proved quite impossible when he came to retire to find another who was prepared to undergo such sustained and prolonged torture.

But while I was there Sir Kenneth still ruled, and on the memorable occasion of my own Shylock appeared suddenly in front of the tabs to quell a near-riot among my fellow students who had found my acting with Tubal so hilarious that they screamed and demanded an encore. Sir Kenneth quelled them with a short speech. "Now," he said, "let us all remember; fair is fair," and indicated the performance was to continue. I have never to this day understood why I was considered so funny as Shylock, and indeed once or twice I have been tempted to play the part again just to find out the cause. Once, after a particularly fine dinner, Peter Hall, who was still at Stratford, urged me to join his company in any role I fancied. "I might do Shylock," I told him and he promised to ring in the morning. It was just unfortunate my phone happened to have been out of order.

I enquired of Mr O'Donoghue whether the legend of my

performance still persisted but he thought not. "You were marked Above Average that term," he told me pushing forward the relevant document. Together we read the names of my contemporaries about whose subsequent careers I was a mine of misinformation; opining for instance that the late and much loved Joan Harben had married a poet. Mr O'Donaghue pointed out that *Who's Who* had her listed as having married Clive Morton, another dear friend who died last year, alas. Far too many of my contemporaries seem to have done just that, but we were back happily in the land of the living with Jean Anderson the ever-ailing but fortunately never actually succumbing Mother of that popular television series *The Brothers*.

I fell to wondering about Alan Webb whom I had seen the night before in a revival of *The Seagull* on the box. "Was he here with you?" asked the Registrar. "He was here before me, I think," I told him, "but no doubt the records don't go back that far." "On the contrary," he reassured me, "I was looking up Athene Seyler who popped in the other day, she was here in 1908 when any performance the students gave took place in the front drawing room, except, of course, for the Public Show."

The Public Show, now discontinued, was the event of our two-year course. It was the day, as the title suggests, when we appeared in public in a real West End Theatre, in my day the St James's, and were reviewed by professional critics in the daily press. The Academy itself awarded Gold, Silver and Bronze Medals to the outstanding students and, reading the roll of honour hung in the entrance hall and signed not only by Dame Madge Kendal herself who penned the immortal advice "To Your Own Self Be True" in the firm hand associated with her own strict code of morals and deportment, one is surprised at how often the judges guessed right. The list is impressive: Charles Laughton, Robert Shaw, Robert Atkins, Athene Seyler, Meggie Albanesi, Alan Badel, Sian Phillips, Gemma Jones. Indeed only in one instance was potential not apparently spotted, I myself being sent for by the Administrator at the end of my first year and questioned closely as to whether I had private means to sustain a further year in the direction of what Kenneth obviously regarded but was too polite to actually designate as a suicidal course. Whenever I met him subsequently and he thought I was about to repeat the tale, he begged me to desist on the grounds that I had not heard him correctly. Besides the medals and certificates to be won annually, there was a feast of other prizes and awards usually bearing the name of the donor (sometimes still extant but more often deceased) who had bequeathed a sum sufficient to keep his name alive by the annual distribution of largesse which in those days usually amounted to about five guineas.

There was the "Kenneth Kent Award for Attack in Acting," "The Hamen Clark Award for Diction in Relation to Dialect," "Mrs Willard's Prize for Spontaneous Laughter" and "V C Buckley's prize For The Wearing of Clothes Period or Modern." None of us in my time was a dedicated pot-hunter but we were encouraged by the staff to enter these gladiatorial contests if only that they might have a further insight into our failings in the field, for instance, of mime or fencing. No subject bored me more than that of the study of the foil, and I seldom attended the great M Bertram's celebrated classes to which like the dance classes I gave as wide a berth as was allowable. There was a good deal of flexibility in the regulations which ordained how many appearances one should put in per term. I was an ungraceful youth and I fear no amount of thrust, parry and tiptoe would have made me otherwise. In any case I never tried. At almost my first session at the dancing class I was singled out as the square boy at the back and made to stand in front of my comrades on the grounds that I had most to learn. I never returned.

Imagine my delight, therefore, when discovering, as I have already boasted, that I was marked "above average" in my first term. Above average, indeed, I should hope so but who were the others? In nineteen twenty-six when I first came on the scene the Academy was still recovering from Charles Laughton, who was to do for Gower Street what John Osborne was later to achieve for Sloane Square. He changed the image. Regarded as unlikely material when he first arrived with his Yorkshire accent and flying yellow mackintosh, he carried all before him including his enormous frame, won every prize, caught every judge's eye and almost immediately after leaving gave in what was then the fringe theatre at Kew the finest performance as *The Government Inspector* London had seen for years.

I was no Laughton, although in bulk and general untidiness of costume I bore perhaps a fleeting resemblance; but Laughton heartened us fatties and the regional types who by the nature of the Academy were in those days still regarded as rather second-class citizens. If Kenneth Barnes was to run the Academy at even the smallest margin of profit, he had perforce to run it first and foremost as a charm school. Mothers who hadn't wanted to put their daughters on the stage were much more likely to continue paying the fees if they noticed a distinct improvement in their child's posture and appearance, in the way she spoke and dressed and brushed her hair. A year at the Academy could often do wonders in turning a dumpy duck into an acceptable cygnet.

"Can't get a quiet pint nowadays without a lot of highbrows spouting poetry at you."

For the men, of course, no such transformation was possible or indeed thought desirable but some parents remained hopeful that at the end of two years their sons would change direction and consider a more serious and gainful career. Indeed had all four hundred or so of the student body who crowded the class rooms been inspired by the staff with unwavering purpose and devotion to its temporary vocation, the profession would have been even more hopelessly crowded than it is today. Many of us fell by the roadside or more properly thumbed a lift to town by way of early marriage or the acceptance of a job in our father's business, but a surprising number of my year remained on the stage to tell the tale or enable me to do so for Mr O'Donaghue who passed me list after list of their half-forgotten names.

Dorothy Dunkels, who along with a girl called Marjorie Playfair, and Plum Warner's daughter Betty, were the three great beauties of our day. Miss Playfair had the prettiest legs imaginable and she would sit swinging them on the dresser of the canteen to the hopeless admiration of most of the fellows and indeed some of the staff. Betty Warner had the most beautiful red hair and Dorothy Dunkels was teacher's pet, at least where Miss Sevening was concerned. Miss Sevening was the formidable power behind and indeed on the scenes. It was generally

admitted that it was she who ran the show. She was Baroness Falkender to Barnes' Harold Wilson. She kept things moving, knew what was going on and on occasions stopped the rot. I suppose what she liked about Dorothy Dunkels was that she was nearly, if not quite, as elegant as herself. Much to our surprise Dorothy didn't carry all before her on the day. I am not certain she even won a prize but I remember her at the Strand Theatre later giving a memorable performance as a manicurist in one of Arthur Macrae's plays and looking the same cool and lovely child

THE STAGE AUTHOR.

It is pleasant to notice the highly satisfactory pecuniary results which nowadays attend the stage literary profession. The modern stage author appears usually to be either very successful or just on the point of becoming very successful. He does not have to wrestle with poverty nearly so much as did his serio-comic predecessors. On the contrary he invariably has a comfortable study, a faithful housekeeper and a set of golf-clubs. In addition to which he is often quite an important dramatic personage. He can scarcely help getting on. The stage publisher must be a nice man.

The faithful housekeeper is a great boon to the stage author, as the latter is generally a middle-aged bachelor. Occasionally he may have a wife whom he does not understand, but it is more likely that he will have no wife to understand; not in the first Act, anyway. For, despite the brilliance and popularity of his novels, the big boyish fellow does not know everything. He does not know much about love; not more than enough, that is, than enables him to be epigrammatic about it. And because he is so big and boyish and handsome (you rarely see a dried-up under-sized novelist on the stage), women in general take to him in a motherly sort of way, though, despite his epigrams, he is rather afraid of them. A few of the more self-sacrificing ones are even ready to marry him for the sake of taking care of his royalties for him; but he cannot work up to tumultuous passion even for them.

Then his lady typist steps in and takes him in hand. The stage literary amanuensis has to be a fairly bright girl. Unlike her real-life sister far more is required of her than mere technical competence. Not the least part of her job is to show authors what is lacking in their lives and in their work, and to teach them what true love is, even at the cost of marrying them herself. And it says a good deal for the efficiency of the stage secretarial training colleges that these conscientious girls rarely fail to do their work well and marry their employers.

Needless to say the stage author puts up a stiff fight, but the girl is too much for him. The poor fellow is badly handicapped in the first place by the fact that on the stage it is practically impossible to engage an unattractive and inefficient lady secretary. Failing that, he tries hard to make himself thoroughly objectionable; but his pose as an unrelenting misogynist would not impress a simple village maiden, and the girl loves him all the more for it. So he has to give in and fold her in his arms. After that, presumably, he becomes more successful than ever.

There can be no doubt that, on the stage, literary success is a very beautiful and mysterious thing, inasmuch as one rarely sees the stage author doing any really solid work. Still, from his conversation (and he talks a good deal) you gather that he has just left off, or is just about to begin, so it is quite obvious that he is a fairly busy man. One sometimes hears him dictating for almost five minutes without being interrupted. The working day of a stage author is full of interruptions. But that does not prevent his being successful. His charming and determined secretary and his genial publisher are dead certain to pull him through.

15 August 1923

HEATH

she had when she sat beside Marjorie but didn't swing her legs.

"You knew, of course," I told O'Donoghue, "That *Grizel* Niven was David Niven's sister and became a sculptress and that Ingaret Giffard married Laurens Van Der Post and that Cheatle committed suicide and so did Sandford who won the Gold!" "I knew about Sandford," he told me, "Barnes wrote R.I.P. after his name." "I don't know what happened to Elizabeth Thynne," I said and O'Donoghue told me Barnes had written R.I.P. after her name as well.

Bruno Barnabe is still going and so is Brian Oulton and, of course, Jean Anderson and Hugh Moxey. I caught him on television only the other day. Esther Thomson, now she married Komisarjevsky or was it Claude Rains? I'm pretty sure it was Rains not Komisarjevsky. Come and seduce me, we used to call him.

Carol Hahn married Llewellyn Rees who became Secretary of Equity, but then afterwards she married Giles Playfair, whose father Sir Nigel ran the Lyric Theatre Hammersmith. "There is a Carol Hahn Memorial Award," O'Donaghue told me, "she was American."

"They were married straight from the Academy I rather think," I told him, "I gave her away, at any rate Llewellyn was *my* best man when I married. I'm afraid it's all getting a trifle blurred. Did you know," I asked, surer of my ground, "that Wallace Finlayson was really Wallace Douglas, Robert Douglas's brother? Robert stepped straight into *Many Waters* as the Jeune Premier and then went into films and still produces them for television. Or than Andre Van Gysegem married Jean Forbes-Robertson? Curigwen Lewis, now she did marry a poet." "Andrew Cruickshank" he reproved me gently. "Joan Hickson is still going strong," I came back at him, "Did you see her in the Ayckbourn play?" *"Bedroom Farce,"* he countered. I began to understand my Aunts and Uncles all those years ago: perhaps it wasn't pretence, forgetting the names.

I was on surer grounds where the staff were concerned. "Miss Elsie Chester had one leg and a crutch she used to throw at us when she couldn't bear it any longer. Helen Haye always acted Grand Duchesses clutching cambric handkerchieves. A great teacher, once after I had been particularly terrible in *The Last of Mrs Cheyney* she firmly opened a copy of the Evening Standard Racing Edition. "I am unlikely," she remarked not unkindly, "to find a winner in this class. We must try Sandown Park."

"There was the great Rosina Phillipi, retired I think by this time, who taught breath control. You were expected to do Mark Antony's speech about Brutus not bringing chariots to Rome in three breaths. For years afterwards I used to test myself. Now if I manage a length underwater in the pool I am content.

"All the staff had their favourite plays, Elsie Chester's was Galsworthy's *The Silver Box,* Herbert Ross (married to Helen Haye) stuck more or less to *Tilly of Bloomsbury,* Norman Page was devoted to one by Dunsany about a Pierrot. Then there was an elocution teacher, or more properly a voice production coach, who made you stand at the end of the room and bounce final consonants off the opposite wall. Hop Poles Unchecked Desire. I still do it."

"Do what?"

Sound the final consonant. None of the young do; that's why I can't hear them, that and because I am a bit deaf."

"Would you like," he said "to go and see the Young People?"

"I'd quite like to go and see the old place."

Like Milton Keynes it had sadly changed. The canteen is upstairs and the basement where it used to be is now a small theatre. It was as if I had never seen the place before. I suppose in a way I hadn't. Once, when I was about to go into the old theatre, I leant heavily against a door which gave way and found myself in the disused box office. Quick as a flash I opened up for business. "It's half-a-crown now for each parent," I told my fellow students as they streamed past. Some of them even gave me their half-crowns. When I had counted up, I slipped inside the auditorium. I couldn't hear the play because of the whispered protests of those who had paid and the gleeful pleasure of those who hadn't. Barnes sent for me later and confiscated the loot for the Building Fund, what was left of it. In those days half-a-crown went a long way, you could eat at Bertorelli's in Percy Street on newspapers for ten pence. A huge bowl of spaghetti and an apple dumpling. Enough for growing boys and girls.

The grown boys and girls were in the basement preparing to rehearse an extemporisation, the sort of thing they do in Hampstead. "At least they don't have to learn the lines," I said to the rather severe young woman who seemed to be in charge. "Indeed they do," she told me, "Once we've decided on the script." "Have you decided on this one?" "Not yet." "Will it be a happy piece?" I asked. "Not particularly," she assured me, "It's about a group of students and their problems. I hope it will be a true picture." I told her I hoped so too and climbed the stairs to retrieve my hat and coat. "What about her," I asked, "is she permanent member of your staff?" "Visiting," he assured me, "after this she is off to the Crucible at Sheffield to stage the same sort of exercise."

"She is leading them down a path only the critics will follow," I told him sagely. There was one chocolate biscuit left on the plate. I munched all the way to the bus stop. Age has its compensations, but then I always had a sweet tooth.

"Your Majesty, this is the Royal Command Performance. You plant the tree tomorrow!"

UNCLE VANYA
(Old Vic)

This play, which begins on a hot afternoon of summer, ends rightly in the dark of an autumn evening. Rightly, because autumn fits Chekhov's mood. He is (for all his incidental humours) pre-eminently the dramatist of nostalgia, of regret and frustration, falling leaf and fading tree, the sunset's smouldering embers, the note of a far violin. "A plague of sighing and grief!" say the sceptics. Let them say. In the theatre Chekhovian melancholy can be a profound enchantment, always assuming—and here lies the point—that the piece is not presented as some esoteric Russian ritual but is left to speak for itself and to move at its own pace.

Mr. JOHN BURRELL, producer of the Old Vic revival, has already succeeded with a Shakespearean history, *Richard the Third*—which partners *Peer Gynt* as the top of the season's performance—and with the Shavian

"Rack your brains, Findlay — I'm certain there's a foundation stone around here somewhere."

Arms and the Man. We gather, alas, that he prefers his Chekhov in slow-motion. No one wants *Vanya* to whirl on a merry-go-round, but Mr. BURRELL has chosen a bath-chair. How it dilly-dallies by the way! Our enchantment frays into a puzzled exasperation. This, we murmur—sadly against our wish—will last out a night in Russia when nights are longest there. The misconception is especially unfortunate because the Old Vic Company, with Mr. RALPH RICHARDSON as *Vanya* and Mr. LAURENCE OLIVIER as doctor and man of the trees, is now the strongest cast upon our stage. It could have done so much with the piece—and can do much still if only the pauses are docked and the action is permitted to flow.

The play, given here in the CONSTANCE GARNETT translation, is a picture of frustrated hopes in the deep south of Russia at the tail of the nineteenth century. Another title is "Scenes from Country Life," but let no stranger to Chekhov look for a Russian equivalent to our English Mummerset. "Such goings on!" chuckles the old *Nurse* as she watches the characters' aimless to-and-fro and listens to them while they sigh for the moon or write sorrow on the bosom of the earth. Feckless, futile? Maybe; but see how subtly they are established, how Chekhov causes us to hope and grieve (and laugh) with them, and how their shadows linger when the piece is done, the doctor has driven off in the gloom, the pens no longer scratch or the crickets churr, and we have heard the last plaint of *Telyegin's* guitar and left *Sonya* piteously affirming in the autumn night: "I have faith. I have faith."

Individually, the New Theatre players are distinguished. *Vanya* is miserable because his life has been wasted and his future is a void. Loyalty betrayed, love scorned: what chance can there be for a man of forty-seven? Mr. RICHARDSON has mastered this introspective fellow who sees himself of all creatures most deject and wretched, and who is slightly ridiculous, entirely lovable,

intolerably pathetic. The tragi-comic flash of melodrama at the end of the second act is as precisely judged as the third-act deflation. Beside Mr. RICHARDSON stands Mr. OLIVIER'S *Astrov*, the doctor in permanent rural exile who has what *Vanya* lacks, one redeeming passion, his deep-rooted love for the kingdom of the trees. Simply, without a hint of flamboyance, Mr. OLIVIER puts the man before us in his failings and his strength: none could excel the quiet eagerness of the speech over the chart to Miss MARGARET LEIGHTON'S unheeding *Yelena*. Two other performances to honour are those of Dame SYBIL THORNDIKE, gruffly tender as the *Nurse* to whom all alarums are merely the children at their game, and of Mr. HARCOURT WILLIAMS as the *Professor* (with a trace of Skimpole), *Vanya's* fallen hope. Mr. WILLIAMS is merciless to the old humbug, little more than frock-coat, voice and beard.

The *Professor* says of the house at one point: "It's a perfect labyrinth… People wander in different directions, and there is no finding anyone." The wanderers compose the familiar Chekhovian pattern. Two of them are the maddeningly indolent *Yelena* of Miss LEIGHTON, and the *Sonya* whom Miss JOYCE REDMAN transforms movingly into a blessed damozel; it is useless for her to pretend that the girl is plain. Miss BETTY HARDY, an obvious relict, burrows into *Mamma's* pamphlets, and Mr. GEORGE RELPH'S *Telyegin*, guest perpetual, is humbly content to listen in the background and to nod over the throbbing of his guitar.

Here, simply, is a play fitted. Miss TANYA MOISEIWITSCH has set it imaginatively. All the makings of a success are at hand, but—and the reservation is serious—the producer has allowed the audience to drowse and droop. Pools of silence, gulfs of thought—is Chekhov really so portentous? We fear that the revival, last of the New Theatre season, needs itself to be revived before we can say from our hearts, as we wish to do: "So, Uncle, there you are."

J.C.T.

Hamlet and Sickle

As actors become more militant, enter (stage left) DICKINSON

"Vanessa has had to cancel — she's having lunch with Bernard Delfont."

"It's hell out there — the critics have joined forces with the National Front mob."

"I'll have less of the 'comrade' from you, duckie!"

"Someone should tell that Special Branch Inspector that the Samuel Beckett season ended last week."

"Look here — when is the Revolutionary Committee going to do something about the frightful price of oysters at the Garrick Club?"

The Royal Shakespeare Company's new production is "Sherlock Holmes". But not the original Shakespearean version, as presented here by MILES KINGTON

THE CASE OF...
THE DANISH PRINCE

ACT I

Baker Street. No. 221b.
Enter SHERLOCK HOLMES and DOCTOR WATSON
  Sherl. Were all the fiery demons in the nether world
To blow their poisonous smoke up into London,
Compound it with a yellow hue and take
Away our light, they could not make a fouler day
Than we have now.
  Wats.   It's foggy out?
  Sherl.   It is.
A wretched, vile and tedious kind of morning,
And nothing in the post but thanks from Scotland
That I did solve the sudden death of Duncan,
Not to mention Banquo. No doubt by now
You've written up the case and had it published?
  Wats. A little five-act tragedy, with notes
On some of the more striking details.
  Sherl.   And blood,
And fights, deaths, witches, ghosts and all
The melodrama that you inflict on logic,
I'll be bound. Once I'd seen the importance
Of having, not two murderers, but three,
The rest was simple. Have you read the paper?
  Wats. Only the "Morning Post". King Lear's
Still lost. A fascinating trial in Venice.
A case of changed identity in Verona,
And sundry goings on in Windsor. Nothing else.
A noise on the stairs
  Sherl. But here, unless I'm much mistook, comes one
That needs our aid. A case at last!
Enter to them HAMLET
  Ham.   Which one...
  Sherl....Of us is Holmes? 'Tis I. This gentle here
Is Watson, my devoted friend and colleague.
  Ham. Good morrow to you both. You do not know me...
  Sherl. Apart from knowing that you are a prince,
From Denmark, I would hazard, a solitary
That you take snuff, have lately been at sea,
Were frightened by a horse at five and now
Are sitting for your portrait, you are a stranger
  Wats. Good heavens, Holmes!
  Ham.   Do you have magic powers?
  Sherl. Sheer observation. You do wear a crown
And are a prince. You have a Danish accent,
Your shoes have late been knotted by a seaman,
There's snuff upon your ruff, and on your doublet
Some Prussian Blue flicked by a careless painter.
That you do not frequent society
Was clear because you did not knock the door

When entering, and then did leave it standing open.

    Wats. But, Sherlock, what about his childhood fright!

    Sherl. Come, come, dear Watson! Lives there yet a man
Who was not frightened by a horse at five?

    Ham. All that you say is true, and yet I fear
You cannot guess my problem. To be brief,
My father was the King of Denmark, where
Now reigns his brother, my uncle, Claudius,
With as his wife my mother, the late Queen
And Queen again. Sir, I implore your aid.

    Sherl. The grammar's convoluted, but I think
I have the picture. I have the answer too.
The wrong man reigns—*you* should have climbed the throne.

    Ham. No, no, that's Danish law, to instate the brother,
Not the son, What I seek to know
Is how my father was so cruelly murdered?

    Sherl. Your father murdered? Are you sure of this?

Ham. Quite sure. My father's ghost has told me so.

Sherl. I see. *(aside)* Quick, Watson, get your gun. This man's
A raving lunatic. *(To Hamlet)* You have a suspect?

    Ham. I fear the foulest of my uncle, Claudius.

    Sherl. No evidence?

    Ham.   Except that he poured poison
Into the ear of my poor sleeping father.

    Sherl. How know'st thou this?

    Ham.   The ghost did tell me so.

    Sherl. Hmm. *(aside.)* A talkative ghost. Would that he were
Admissible in the court of British justice.

    (To Hamlet) This case is not without its points of interest.
Within a day or two, sweet prince, I may well be
With you in Denmark.

    Ham.   My thanks! *(Exit)*

    Sherl.   Or there again
I may well not. I've better things to do
Than listen to the babblings of mad youths.

Enter CLAUDIUS, disguised

    Claud. Have I the honour to address the well-known
                Holmes?

    Sherl. You do not. That is my trusty colleague Watson.

    Wats. Hello.

    Claud.   Hello. And was that man outside
Young Hamlet, Prince of Denmark?

    Sherl.   So he said.

    Sherl. So he said.

    Claud. And did he spin you some far-fangled tale.
Of how his uncle had contrived his father's death?

    Sherl. That was the drift.

    Claud.   Pay him no heed. He has
A most ingenious mind, but little sense.

    Sherl. Indeed, your Majesty?

    Claud.   You guessed?

    Sherl.   Of course.
You too did leave the door ajar, and wear a crown.
Are there many more like you at home?

    Claud. Nevertheless I swear there's nothing to it.
Remember—you come to Elsinore at your peril.

Exit CLAUDIUS.

Sherl. Better and better! I think it would not hurt
To spend a day or two at Elsinore.
Watson, look up the boats and see which leaves
Tomorrow morning on the Danish line.

Wats. Right ho.

ACTS II, III, IV, and V

Denmark
Enter SHERLOCK HOLMES and WATSON

Wats. A draughty castle this, Holmes, where a man
Could catch his death of cold. I'm glad I brought
My tartan rug.

Sherl. I thought your kilt looked odd...
I wouldn't be surprised if Hamlet's father
Froze to death. But look! What shape is this?
Enter HAMLET'S FATHER'S GHOST.

Ghost. For you to be in Denmark is not meet.
Go now, and get you back to Baker Street.
GHOST vanishes.

Wats. I think he's right, Holmes; I do fear that he
Came from the other world to give us warning!

Sherl. *(With lens)* Then why did he leave prints
                           in this soft earth
Of hunting boots, size ten, one broken heel
And marks of clay upon the instep? Tell me that.
Enter HAMLET.

Ham. 'Tis good to see you, Mr Holmes. Have you
Found aught that might reveal the murderer?

Sherl. A clue or two. But tell me, Prince, is there
A man who served your father at the court
Of whom I might a few light questions ask?

Ham. Alas, alas, one such there was, but he
—Polonius, I mean—has just been stabbed i'th'arras.

Wats. Sounds painful. Is this a Danish malady?

Sherl. And does he live?

Ham.   No, sir, his life has ebbed.

Sherl. Most interesting. And tell me, Hamlet, too,
If Claudius should die, have you a queen?

Ham. I would have had, in fair Ophelia.

Sherl. You would have had? You mean...

Ham.   She's also dead.

Wats. I told you that the castle was unhealthy.

Sherl. I think I start to see some light amid the gloom.
I'll take a walk and meet back in our room.

A graveyard with diggers
Enter SHERLOCK HOLMES

Sherl. Good fellows, may I talk with you and ask
What is't you do?

1st Dig. Why, sir, 'tis meet we dig, though 'tis not meat
We dig, but bones, of that we make no bones,
And then into this hole we place the bones,
Though being bones they are not whole...

Sherl.   Here's five bob.

2nd Dig. To answer questions?

Sherl.   No, to stop thy puns.
Here's five bob more to answer questions with.
Now, tell me straight, is business good or bad?

1st Dig. Not bad, not good. Not good for us, but good
For those that stay alive. 'Tis many a year
Since we did have good digging, people live so long.

Sherl. Except for Hamlet's father.

2nd Dig.   A one-off job.
Since then, nothing. Still, it may pick up.
Ours is a dying business...

Sherl.   I said, no puns!

1st Dig. We're sorry, guv. That's one of our favourite on—

In Elsinore Castle
Enter SHERLOCK HOLMES and WATSON.

Sherl. You know my methods, Watson; when in doubt
Eliminate th'improbably—what is left
Must be the truth howe'er unlike it seems.

Wats. So you have always said, but still I am
In some uncertainty over the murderer's name.
Who was it?

Sherl. I'll tell you presently.
But first I expect some news. This may be it.
Enter to them FORTINBRAS

Fort. Alack! What a dreadful day! The heavens themselve
Could no more cease from weeping than the sea...

Sherl. Come, pull yourself together. I have not time
To listen to long speeches. What's your news?

Fort. Hamlet is dead!

Sherl.   I thought as much. Go on.

Fort. And Claudius! Laertes! Also Gertrude!

Sherl. The whole bang shoot, in fact. That's life.
Or, as my digger friend would say, that's death.

Wats. You have an Australian friend?

Sherl.   Sometimes, Watson.
I wonder if I'm really in detection
Or the better half of an awful music hall act.

Fort. O heavens, weep!...

Wats.   He's off again.

Sherl.   You asked
Just now what was the murderer's name.
I told you. Eliminate all else
And what is left...

Wats.   You mean, its Fortinbras?

Sherl. No, no, he's just the man who brings the news.
The gravediggers. Their trade was bad and threatened by
Redundancy, so they conceived a plot
To slay the highest in the land and profit
By their piecework. Only one mistake they made,
To imitate the ghost and wear their boots the while.
I wrote a monograph on soles you may have read.

Wats. May God have mercy.

Sherl.   Mercy on what?

Wats.   Their soles.

Sherl. That settles it—let's leave this cursed place
Where none do ope their mouths but they do utter puns.
Besides, I have a telegram from Lestrade in the Yard,
Begging for my help in some new case.

Wats. What says he now?

Sherl.   "Othello's wife is dead.
We found her lying lifeless on her bed."

Wats. No sooner is one case accounted for,
Than we go chasing after...

Sherl.   Don't say it!

Wats.   ...some Moor.
SHERLOCK HOLMES knocks Watson to the ground.
Exeunt omnes.

CURTAIN

Mr. Ivor Novello gives a Christmas-Party

Mr. Bernard Shaw impersonates Father Christmas under protest. He says, "My beard is too true to be false."

Miss Elizabeth Pollock gives an imitation of herself imitating a child reciting "Casanovabianca."

The Aldwych Quartet play Blind Man's Brough.

Miss Edith Evans adapts herself to the occasion.

Mr. Ivor Novello gives an extract from Mr. Cochran's coming novelty, "Songs Without Words or Music."

Mr. Noel Coward (to waits singing "Noel! Noel!"), "Well, what is it?"

A Pas de Deux by the Dubarry and the Jimmiebarrie.

Mr. Sydney Howard circulates refreshment (Honi Soit Vintage, 1932).

BEHIND THE
SCENES AT LAST
Janet Suzman

"I lived with down-and-outs to get the correct feeling of what it was like, wrote a play, couldn't sell it, now I'm down and out."

Hot Flushes, Exercise, Diet, Respectability, Courtesy, Breakdown, Morale, Perspective, Humility, Self-Help—if these sound like exhortations to a Fuller Life for menopausal widows, you're wrong. They are just a few of Clive Swift's unexpected sub-headings in his book *The Job of Acting—A Guide to working in the Theatre* (£2.95 from Harrap and worth it).

This is a handbook for beginners; amusingly illustrated by Heath, carryable, and with a useful margin on the left for scribbling in. It's as wholesome and gritty as a brown loaf, and Swift (an actor himself) has clearly used his in thinking to write it in the first place. He saw that the daily banalities, aggravations and unwritten laws (lores?) of the acting profession needed chatting about and he has done just that. Quite on purpose, he leaves out what Arthur Koestler has recently described as the "oceanic" side of things, and sticks to the title he chose. Consequently the book is utterly readable, bereft of claptrap, and chocablock full of useful information. Not for me so much, because I'm an old hand (well, oldish), but I can see how positively biblical this book will be to young people wanting to become an actor. It should be on every Careers Office shelf.

Who on earth has ever bothered to tell a kid how their VAT and Income Tax Schedules will work, whether to tip dressers, which answering service to have, what agents do (or don't), games to play when you're bored stiff, and even whether marriage is an advisable contract to enter into given the inhospitable hours of work? More pertinently, he describes the functions of the people who make a theatre/TV/film production happen, so that the trembling newcomer won't land up asking the prop-man for a Kleenex. Most pertinently he advises "Don't go straight from school to Drama School; taste the world first."

I quibble, though, with a couple of his ideas. "Why is there no school … that tries at least to put students through a real situation…?" Well, money for one thing, and for another I'm not sure that Drama School is simulated-command-module time. With a touch of native cunning and an eye sharply out for pseuds (which he should be pretty good at, after all, being a drama student), when he goes out into the big, bad, unemployed world, he should be able to cope with his professional weightlessness. No, it's the Miss Havershams who do the damage. At one of our big drama schools, I once witnessed a class in something designated Period Movement. As if there were such a thing! Every ninny knows that you move like you do because of what you wear. Try slouching around in a Restoration corset and you'll soon squeeze your lungs and liver to perdition!

However, Swift's swipe at the DES's financial neglect of Drama Schools, which do not have the status of "further education" that Art and Music colleges have, is justified. Do we not have the greatest dramatic literature in the world? Is not British theatre a huge tourist attraction blah blah? Yes. He swipes, too, at the annoying little pimples of "Mrs. Pennywhistle's Acting Academies" on this grandiose visage, which are "rife in the British Isles", but which, I daresay, haven't done all that much harm in the long run. A big talent is rare, as in every profession, and it won't be crushed too easily by her dainty feet. Still, the Gulbenkian Foundation's Committee of Enquiry into Drama Schools might help to streamline the nonsense, as Swift points out.

He proposes—quibble number two—that actors "ought to be paid expenses when attending auditions and interviews: certainly when no work results". On the very next page he notes that "auditions and interviews are part of our way of life". Exactly. And anyway travelling expenses for such things are tax-deductible. The strain on our *amour propre* is part of *la guerre,* even if it's not too *magnifique.*

He seems to have left nothing out, even down to spending a moment on dressing-room behaviour: "It is advisable to stay away from dressing-rooms if enthusiasm and even gratitude is not the driving force of your visit." Right on! I would add that all who enter, unexpected, should treat the incumbent as if he were blind and senile, and announce themselves loudly and *in full.* It is agonising trying to place a face when the asp is still metaphorically stuck to your bosom. Like people who sign Christmas cards with their first names only.

I like Swift's laconic style: "Brecht (Berthold, wiry, intellectual, German)"; his simplicity: Shakespeare's "the most commercial dramatist we've got"; his warmth: "Critics take the place of Mother (will she, won't she approve?)." Gosh, I never thought of that. I like his odd anecdotes: Francisco Goldblatt interviewing Athene Seyler—"Tell me what you've done?" "You mean this morning? I went shopping", his common sense: "Don't spend top prices at top photographers, they are rarely worth it".

He scatters definitions like corn and they are all acceptable. "Acting is performing in a disciplined and rehearsed way, and being able to do so in a variety of styles." "You are the spokesman for your character, you put his case." "Acting is a sport ... Play, players, playing." "The best theatre is produced by the best team." "Acting is energy. In the theatre you pay to see energy." "Actors seem to have power over other people." "Actors are like mercenary soldiers. We sell our skills to all comers but the choice of commitment is ours." "The best shows are the ones that give more life to the audience." "Good theatre grows like a plant. It is impossible to say exactly who was responsible for which cleverness." "We make the truth." "Acting is stopping people coughing", and again "Acting is partly dreaming" (both attributed to Sir Ralph Richardson). "We act, a lot of us, to exceed our grasp." "We all perform all the time...life is a business of role-playing." "The theatre is the lay-church. The actor is a priest" (Peter Brook). "When acting is an art it has the quality of redemption which is of more value than money". This last, I would guess, lies closest to Clive Swift's heart.

Out of this amiable but dense little book there seem to be two vital themes to be extracted. Swift repeatedly stresses his dislike of the actor being a passive pawn on the managerial chessboard. Self-help. And if acting is to be perceived as something more than sheer entertainment, it is redemptive because only through the ritual assumption of a role can the truth be told; a paradox which often eludes the layman.

HOW TO BEHAVE AT THE THEATRE
Kenneth Dear
1946

Before making your way to the theatre, examine your tickets to see when the performance is due to begin. If you discover at six-twenty that the play is timed to start at six-thirty, and if your journey to the theatre will take ten minutes, your party obviously has time for some more drinks. Pour stiff ones; they will help you later to forget that you are sitting through a Shakespeare thing instead of that wizard show Bunny just couldn't get tickets for.

You should reach the theatre at six-fifty or, with luck, even later. On entering the foyer the ladies should scamper away, shouting that they will only be a minute, and the men should leave their hats and coats with the little woman in the cupboard up the stairs. One man, however, should retain his overcoat; *this is important.*

When the ladies eventually return the party should advance into the auditorium. The noiseless progress of the attendant who leads you to your seats is intended to ensure that no one misses a single decibel of your conversation, so stop in the gangway and discuss who is going to sit next to whom. Ignore any suggestions proffered by members of the audience; they do not know in what order you wish to sit, and in any case you should not make a hasty decision, for sitting next to the wrong person may spoil your entire evening—particularly at a Shakespeare thing.

The last member of your party to enter the row should be the man with the overcoat. While the rest of you are rattling your seats he should remain in the gangway with the programme-girl. He should say *"How* much?" and drop a handful of silver on the floor. After he has collected most of it he should say "There's another half-crown somewhere" (this encourages people to move their feet surreptitiously), and then wriggle towards his seat, making sure that his overcoat is hanging over his arm. This manoeuvre enables the coat to brush people's hair the wrong way, and gives them something to think about until the interval.

When the people in front have stopped fidgeting, someone with a cigarette-lighter—preferably one that does not work until it has been clicked twenty times—should hold it over his programme and announce the title of the play, before saying "Elsinore," "Rome," or "Act One." One of the ladies can then say "We went there with the Tonghams, darling," or "What a pity we haven't any chocolates!" or make any other comment likely to interest the audience.

After a few minutes, which can be spent in coughing or shaking a bunch of keys, a member of the party at one end of the row should ask, "Is Gielgud in it?" This question should be passed along to whoever is at the other end of the row, and he should say "No," "Yes," or "I don't know" as the case may be. His remark should be passed back to the original enquirer, who should then say "Oh" *indistinctly,* so that the original answerer can ask "What did Bunny say?" What Bunny said should then be transmitted along the row, as before.

In front of your party there is certain to be a woman wearing a small hat. When someone on the stage is soliloquizing, one of the ladies

*"Well, they **are** from Verona but I'm afraid that's about as far as it goes."*

should demand the removal of the headgear—conveying by the tone of her voice that she objects to the hat primarily because it is too hideous to be worn in public, even by the terrible woman who is wearing it now.

When the hat has been removed members of the party should exchange cigarettes, and after a lively discussion on the merits of Virginian and Turkish the man with the reluctant lighter should circulate his handy little gadget among his friends. You should be able to make quite a nice smoke-screen before an attendant tells you that smoking is not permitted in the auditorium. Take your time over understanding what the attendant says, then drop your cigarettes and allow them to burn the carpet before extinguishing them.

If you are fortunate, one of the men will know when to expect the first interval, and this knowledge will enable you to reach the bar well ahead of the unimaginative people who wait until the curtain falls. Drink, relax, and refill your glasses; there is no hurry.

When you decide to return to the auditorium, stroll down the gangway saying "Oh, it's started," and push well into row K before discovering that row G is further down. Arrange yourselves at your leisure, then look at the stage; one of you may notice an actor who resembles a friend, and this amazing coincidence should be the subject of general comment and unrestrained hilarity.

Remain seated during the second interval, and if anyone tries to surmount your outstretched legs allow your expressions to indicate that *some* people just don't seem to know what moderation is.

After part three has been in progress for about twenty minutes you should all whisper that if you don't leave now you'll be late for your table. Fidget until a love-scene is in progress, then surge desperately into the gangway.

When you are all at the door marked "Exit," the man who had the overcoat should remember that he has forgotten to bring it out. He can then run down the ganway, wriggle back into row G, and return dragging his coat so that it brushes everyone's hair the *other* way, and you can all have a good laugh about it as you stand outside waiting for a taxi.

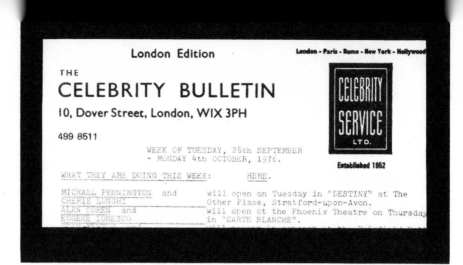

BARE ESSENTIALS
Alan Coren

If you ring the number listed above, and if you ask how it comes about that Alan Coren and Eugene Ionesco should be appearing in Mr Tynan's latest flesh-mortifying erotorama, a very nice lady will—as far as it is possible to do so over the telephone—blush, and tell you that it is all a terrible mistake for which they have already apologised to an incensed Mr Coren, whose relatives have been jumping out of high windows rather than face the opprobrium attendant upon the scion of their ancient line running round in public with his clothes off.

Yet despite her fulsomely apologetic denials, may there not still be some unkind souls out there who, when they see smoke, shout 'Fire!'? Is it not possible, I hear some of you say, that literati eke out their paltry livings by leading such devious double lives?

Should I, in short, come clean?

How strange that history is almost invariably made in inauspicious places! To think that the revolution which was to change not just the theatre but the whole tone and temper of modern convention should have undergone its birth pangs at that lowly environ, the Alhambra, Bradford!

We had been engaged to open the second half on that chill February Monday, just a few short years ago: IONESCO & AL, A JOKE, A SONG, A SMILE. We were in our bleak little bedsitter in Mrs Compton-Burnett's Theatrical Boarding House, wiring our revolving bow-ties to the batteries in our hats and polishing the climax of our act (Ionesco: 'My dog's got no nose.' Me: 'Your dog's got no nose? How does he smell?' Ionesco: 'Awful!') when there was the most fearful thumping and barking from the floor above.

'Stone me!' cried Ionesco, snatching off his rubber conk in justifiable irritation. 'How do they expect us to rehearse with all that bleeding racket going on? Are we artistes or are we not?' He hopped to the door on his giant shoes, and wrenched it open. 'IVY!' he roared.

Mrs Compton-Burnett came heavily up the creaking stairs. She pushed a wisp of ginger hair under her mob-cap with a dripping soup-ladle.

'Madame,' said Ionesco, hand on hip, left profile tilted to the

"Who's the pretty little filly in the second row?"

bulblight, 'us acolytes of bleeding Thespis are at pains to...'

'It's T.S.Eliot,' said Mrs Compton-Burnett, 'he's got that bloody seal upstairs with him again. I don't know how many times I've told him.' She leaned into the stairwell. 'YOU BRING 'IM DOWN OUT OF THERE, MR ELIOT!' she shrieked. 'I GOT ENOUGH TROUBLE WITHOUT CODS' HEADS IN THE S-BEND!'

An upstairs door opened, and T.S.Eliot's top-hatted head appeared over the banister.

'Boris is an artiste,' he shouted. 'You cannot expect him to spend his days juggling jam-jars on his hooter and his nights in a bloody toolshed! A seal has his pride, too.'

'Well, some of us is trying to synchronise revolving bows and funny walks down here,' Ionesco shouted back. 'Don't bloody mind us, mate!'

'TENANTS OF THE HOUSE!' yelled Eliot. 'THOUGHTS OF A DRY BRAIN IN A DRY SEASON!'

He slammed the door again.

'Patter!' snapped Ionesco. 'That's all he is, bloody patter. First house Monday night at Bradford, who gives a toss whether he should have been a pair of ragged claws scuttling across the floors of silent seas? Get the seal on, get your plates up on your sticks, tell 'em the one about the one-legged undertaker, and get off. Never mind your bleeding patter!'

The door across the landing opened, and two fat men in fright wigs emerged. Between them stood a balding midget.

'I don't think you've met Evelyn Waugh's Harmonica Fools,' said Mrs Compton-Burnett. 'Evelyn, Alec, and little Auberon.'

We all shook hands.

'Only trying to rehearse the bloody *Thunder And Lightning Polka*, weren't we?' said Evelyn, testily. 'Got into the middle twelve and going like the bloody clappers, suddenly there's all this shouting, Morris the Musical Dog bites Alec in the leg, little Auberon falls off his shoulders, bang!'

Mrs Compton-Burnett stroked the midget's pate.

'Did he hurt himself, then?' she murmured.

The midget opened its mouth, and a strange discordant wheeze came out.

'Only swallowed his wossname, hasn't he?' snapped Evelyn. 'His organ.'

'What will you do?' I said.

'I'll have a heart attack, that's what I'll do,' said Evelyn. 'I'll bang my head on the wall. Better ideas you got?'

'We should never have left Poland,' said Alec.

They went back inside.

'Come on,' said Ionesco, 'we're on in half an hour, and J.B.Priestley's borrowed my bloody monocycle, we'll have to take a short cut across the allotments.'

A far door opened.

'*Across the allotments?*' cried a voice. 'Why, as you wend your way 'twixt elm and privet, who is this bounding up to you? "Arf, arf!" it goes. "Why, it is Rover the dog!" you cry, "and who is this with him?" "Baa, baa!" "Goodness me!" you exclaim, taken somewhat aback, "what is this little lamb doing so near the pig-sty?" "Oink, oink!" the pigs inform us, their little...'

We went back to our own room, and shut the door.

'C.P.Snow,' explained Ionesco. 'A professional to his fingertips. Ever heard his starling?'

I shook my head.

'A masterpiece,' said Ionesco. 'I seen him do it riding bareback at Bertram Mills' one Christmas, I'll never forget it. 'Course, I'm going back a bit now. It was when he was with Compton Mackenzie's Elephant Ensemble.'

'They were great days, I understand,' I said.

'The best, son,' said Ionesco, his eyes moistening. 'Remember Graham Greene & His Krazy Kar? That was one of the Queen Mother's favourites, you know. She used to send Graham a pound of cobnuts from the Sandringham estates every Guy Fawkes' Night. We go back a long way, him and me. I knew him when he was Brian Breene.'

'I didn't know he'd changed his name,' I said.

'Had to,' said Ionesco. 'Started out as a ventriloquist. The dummy used to introduce him, and afterwards people'd come up to him in the street and say "I know you, you're Grian Greene" so he decided to make life easier for himself.'

We packed our props and stage suits in our hold-alls, went downstairs through the reek of cabbage and dove-droppings, and walked briskly through the sleet to the theatre.

Stone-faced matrons thronged the foyer, and bronchitic British Legionnaires, and drunks with Brasso bottles in their hip-pockets, and malevolent small boys a-gleam with bright acne. There was a smell of rainsoaked dandruff.

'Bloody hell!' said Ionesco, the seams lengthening in his sad Rumanian face. 'I'd rather be opening the first half, son, before they've had a chance to get their eye in. It'll be like the bloody Somme after the interval.'

We crept past them, and down the back stairs to the mean little dressing-room we shared with Angus Wilson. He was sitting slumped in the corner, in his horse's head. There was despair written all over the little white legs poking out beneath the dappled torso.

'What's up, then, Angus?' said Ionesco.

"Give us a quid or I'll tell you who dun it!"

The head turned, very slowly, towards us. Its glass eyes rolled.

'Me hindquarters,' it said, 'have gone down with sciatica. I just heard.'

'No!' cried Ionesco, 'old Betjeman not turned up?'

'Crippled,' muttered the horse. 'Lying there like Gregor bleeding Samsa. What am I going to do?'

'*We're* not on till the second half!' I cried, in true showbiz tradition. 'Why don't I do the back legs for you? It's the easy bit, no singing or juggling involved, just the tap-dance at the end.'

'It's very nice of him, Eugene,' said the horse, 'but he doesn't understand, does he?'

'You don't understand,' said Ionesco, to me. 'Angus can't get in a horse with any Tom, Dick or Harry, no offence meant. It's a very intimate relationship. It's got to be built up over the wossname, years.'

'It wouldn't feel right,' said the horse.

'Look,' said Ionesco, 'Suppose we both got in?'

'Don't talk bloody daft,' said the horse. 'Six legs hanging down? We'd look like a giant ant. I'm not billed as ANGUS THE WONDER INSECT, am I?'

'I didn't mean that,' said Ionesco. 'You go off home, me and him'll do your act. The management'll never know.'

'Would you really?' cried the horse.

'Say no more!' replied Ionesco.

We went on fourth, after H.E.BATES, WIZARD OF THE XYLOPHONE, and we managed well enough, despite some personal embarrassment during the somersault, but when we returned to our dressing-room, we found ourselves to be so sweat-wrung that there was nothing for it but to take off the underwear in which we had performed the act and hang it in front of the electric fire to dry. After which we turned to our mirrors, in order to make up for our own act. So intent was I upon this, that I did not notice the smell until Ionesco suddenly turned from his dressing-table and said:

'What's burning?'

'Burning?' I said, 'I don't…'

'FIRE!' shrieked Ionesco, and I looked round, and our underwear had not only ignited, but had also set fire to the curtains! As the flames licked the pelmets, Ionesco and I rushed, naked, for the door.

The corridor was packed. C.P.Snow was mooing expertly to himself, The Singing Pakenhams were combing one another's coifs, Cyril Connolly and Doris were shoving cards up one another's sleeves—the exit was completely blocked!

'Come on!' cried Ionesco, and we took off in the opposite direction, not knowing, in our panic, where we were going, until, suddenly we burst through a door and found ourselves in the middle of the spotlit stage, from which the previous act (W.H.AUDEN, HE FILLS THE STAGE WITH FLAGS) had just made his exit.

The audience roared!

The audience shrieked!

The audience cheered!

'Come on!' I hissed, grabbing his bare arm. 'Let's get off!'

'*Get off?*' cried Ionesco. 'GET OFF? Laddie, we'll never get a reception like this again!' He threw an arm around my naked shoulder. 'I say, I say, I say!' he shouted. 'What's got nine legs, three ears, and walks like my Uncle Bert?'

It was still not too late for me to run, but the applause of the crowd filled my ears, and the smell of the greasepaint, and the blaze of the lights, and all those wonderful things ravished my senses, and…

'I don't know,' I replied, 'what *has* got nine…'

And after that, we never looked back.

AT THE PLAY

LOOK BACK IN ANGER
(Royal Court)

John Osborne, the author of *Look Back in Anger,* makes it clear from the start that he intends to kick us in the teeth, and go on kicking us. "Squeamish, are you?" we can hear him saying, "you just wait!" So he draws liberally on the vocabulary of the intestines and laces his tirades with the steamier epithets of the tripe butcher. His hero, who for most of the evening is roaring his contempt for the middle and upper classes and indeed for any orderly plan of living, is a very tiresome young man, an exhibitionist wallowing in self-pity. He bullies and humiliates his wife, whose prim parents have not unnaturally opposed the marriage, and when his social rage is temporarily exhausted he weeps at the infinite sadness of his life. If you ask why he behaves like a spoilt baby, the answer is hard to find, except that this is Freud's centenary and I suspect Mr. OSBORNE of an over-dose of Tennessee Williams; all that can be claimed in the man's defence is an unhappy childhood, but otherwise, in spite of having a degree behind him, he has chosen to quarrel with everyone, run a sweet-stall and live in an animal way in an abysmally sordid one-room flat.

The very odd thing is that Mr. OSBORNE seems to expect us to sympathize with this creature, as if he were a reasonable representative of a betrayed and bewildered generation. Anyone less deserving of sympathy I cannot imagine; self-pity hardens the most charitable heart. One is sorry for his wretched little wife, pulverized by his verbal artillery (one began to feel bruised oneself) and delighted when she leaves him; but I could have smacked her for her final grovelling return, in hysterical renunciation of all the creeds black-listed by bed-sitter nihilism. Is this supposed to be a splendid gesture on behalf of the self-oppressed? In any case it is no end to the play, for the whole silly cycle of torture and collapse will clearly begin again.

This is a first play, and if I have been hard on it it is because Mr. OSBORNE has not done justice to his own powers. He has a good turn of wit and phrase, and an ability, when he is not over-writing, to express himself with force. There are moments here, swamped by bitterness and hysteria, that might have been moving; and though the dialogue holds up the action by trying to be too clever, it is not without quality. Having got this gall out of his system he should write a more interesting play.

The heavy burden of almost constantly addressing a public meeting is carried by KENNETH HAIGH, slightly monotonously but with spirit. Pale and crushed, MARY URE dumbly conveys the nervous strain of living with a masochist, and there is a good performance by ALAN BATES as the simpleton friend who stands by faithfully. HELENA HUGHES plays the upright visitor who loathes her host and then, when his wife leaves him, suddenly becomes his mistress. One moment she is smacking his face in fury, the next, to our great astonishment, they are locked together. I felt she would never have stayed five minutes in such a zoo, but Miss HUGHES went some way to persuading me.

"Well, I'm glad to hear your stage-struck daughter is thriving, but you know, dear, a call-girl isn't quite the same sort of thing as a call-boy."

94

AT THE READING OF A PLAY

CHAPTER I.—DIRECTIONS TO ACTORS.

HE Handy-book will deal first with the Actors, not only because they are the objects of most public interest in a theatre, but because they are the real foundation-stones of the theatrical edifice.

"THE ACTORS MAKE THE THEATRE."

Let this fundamental principle be deeply impressed on the mind of every one who follows that noble profession, which can boast the names of a SHAKSPEARE, a BEN JONSON, and a GARRICK. It will encourage self-respect, which the lingering influence of a wretched social prejudice might otherwise impair in the Actor, and teach him a lesson he needs above all men—to set a proper value on himself. Besides, a conviction of this truth is, in a great measure, the secret of the Actor's public importance—the key-stone of his position. We may be told that the Manager and Author are just as essential to the fortunes of a theatre as the Actors. But where would the Manager or Author be without the performers? The one has merely to settle the plans of his theatrical campaign, to find pieces and capital, to pay his company, to hear their complaints, arrange their little difficulties, protect their interests, and find them proper opportunities for the display of their abilities. Anybody can make a Manager. Don't we see, every day, men who have failed in every other calling, taking up this, and doing just as well in it, apparently, as those who have been at it all their lives? In comparison with the Actor's the Manager's work is child's play. And besides being easy, it is mole-like, dull, obscure, and mechanical. You can no more put the two on the same parallel than you can level distinctions between the crawling grub or torpid chrysalis and the brilliant butterfly. As for putting the Author before the Actor, you might as well say the tailor was greater than the man who wears clothes. The Author is the poor drudge who laboriously fashions the pale outer husk and dead case of the part, which it is the Actor's business to endow with life, colour, and motion. *He* is the true creator, who breathes over the dry bones of the play-wright, and bids them put on flesh, and rise and walk. That this is the right estimate of the two callings, is shown by their relative position and remuneration. Compare the social position of the Actor—courted, *fêted*, caressed, the darling of the public—with that of the Author, an obscure drudge, too often shy, shabby, altogether the sort of person to fight shy of rather than *fête* or ask to dinner. Put the rewards of the successful Play-actor by those of the successful Play-writer. The one shall be receiving his £50 a night, perhaps, for his performance in a play the Author of which thinks himself well paid by a fiftieth part of that sum. Look at the Author—even the successful Author—before the Manager. What do we see? A poor creature, submissive, if not abject, thankful for an audience, grateful for a payment on account, submitting to snubs and sneers, glad to clip, and carve, and remodel his work at his customers' dictation—too thankful to have it tried upon any terms, and the bill paid. Then see the Actor in the Manager's room, dictating the terms of an engagement—throwing up a part, or exacting satisfaction for a grievance or failure of proper respect. You find in him a man animated by a becoming sense of his importance to the theatre, dealing with his Manager rather as a superior than an equal, imposing his own terms, buoyant, and self-confident with that noble assurance which springs from the proud sense of power, and the invigorating consciousness of universal recognition.

As, then, the Actor is the back-bone of the theatre—the working pivot of the whole stage machinery—it is with the Actor that our Handy-book first deals.

But the reading and rehearsal of a Play must precede the acting of it, and in both the Actor has some concern.

A few rules, therefore, for his guidance on these occasions, may properly precede our hints for his conduct on the Stage :—

Do not trouble yourself to be punctual to a few minutes—if your position in the theatre renders you safe from a fine. Nothing is so foreign to the spirit of an essentially artistic calling as a mechanical, business-like exactitude. Time was made for slaves—such as clerks, men-of-business, lawyers, tradesmen, and railway guards—not for the volunteers enlisted in the delightful service of the Arts.

Besides, a little waiting will give the Author time to collect himself. If he know his place, he will feel timid and nervous, as inferiors must be expected to feel in the presence of their betters; if he do *not* know his place, it will be wholesome to teach him; and for this purpose nothing is better than to let him kick his heels for a little time on a cold stage, or in an empty green-room.

Be careful in your demeanour, and in any remarks you may address to the Author—I do not object to your speaking to him, though I must caution you against any undue familiarity, *which is pretty sure to be presumed upon*—to show that you thoroughly understand his position and your own. Do not let him for a moment forget that he is conversing with a superior.

When summoned to the reading, do not take your seat hurriedly, and never submit to any discomfort, such as a place near the door or the fire, or a possible exposure to draught. To do so, shows a disposition to put up with slight and disrespect, which is fatal in a theatre. Always take the best place, and then find fault with it. This will show you are not a person to be put upon, and will prepare the Author for that critical severity in your judgment of his piece which is the kindest service you can render him.

If a lady, you will, of course, take the opportunity of the Author's opening his manuscript, to recognise your particular friends in the company, exchange the civilities of the morning—which should never be omitted in a theatre, where good-breeding ought ever to find a home—and any remarks which may be naturally suggested by last night's performance, the play-bills of the day, or the morning papers. These little neighbourly attentions cannot be so well paid later in the reading, and they will help to put the Author at his ease, and show him he is among friends who make no ceremony with him.

Be careful how you choose your place. Always command a mirror, and avoid a strong light. You will thus be able to observe the play of emotion on your own features during the reading—the most improving study for the Actor—and you will avoid exposing your complexion to that disagreeable observation, from which even the cordial good-feeling and mutual forbearance generally to be found among members of the same company will not always preserve you.

I need hardly caution you against feeling—much more showing—an interest in the scenes as the reading proceeds. Interest is the most uncritical of all possible moods of mind, and as completely unfits you for clear judgment, as a keen appetite for the appreciation of refined cookery. If you feel an interest growing up, in spite of your better judgment, struggle against it. Think of something else. Blow your nose noisily. Shift your position. Whisper to a neighbour. Rise to shut or open the window . . . or pretend to fall into a doze, and wake suddenly, with an exclamation. You will thus break the chain not only of your own ideas, but of your companions', and, probably, the Author's, and recall him to the region of hard fact, from which he may be beginning to stray under the united operation of his self-conceit and the mischievous excitement of reading.

One useful rule for destroying any interest the piece may be awakening is not to listen to any part but your own. The unerring instinct of the artist will, of course, soon guide you to the character intended for yourself. Follow that closely and critically, and see that, in justice to himself, as well as to you, the Author does not trifle with it. Remember that golden rule of your art—to think that the success of the piece rests entirely on *your* shoulders. In this way, only, can thorough devotion to your part be secured. Any attention to the other parts will naturally weaken your interest in your own, and so diminish your contribution to the effect of the piece.

If every Actor follow this rule, the result will, of course, be, that all the parts will be strengthened, and the effect of the *ensemble* raised in proportion.

But even if your part should leave nothing to be desired, you will, of course, be careful not to let the Author see that you think so. Besides the general impolicy of encouraging a class at all times too ready to presume, it is clearly against your interest *ever* to be satisfied, as you may thus bar the way against future requirements. The best part is likely to have its weak points. Carried away by the general effect, you may at first overlook these. But be cautious how you yield to your first impression. Never commit yourself to strong approbation. Shrug your shoulders; grumble inaudibly; tell the Author you have failed to discover the part meant for you; and when he tells you, smile, and appear surprised, and say that somehow you do not see yourself in it.

You will thus prepare the Author's mind for any demands you may afterwards find it your duty to make upon him for the enrichment or strengthening of your part; or in the improbable event of your remaining satisfied with it as written, his mind will be more relieved than if you had never grumbled.

TAILS OPTIONAL
Eric Keown

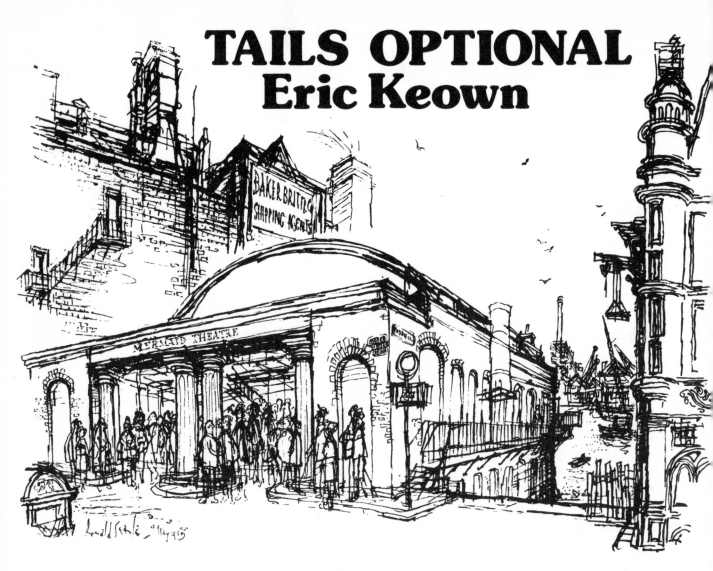

© **Ronald Searle**

Puddle Dock is a tiny tidal inlet, a few yards across, in the Thames just below Blackfriars Bridge. Behind it is the site of the Blackfriars Theatre. Inland, a little way down on the opposite bank, was the Globe. In a neighbouring street Shakespeare bought a house for £140.

Next week, on this amply historical site, a theatre will open which will be new in every way. The Mermaid is the first playhouse to go up in London for twenty-six years, and the first in the City for two hundred and fifty. It has been built by public subscription, with a lease from the City Corporation of £100 a year, and it owes everything to the vision of one man—Bernard Miles.

It all began eight years ago in his back garden in St John's Wood, where Miles built a small Elizabethan theatre in an old schoolroom and gave us Shakespeare as nearly as possible as it was done in Shakespeare's time. Here he persuaded Kirsten Flagstad to sing thirteen performances of *Dido and Aeneas* for a fee of a bottle of stout a day. A second season followed, and during it the Lord Mayor was so impressed that he offered the Piazza of the Royal Exchange to brighten the City for the Coronation. The stage of the first Mermaid was dismantled and re-erected, and during thirteen weeks in the summer of 1953 seventy thousand people flocked to see Elizabethan plays.

Bernard Miles has a sly sense of humour, and it delighted him to think he had overthrown the last prejudices of the City against his profession. Rogues, whoremongers, coney-catching rascals, the City had called the players; but here it was, acting as a benevolent godparent. This was a miracle. It linked up with his dream of a popular theatre that would bridge the classes and the -isms, it confirmed his belief that the City held a vast audience of starved theatre-goers, and it woke him to the delicious possibilities of industry as patron. In fact it was a very useful practice run for the next edition of the Mermaid that was now taking shape in his mind.

In 1941 a bomb had cleared the site. In 1946 the Corporation granted a lease, and then Bernard Miles went into action. He began to sit on industry's doorstep in a big way, and industrialists found this soft-spoken idealist irresistible. Fat cheques started rolling in. Many gifts in kind came from manufacturers, and at the same time a tide of small contributions began to arrive. A carpenter from the warehouse next door has called every week with his half-crown, and thousands like him have given because they were thrilled to think they were building their own theatre. The Mermaid has bitten the imagination of the ordinary Londoner far more than anything for a long time. It will have cost £70,000, including a small reserve for productions, and there are still a few thousands to come in.

Since building began Bernard Miles and his loyal wife, Josephine Wilson, have been almost daily hosts at luncheons on the site at which, recklessly and with complete success, they have mixed industry and the Arts over wine, cheese and sausages cooked on a spirit-stove. Bankers have passed the mustard to rising dramatists with decreasing suspicion; men in beards and sweaters have found sympathetic listeners in men in faultless waistcoats. Much good will has been generated on both sides.

The theatre, designed by Elidir Davies, is really exciting. You are very conscious of the river. When Lennox complains, as he will in due course, that "the obscure bird clamour'd the live-long night," it will almost certainly have been a tug. The old warehouse walls have been retained, covered by a span barrel roof. First, a paved courtyard, from which one enters the main foyer, with bars and cloakrooms. Then, the auditorium, its five hundred seats on a sharply raked single tier. Bernard Miles has always been an open-stage man, and now he has got the finest in England, coming right down to the front row. It is a big stage for so small a theatre; it will put the actors in touch with the audience and is designed for big casts. In the middle is a revolve that goes round as easily as a bicycle wheel.

After that, still going towards the river, is the restaurant (with a marvellous view of the whole reach from Blackfriars to Tower Bridge) and the snack bar, and above are dressing-rooms. The whole thing is planned down to the last light-plug. The stage-door opens on a little gallery above the river; the villain can escape down a rope-ladder into his hissing pinnance.

Bernard Miles took us round himself.

"Policy? I want to bridge the gulf between highbrows and lowbrows. It's largely artificial. They're afraid of one another. So I'm starting with a roaring musical based on a Fielding play—he called it *Rope Upon Rope* but we've changed that to *Lock Up Your Daughters* in deference to the sterner City fathers. It'll run for six weeks, twice-nightly, at 6.10 and 8.40. After that *The Antigone* of Sophocles, *Journey's End*, a new comedy, an Elizabethan play, and *Great Expectations* adapted by Alec Guinness. You see, a complete mix-up. I'm negotiating for a Brecht. We want to broaden people's taste, to stop them taking a narrow view of the theatre."

He dodged nimbly over a boa-constrictor of cable.

"We plan to have half the seats at the first house at only five bob, and to give a reasonable meal for the same price, so that a couple can have a night out for a pound. I believe there's a huge audience

waiting at our door. We won't only give them plays—but ballet, jazz, opera, and the theatre's wired for cine. In fact, the lot. It's incredible to start free from debt. All the money that comes in from the box-office can go straight into the production kitty. No bricks-and-mortar men waiting for their whack."

We reached the stage.

"I've a theory that audience and actors have lost each other. Whatever you may say about TV it does project the player bang into the middle of the audience. That's what the Elizabethans did, and that's what we're going to do here, so that everyone can share in the play."

What kind of man is he, this Shakespeare-worshipper, dialect-expert, agricultural music-hall comedian and accomplished entertainer, this single-minded missionary responsible for the astonishing achievement of persuading the City to build its own playhouse? Fifty-one, slight, gentle, horn spectacles, a good listener. He is so modest that you have to be with him a little while before you realize that inside him is an unquenchable fire of enthusiasm.

London has reason to be mightily grateful for it.

THE NEW PLAY.

Low Comedian. "HAVE YOU SEEN THE NOTICE?"
Tragedian. "NO; IS IT A GOOD ONE?"
Low Comedian. "IT'S A FORTNIGHT'S."

24 May 1922

DRAMATISTS AT PLAY

The practice, inaugurated by Mr. ARNOLD BENNETT and Mr. FRANK VERNON, in connection with *The Love Match,* and brilliantly carried on by Mr. GALSWORTHY and Mr. LEON M. LION in connection with *Windows,* whereby author and manager engage in a correspondence in the Press upon the merits and significance of the play, and debate as to whether it is in need of alteration, is about to be followed by a number of other well-known authors and managers.

Thus, with reference to a letter from Mr. NORMAN McDERMOTT, purporting to identify the *Leit-motif* of *Misalliance* with that of *You Never Can Tell,* and suggesting that it would be an improvement if the play could be re-written so as to make it possible for the parts of *John Tarleton, Lina Szchepanowska* and the would-be murderer to be played by the same actor (preferably Mr. GEORGE ROBEY), Mr. BERNARD SHAW proposes to write as follows:—

DEAR SIR,—What Mr. NORMAN McDERMOTT thinks of my plays is not of the slightest interest to me, you or anybody else. His reading of the character of *John Tarleton* shows him to be a Rosicrucian, and his views on *Lina Szchepanowska* mark him down as a supporter of the Nebular Hypothesis in its crudest and most puerile form. Otherwise there is nothing to say except to offer the usual condolences.

I wonder what Mr. McDERMOTT would think if I wrote to the papers giving my views (which as a matter of fact are particularly sound) on the decoration and management of the Everyman Theatre? No doubt he would thank me for the free advertisements; but he would say with perfect justice that it was a damned piece of cheek on my part.

So is his letter to you.

Yours, etc.,   G. BERNARD SHAW.

SIR ARTHUR PINERO is contributing to this symposium, in reply to an appreciation of *The Enchanted Cottage,* contributed to *Form* by Mr. OWEN NARES (on behalf of himself and Mr. MEYER), emphasizing a number of subtleties beyond the comprehension of the ordinary play-goer and throwing out the suggestion that a small modification to the play to make the hero a young Red Indian, the heroine a Russian Princess and the scene of the play a Patagonian village, together with the introduction of a troupe of performing seals in the dream scene of the Second Act, and an exhibition of pemmican-pounding in Act III, would instantly transform the play into a prodigious success. Sir ARTHUR'S reply is too lengthy for reproduction in full. The following is an extract:—

DEAR SIR,—Accustomed as you doubtless are to the eccentricities of the theatrical profession, it must have come, even to you, with something of a shock that Mr. OWEN NARES, for whose qualities as an actor-manager I hasten to express my unbounded admiration, should have contributed to your columns what seems to purport to be a critical examination of the merits and meaning of my play, *The Enchanted Cottage.* I am well aware...and nothing could be further from my thoughts than...which moreover...greatly to be deprecated. Furthermore...and indeed such a course...although I would be the last to deny...deep and entire satisfaction.

But I feel it is incumbent on me to say this: *The Enchanted Cottage,* as its name implies, is an enchanted cottage and not a circus or a menagerie. It is moreover entirely self-sufficient and self-explanatory. And I must add that commentary and suggestion for members of the distinguished cast who were privileged to appear in it, however interesting to their own immediate little circle of friends and relatives, is hardly of such value to the public as to justify its appearance in the great organs of the Press. I am, Yours faithfully,

ARTHUR WING PINERO.

The following letter, which explains itself, will shortly reach us from Sir JAMES BARRIE:—

DEAR SIR,— Mr. HARRISON, in taking off my play, *Quality Street,* has probably written to you explaining that only my refusal to alter the title to *Calamity Street*— a concession to the public demand for strong plays—has induced him to end the run before the full year was up. Sir GERALD DU MAURIER at the same time writes urging me to introduce a scene into *Dear Brutus* in which he may have an opportunity of giving an impersonation of a foreign Prime Minister at the Genoa Conference.

This is the kind of demand that impetuous youth so constantly makes upon its Betters; and it needs courage of a kind that I, alas, do not possess to grant it. I could never again face *Old Lob* if I changed him in the smallest respect; nor can I bear to think of *Quality Street* except as *Quality Street.* No, such as they are, my plays must remain.

Yours sorrowfully,
J.M. BARRIE.

' P.S.—I ought to add that, as usual, that unruly devil, MACCONACHIE, is on the other side, and not only wants to grant Mr. HARRISON his point, but is actually urging me to give Sir GERALD his scene at Genoa and throw in a scene in Purgatory as well.

Works
Pantomime

THE CARETAKER ... or PRIVATE LIFE

The National Theatre in 1976 presented their first revival of *Blithe Spirit* by Noël Coward, in a production directed by Harold Pinter. Were Coward still alive, he would doubtless wish to repay the compliment by directing a Pinter play...

LONG DAY'S JOURNEY INTO NIGHT

LAURENCE OLIVIER as James Tyrone
CONSTANCE CUMMINGS as Mary Tyrone
DENIS QUILLEY as Jamie
RONALD PICKUP as Edmund

ACT ONE

A basement. Dingy perhaps, but not actually dirty. Old furniture, but tastefully arranged. ASTON is alone in the room; he wears an old leather jacket but well-cut trousers off which he's elegantly flicking the cigarette ash. (Nigel Patrick, perhaps?). Enter DAVIES, a tramp but picturesquely dressed and with rather distinguished greying hair. (Wilfred Hyde White?).

ASTON: Hello, matey, who are you?

DAVIES: I came, er, I come for my papers. Here, they said, or Sidcup.

ASTON: Very flat, Sidcup.

DAVIES: There's no need to be unpleasant.

ASTON: It was no reflection on the papers, unless of course they made it flatter. Do you come here often?

DAVIES: No, Budleigh Salterton, mostly. A better class of papers, there, and the moonlight on the bus-station roof is peculiarly attractive.

ASTON: Moonlight can be cruelly deceptive. How will you recognise it?

DAVIES: The moonlight?

ASTON: No, no. Sidcup.

DAVIES: There's bound to be a sign. If not, I shall ask. I'm told that people at bus-stations, if asked, often reply.

ASTON: In what?

DAVIES: English, mostly, or so they tell me: nowadays one must never be too hopeful.

ASTON: I remember a station. Long ago, it was, and terribly far away. Up north, well past Watford. Maybe even Berkhamsted. Or Bletchley. It was in the war—everyone terribly busy with rationing and rock cakes and killing Germans and dressing up in those funny tin hats and there, quite suddenly, unexpectedly, almost surprisingly, there was this woman. An ordinary, middle-aged woman, terribly ordinary and terribly, terribly middle-aged and with a funny sort of look in her eye as if she was really supposed to be wearing glasses. We knew at once, of course.

DAVIES: Knew?

ASTON: That we were terribly, terribly in love. *(He goes over to the piano, old but Bechstein, and starts to play softly).* It was impossible, of course—too, too impossible for words and I suppose that was why we never actually spoke. Just stood there and stared and stared and wished the platform announcer could also have been to elocution classes. Then a train came—quite unexpectedly, really, out of a tunnel and with no sense of timing, and suddenly we knew it was all over. But sometimes, even now, I wake up in the night and wonder somehow if it could all have been different; if there hadn't been that awful fire at the Reichstag and then that common little man with the strange haircut shouting so much, would we have managed to speak? It all seems so terribly terribly sad and often, in the sudden chill of an autumn evening, or whenever Spring breaks through again, I know...

DAVIES: A dark, secluded place, where no...

ASTON: Did you say something?

DAVIES: No, no, I was just wondering about the papers and Sidcup and somehow everything seems so terribly complicated nowadays.

Enter MICK, younger than the other two, suave, Simon Williams perhaps?

MICK: You can't stay here: it's mine. Besides, who are you?
DAVIES: I'm Davies—there's an e before the last s. So important, don't you think? It makes me feel so terribly Welsh, and I always think that's what matters. It's no good feeling just a little bit Welsh.
MICK: What are you doing here?
DAVIES: I'm on my honeymoon.
MICK: Enjoying it?
DAVIES: It hasn't really started. What about you?
MICK: India, just back.
DAVIES: And the Taj Mahal, how was the Taj Mahal?
MICK: Incredible—a sort of dream. You'll have to go.

"More newts - Macbeth is staying to dinner."

DAVIES: So you've said. It's just a question of the fare. Sidcup's not a day-excursion, whatever that might be. People seldom seem to come back.

MICK: Perhaps you'd better stay. I need a man to look after this place—is there anything you can do?

DAVIES: I play the piano a little, look rather good on balconies in evening dress, expanding cigarette holders, that sort of thing. What did you have in mind?

Curtain

ACT TWO

The same, a few seconds later.

MICK: Well?

DAVIES: Not bad, considering the state of the piano. Strange how potent cheap music is.

MICK: I mean, are you staying?

DAVIES: I often think perhaps I should: not terribly, terribly long, just a day or two or until I find her, moonlight behind her, true to the dream I am dreaming. As she draws nearer I'll smile a little smile, for a little while, we shall stand, hand in hand...

MICK: I mean do you want to be the caretaker here, yes or no?

DAVIES: Caretaker? But I've always taken terribly, terribly good care of everything: you don't end up looking like me just by chance, you know. It's in the blood: that and the profile; Elvira always said I had the best cheekbones in Shaftesbury Avenue. Sex, you know, is just a matter of cheekbones. So, of course, is Life.

ASTON: But what about me?

DAVIES: We can all be terribly, terribly good friends and sing little comic songs at the piano and open cigarette boxes and do wonderful things together. It'll be new and gay and terribly exciting, for how ever many others we may have loved in the meantime, and however old and tired we may be, we shall have between us a perfect memory.

MICK: You mean all three of us? Here, in this basement, forever?

DAVIES: Why not? It's London, isn't it? Cockney pride? Jokey barrow boys? Mayfair in the morning, hear your footsteps echo on the empty streets?

MICK: I suppose it's an assumed name, yours?

DAVIES: Assumed, dear boy? Everything is assumed, that's what wrong with the twentieth century—no reasonable assumptions refused.

ASTON: Here we are, then. Forever.

DAVIES: Not necessarily. Maybe only a month or two; then they'll be the tour, after that the film, perhaps even the musical version. At least with nostalgia you know what you've got to look forward to.

Curtain

THE RAKE'S PROGRESS:
THE ACTOR
Ronald Searle

1. OVERTURE *A bonny lad, but witless. Shines in fit-up tour of Private Lives. Sends press cuttings to Old Vic. Gets them back. Complains to Equity*

2. SUCCESS *Finds old "Stage" in the Salisbury-lands job with Donald Wolfit. Spotted by talent scout. Praised by Harold Hobson. Flown to Hollywood*

3. TRIUMPH *Dr Johnson in musical version of Boswell. Oscar. Life story in "Colliers". Man of Distinction. Sends donation to Old Vic.*

4. TEMPTATION *On location in Capri with prominent Continental Starlet. Weds. Immediate offers from Jack Hylton and Old Vic. Chooses Old Vic.*

5. DOWNFALL *Insists on Lear. Underplays in American accent. Ivor Brown carried out screaming. Divorced for mental cruelty.*

6. RUIN *Sells ex-wife's life story to "Reveille". Starts own repertory company. Reserve Hoop-la attendant at Theatrical Garden Party*

RESERVED SEATS WITH A RESERVATION.

Most visitors of the theatre go there to be amused; but they very often meet with diversion besides amusement. Seated in the second or third row of the boxes, after the play has begun, whilst they are closely following the performance in a peculiarly effective part of it, their attention is suddenly diverted therefrom by a party of people who have taken places in front, and who, coming in late, oblige everybody intervening between their seats and the door, to get up and make room to let them pass. This is a diversion which is not only additional, but entirely opposite to the amusement which is afforded by the players; it provokes grins and not laughter; clenched teeth, which hold in language that if uttered would perhaps incur the penalty of a crown.

Ladies and gentlemen who prefer the amusement of listening to the drama to the diversion of mind occasionally, as above described, experienced in theatres, will read with some satisfaction the annexed brief report of a little lawsuit, the result of which affords them hope of future deliverance from that unwelcome diversion:—

"MANAGERS AND PLAYGOERS.— On Saturday, at the Westminster County Court, was tried an action of YOUNG v. BUCKSTONE, lessee of the Haymarket Theatre. The plaintiff, on the 3rd of February, took certain places in the boxes, for which he paid 35s., and received a printed receipt bearing on it the numbers of the seats. Plaintiff and his friends arrived at the theatre after the first act was over, and found his engaged seats occupied. He was offered others, but he declined, and demanded back his money, which was refused, and he brought his action for the amount. The attention of the Judge was called, on the part of the defendant, to a note in the receipt, which said, 'Places secured until the end of the first act only.' The Judge, Mr. F. BAYLEY, held this to be fatal to the plaintiff's case, and entered judgment for the defendant, calling upon the plaintiff to pay the costs of four witnesses who were in attendance from the theatre to give evidence, if necessary."

Playgoers, who are accustomed to go to the play really for the purpose of seeing and hearing it, ought to be greatly obliged to MR. YOUNG, the plaintiff in the above-cited case of YOUNG v. BUCKSTONE, for having generously, out of his own pocket, obtained a legal decision which, if MR. BUCKSTONE'S good example is generally followed by managers, will, in some measure secure them in the undisturbed pursuit of their object. Of course the plaintiff did not happen to notice the condition under which the seats were reserved, noted in the receipt of his 35s., and his lawyer, doubtless, overlooked it also. MR. YOUNG, doubtless, never expected, or was advised, that the letter of the law would bear him out in ignoring so just a stipulation. Otherwise we should most heartily congratulate him on having lost his cause, and had to pay MR. BUCKSTONE'S costs as well as his own, and the costs of MR. BUCKSTONE'S four witnesses, besides having lost his £1 15s., and being deservedly laughed at for his failure in a mean and shabby attempt to "County-Court" MR. BUCKSTONE.

"JOURNEY'S END" (SAVOY).

I WONDER how many of the Wise Men of the West-End who gamble on the London Theatre Exchange told Mr. R. C. SHERRIFF or his agent that the public didn't want to hear anything about the War, couldn't stand seriousness, required happy endings, and anyway went to the theatre to see the well-known player in the star-*rôle*, and here was a play with five equally-balanced parts; told him to take it away and not waste business men's valuable time. Many, I hope, and that they are now gnashing envious teeth. For *Journey's End*, besides being an acutely observed, excellently restrained, poignantly tragic piece of work, is also a box-office winner. I have seldom seen and heard such an enthusiastic first-night reception. I am told that the audiences on succeeding nights have been as deeply moved. The Arts Theatre Club, which gave it a first hearing, has again proved itself a good friend of the theatre.

Journey's End, moreover, is the more effective as a reinforcement of the arguments against war which serious minds are constantly shaping and re-shaping in that it does not concern itself directly with propaganda at all. It simply presents a picture in detail of a small corner of the scene of the greatest of Mankind's Follies as viewed for a few hours from a dug-out, before St. Quentin in the March of 1916, through the actions and reactions of the six officers concerned: *Captain Stanhope*, most efficient, trusted and beloved of company commanders, a highly-strung youngster made old by grave responsibilities, keeping himself by overdraughts of whisky from the terror that walks by day and night, the fear of showing fear and of letting down his job and his men by breaking under the strain; *Captain Hardy*, his stolid, unimaginative and rather slack second, about to go on leave; *Hardy's* relief, *Osborne*, a schoolmaster in the forties, *Stanhope's* trusted deputy and understanding friend; *Trotter*, promoted ranker, plumber in civil

life, magnificent in his work-a-day courage, shrewd unstudied humour and dependability; *Hibbert*, with a mean obscene little mind, a shirker shamming sick in order to get away to the base, untouched by any sense of the shame of letting another bear his burdens—that magnificently human support of courage tending to falter under strain.

Hints of each man's private life, so far as they dare dwell on these sacred far-off things, are given with admirable economy of means by the perceptive author. We catch a glimpse of the girl *Stanhope* loves (he will not go on leave as his turn comes, partly because of his job—you see the born soldier and leader in him—but mainly because he dare not let her see him as he has become, a weakling dependent on a bottle of strong drink); of *Osborne's* wife and child at home and his leave spent in making a rockery by day and reading in the evening by the fireside—the wife sustaining him by her equal courage and her brave reticence; of *Trotter's* missus in Battersea watching behind her Nottingham lace and aspidistra; of *Hibbert's* cherished picture-postcards and squalid pleasures. And, with the coming of the new sub, *Raleigh*, a babe just out of school—*Stanhope's* old school, where he had been a general favourite, hero particularly and friend to young *Raleigh*—

we learn that it is *Raleigh's* sister that *Stanhope* loves. The boy has wangled himself into his hero's company and is aghast at the bitter unfriendliness of *Stanhope's* reception of him.

There does not seem to me one touch of false sentiment or exaggerated emphasis in the author's treatment of his characters. Those who have been through the great adventure assure me of the fidelity of the general picture of the War at this period. The author is wisely restrained in the use he makes of mechanical effects. The clamour of war, the signal lights, the effect of the shells on the fabric of the dug-out are adroitly indicated—no more. The tragedy is very properly set forth in the minds of his characters as betrayed in their speech and necessary actions. In the relief of humour, too, the author shows an admirable restraint. This play may not conform to classical pattern, but it has the ring of authentic tragedy, an epic quality, showing forth the grandeur of human suffering, the magnificence of human courage.

I have left myself little space to speak of the players. I can most truthfully say of the five principals (Mr. COLIN CLIVE, *Stanhope*; Mr. GEORGE ZUCCO, *Osborne*; Mr. MAURICE EVANS, *Raleigh*; Mr. MELVILLE COOPER, *Trotter*; Mr. ROBERT SPEAIGHT, *Hibbert*) that they all rose to the full height of their admirable opportunity both individually and, what is almost better, in the finished co-operation of their teamwork. Nor did Mr. DAVID HORNE'S disgruntled *Hardy*, Mr. REGINALD SMITH'S stolidly efficient *C.S.-M.*, Mr. H. G. STOKER'S quiet simple-minded *Colonel*, and Mr. ALEXANDER FIELD'S humorous batman in any way fail in support. The whole must have owed much to Mr. JAMES WHALE'S most intelligent and sympathetic production. Mr. SHERRIFF in fine has done a very noble piece of work and he has found all but perfect interpreters. Critical detachment has no place here, and I am not ashamed to lay it aside. What poignant memories of dead friends, of keen yet fearful regrets for a great adventure missed, of hopes and fears for England

THE SERIOUS SIDE OF WAR.
No PEPPER!

Second-Lieutenant Trotter.	MR. MELVILLE COOPER.
Private Mason.	MR. ALEXANDER FIELD.
Captain Stanhope	MR. COLIN CLIVE.
Lieutenant Osborne	MR. GEORGE ZUCCO.

As They Might Have Been

John Osborne

Who better qualified to choose than he
Which dramatist to damn, and which exhort,
Whose fiat carries the authority
Conferred upon him by the Royal Court?

BOX SET

"If only someone would make an attempt on your life
we'd have a good excuse for leaving."

"Don't be silly, Gladys...
everybody **isn't** looking at you."

AT THE PANTOMIME.

Uncle. "WELL, SONNY, HOW DO YOU LIKE IT?"

Nephew. "OH, TOLERABLE. BUT I FIND THE HUMOUR SOMEWHAT VITIATED BY THE TOO-FREQUENT REFERENCES TO THE LONDON COUNTY COUNCIL."

"You and your 'One day one of those diamonds
is bound to work loose'!"

THE THEATRE FOR THE PEOPLE.

26 March 1870

RUSSIA may well be described as a benighted country! But of all the queer notions ever bred of barbarism, commend us to one in the *Pall Mall's* latest "notes from Russia." Conceive a Commission appointed to examine the question of the establishment of a "Theatre for the People!" And more; imagine the Commission reporting strongly that such a theatre should be constructed! A theatre with a moral object! A theatre meant "to divert the people from foolish, vulgar and gross amusements, by providing them with healthy and elevating spectacular entertainments at a cheap rate"! A theatre to contain seats for 2,350 people—say something between Drury Lane and the Lyceum—with 1,300 of the seats, at prices varying from *2d.* to *4d.*, and the others from *4d.* up to *3s. 2d.*! This infuriated Committee further report that such a theatre might be made to bring in a profit of £5,000 a year—or ten per cent. on the capital employed. They recommend that the management should be entrusted to a competent private person, of experience, taste and refinement, and have prepared a *répertoire* of 140 pieces in the Russian language, original and translated, calculated, they think, to forward their object of entertaining and elevating.

They further recommend that lotteries, masked balls, and the sale of spirituous liquors be forbidden in the "Theatre of the People."

Hear that, ye stunning sons of the music-halls—hear that, frequenters of our splendid saloons and brilliant bars! Contrast, this barbaric dream of a Russian Blue Book, with the civilised reality of London, where Free Trade in theatres does its work, and the demand is allowed to create the supply of theatrical *pabulum* for the people, from the Victoria to the penny gaff! The idea of the people being condemned to "healthy and elevating" entertainment; when their betters can revel in the SCHNEIDER, the MENKEN, the *Cancan* and the *Opéra Bouffe,* the indecent burlesque, the breakdown, and the Sensational drama!

The next thing will be some idiot proposing a Joint Stock Company Limited, of other idiots, who think that the theatre might be made a means of education for the many and of culture and delight for all! Imagine these idiots subscribing their money—of course they would dispense with dividends—to realise their idea, by hiring a theatre, paying a competent and cultivated manager charged to select the best actors, and to produce the best plays, old and new, the shareholders' subscriptions, supplying a financial backbone; and the shareholders giving to the undertaking their countenance as well as their cash! And all this under the idiotic idea, that the English theatre is not what it ought to be, either in the way of art, entertainment, or education; that it might be made better, but never will be so long as managers are left to live from hand to mouth, by catching the crowd, and going ever lower and lower to catch it.

Dreams, silly dreams!

*"It would be a tragedy for this country
if the live theatre completely disappeared."*

113

LARRY THE HAM?

A Profile of Olivier by John Wells

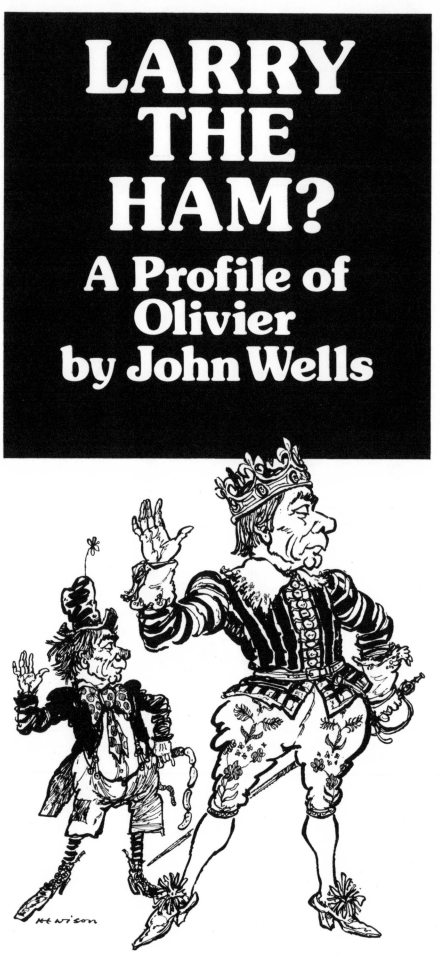

On the only occasion I have ever met Sir Laurence Olivier—I tried to arrange an interview with him for this piece and got a note to say he had to be in America for a tour with the National Theatre Company—I remember being impressed first of all by the military glamour of his entrance as he exploded through the double doors of Sean Kenny's old office above the Establishment, scattering a fall-out of staff-officers and dogsbodies, and secondly by the way he called the Irish designer "Shawnie"—even, I think, "Shawnie, Darling"—without having his nose smashed flat by a man who occasionally lifts cars on to the pavement with his bare hands.

He is the Archactor in the same way that Dr. Ramsay is the Archbishop, as anyone who saw his seventieth-birthday tribute to Noël Coward—also Noëllie in more informal moments—will have observed, and there is no doubt about his glamour or his stature. For over fifty years now—he was first spotted before the First World War playing Katharina in *The Taming of the Shrew* at a school hall in Margaret Street, Marylebone— he has drawn trembling moans from deep in the bellies of his audience with a mere turn of his head, he has thrashed them into empathetic hysteria as he has leapt and tumbled and fought about the stage, and he has coaxed them to one emotional orgasm after another with the brutal, tender or perverse use of his honeyed and skilful tongue.

His greatest and most original achievement, and the one generally overlooked in more sensitive assessments of his art, is to have survived as a popular idol since the 'thirties. There have been dissenting critics who have called his work mannered and artificial, but the great volume of world reaction, from weeping fans in Moscow to screaming teenage ravers in New York right through the great fat smug majority of fashionable theatre-goers, has been devout worship. He has never hoarded his reputation, he has worked in films like *The Sleeping Prince* with Marilyn Monroe and splashed about in a massive communal bath in *Spartacus*, but the breathless mention of his name by the old lady at the box-office still has the same note of girlish wonder in it that it had when he was throwing himself down the staircase every night in the death scene in *Coriolanus* in 1938.

This apparently reckless physical abandon, like that of a crutch-happy, microphone-stroking lead singer in a pop group, may well lie at the root of his massive popular acclaim as distinct from his critical success. The local newspaper reporter who saw his performance as Puck in A

Midsummer Night's Dream at St. Edward's Oxford described it as "a little too robust," and Elsie Fogerty, his voice teacher, reacted to his ranting and armwaving by saying that "she didn't think we needed *that*," but neither piece of early advice has been taken too seriously. He has hurled himself bodily into every part he has ever had, he once broke both ankles leaping over a balustrade, he has sustained numerous other injuries over the years, and he is still threatening to "bust a gut" on the opening night of his forthcoming

Shylock under the direction of Jonathan Miller.

The other and even more solid basis of his popular appeal is the singer's liberties he takes with the English language. Apart from being as memorable in their intonation and accent as the best pop songs of their day, his settings of 'Cry God for Harry...'' or "Now is he winter of his discontent...'' have the same mad extreme uninhibited commitment to the particular rave-up under way and the same voluntary suspension of critical self-control as the falsetto

"It was when Mr Masterman said he was going to the station, I knew it couldn't have been George Bender who did the murder. Remember the station is thirty miles away and the vicar's car was out of order, so whoever went to the booking office had to go on foot. Mrs Benwell said she had sprained her ankle that morning but couldn't say at what precise time because all the clocks had stopped..."

wailing of a modern group. He himself has said that people will be laughing at his interpretations of parts in twenty years' time, and with a piece of unrestrainedly romantic popular entertainment like his West Indian *Othello*, as extreme and camp in its fashionable way as the wildest eyerolling of the silent film stars, he may well be right. But to create any fashion somebody has to go over the top, and he has gone over the top again and again with the courage and apparent invulnerability of a multiple VC in the trenches.

He is now a sixty-three-year-old pop star. He is about to see his life's ambition fulfilled in the building of the seven and a half millions pound National Theatre on the South Bank, and perceptive observers describe him dominating the Theatre's temporary premises, supported and impelled by his wife Joan Plowright, with the sensitive pride of a stag dominating its own territory. Without his glamour and stature it might well not have been possible, but there are signs that the years and years and years of adulation have taken their toll. He is after all a public-school man, a member of the Beefsteak, Buck's and the MCC, and the descendant of a line of Huguenot administrators in Church and State, and it is not surprising that he feels himself from time to time uneasy in his role. He has covered his face with putty and dyed his hair so that people should see the character and not the actor. He has frequently complained that he has "never stopped feeling a resentment that an actor should have to live in a goldfish bowl." Being mobbed by fans has also caused him intense misery, and he has said in public that "these people hover on a very thin line between love and loathing." But one consistent means of escape or possibly of revenge recurs again and again, and that is his still unfulfilled ambition—only glimpsed by his public when he played Archie Rice in *The Entertainer*—"to make people die laughing." It is comforting, at a time when so many public clowns bore us to death with their desire to play Hamlet, to think that Hamlet himself nourishes reciprocal ambitions

ANECDOTES OF ACTORS.

BY ONE WHO HAS WHISTLED AT THE WING.

ANECDOTES of Actors are the *cacoethes* at present with almost all the Magazines, we have, at great expense, collected the following from a stage-doorkeeper, who, having retired from the portico of public life, has given us permission to state, he received them from the copyist of the Grecian Saloon, to whom they had been told in confidence by a bill-of-the-play woman of the last century, who had them direct from the above gentleman (a deceased call-boy, candle-snuffer, and scene-shifter,) during his memorable engagement at the Globe Theatre. We can assure our readers that not one of them has ever been published before.

GARRICK used to drink nothing, when he was acting, but water-gruel. His *Romeo* averaged four pints; but for the curse in *King Lear*, I have known him to take as many as three quarts in one evening. When he performed the " Walking Gentleman," however, he preferred a glass of ginger-beer with the white of an egg in it.

DICKY STONE was the first to dress the "fools" in their present costume. Before his time, the fools were always dressed like courtiers ; but the Earl of Essex having complained, ELIZABETH got her "faithful Commons" to pass a law for the alteration.

An actor of the name of SMITH had a celebrated dog, called "Towser." They performed once in a piece entitled, *The Dog of Deal*, or *Dover*—I forget which—in which the dog had to spring at SMITH's throat, SMITH being a murderer. HARRY SAWYER, however, was in a private box the first night; and, just as the dog was making the fatal spring, he threw on the stage a large piece of cat's-meat : the consequence was, Towser rushed immediately to the tempting morsel, and nothing would induce him to leave it to revenge his master's murder. An apology was made for the dog, but all to no purpose ; the piece was unequivocally condemned.

GRIMALDI was anything but funny off the stage. I have seen him at the wing so affected in *George Barnwell*, that he has been obliged frequently to chalk his cheeks three times in the same evening, on account of the tears washing all the paint off. His " Here we are !" never failed to make GEORGE THE THIRD laugh. The merry monarch would say—" Yes ; here we are ! —very true !—we are here ! Capital !—Yes: here we are ! Ha ! ha !"—and he would go on so for five minutes, till something else was said—" Somebody coming !" perhaps,—which he would repeat in the same facetious way, loud enough for the whole house to hear him.

DANDY SMITH used to wear shirt-collars made out of letter-paper. LORD BYRON was one night behind the scenes asking for an order, but nobody had any paper on which to write one. SMITH immediately pulled out, with great presence of mind, one side of his collar ; and, filling it up, presented it to LORD BYRON, saying, " Allow me, my lord, to invest you with the Collar of the O. P. Order."

HARRY SIMPSON never would take any medicine ; and his medical man was often obliged to resort to some stratagem to impose a dose upon him. There is a piece,—I do not recollect the name,—in which the hero is sentenced in prison to drink a cup of poison. HARRY SIMPSON was playing this character one night, and had given directions to have it filled with port wine ; but what was his horror, when he came to drink it, to find it contained a dose of senna ! He could not throw it away, as he had to hold the goblet upside down, to show his persecutors he had drained every drop of it. SIMPSON drank the medicine with the slowness of a poisoned martyr ; but he never forgave his medical man this trick, as was fully proved at his death, for he died without paying him his bill.

ASTLEY was the first to originate jokes by the *Clown* in the ring. The celebrated conundrum of " When is a door not a door !" made its *début* under his management ; and was so popular, that places for the boxes were sold like stock on the Royal Exchange, and fetched a higher premium than any of the funds. A private box for the Amphitheatre was considered at that time the most valuable wedding-present in a lady's *trousseau*.

BETTERTON had the gift of a very beautiful whistle. He would take a piece of wood, and whistle upon it with such intense feeling and melody, that a whole theatre has imagined he was playing upon the flute. He has often played in this way in the orchestra when the flute has been suddenly indisposed. When he was a strolling player, he has lived for days upon his whistle, paying his expenses, with nothing else, from town to town. The recollection of his shake is still cherished in many of our northern counties.

MRS. HUBBARD (the original "Old Maid" in *Have a Cap and Set a Cap*) was a very great favourite in pathetic parts; as she was known to cry more naturally than anybody else. The secret of this was never known till her death, when there was found a bequest in her will of ten pounds, to be divided in onions every Christmas-Day amongst poor undertakers out of prison.

An elephant was never introduced on the English stage till the production of *Blue Beard*. This is a positive fact; for FAWCETT made his first appearance, I recollect, in one of its hind legs. He was so nervous at the time, that in going over one of the traps it gave way, and FAWCETT and his companion leg were precipitated through it. The result was that *Blue Beard* and his black attendant were brought to the ground; and the two front legs of the elephant were seen lifted up in the air kicking away most violently, whilst the two hind legs, with FAWCETT in one of them, were kicking no less violently under the stage. The curtain was obliged to be dropped before FAWCETT, or the elephant, could resume his natural footing. He afterwards attempted to put down elephants when

he was stage-manager, but they were always too strong for him.

MRS. BILLINGTON had ninety wigs. They were of all colours, and of all ages. She was offered as much as two thousand pounds for them by TALMA, who wanted to present them to NAPOLEON; but she refused the offer, as she was determined they should not go out of the country. She kept her word; for she bequeathed them to the British Museum, where they may still be seen on referring to the head of "Fossils."

QUIN was a very great *gourmand*. He would have his mustard from Durham; and his salt was sent to him regularly from Epsom. A box, hermetically sealed, was left at the stage-door for him every morning from Richmond, full of Maids of Honour; and he never travelled without carrying behind his carriage a tank of sea-water, made in the shape of a trunk, filled with shrimps or periwinkles. When he was ill, he would touch nothing but a Pope's-eye boiled in ketchup.

I recollect CHARLES THE SECOND coming *incog.* to the King's Theatre, to see NELL GWYNNE act *Policotia* in *Not such a Fool as He Looks*. Unfortunately, in those days, there was no Free List; and the KING had not sufficient money about him to pay for a seat in the gallery, much less in the boxes The consequence was, he was obliged to send BUCKINGHAM to a pawnbroker's with his hat and cloak; and, with the money that was advanced upon them, he paid for his own and his friend's admission. Nobody would have known anything about this, only a Welch gentleman, happening to hiss NELL when she was dancing, between the acts, the Highland Fling, CHARLES picked a quarrel with him; and, in the heat of passion, struck him. Cards were instantly exchanged; but

CHOCOLATES.

HERE the seats are; George, old man,
Get some chocolates while you can.
Quick, the curtain's going to rise
(Either Bradbury's or Spry's).
"*The Castle ramparts, Elsinore*"
(That's not sufficient, get some more).
There's the *Ghost:* he does look wan
(Help yourself and pass them on).
Doesn't *Hamlet* do it well?
(This one is a caramel).
Polonius's beard is fine
(Don't you grab; that big one's mine).
Look, the *King* can't bear the play
(Throw that squashy one away).
Now the *King* is at his prayers
(Splendid! there are two more layers).
Hamlet's going for his mother
(Come on, Tony, have another).
Poor *Ophelia!* Look, she's mad
(However many's Betty had?).
The *Queen* is dead and so's the *King*
(Keep that lovely silver string).
Now even *Hamlet* can no more
(Pig! You've dropped it on the floor).
That last Act's simply full of shocks
(There's several left, so bring the box).

20th May 1925

the KING made a sad mistake; for instead of giving his proper name and address, he presented to his opponent the very duplicate (made out in the name of "SMITH") which BUCKINGHAM had received for his hat and cloak. CHARLES would certainly have been turned out of his own theatre, neck and heels, had he not been recognised by his greengrocer, just in time to be saved the *exposé*. PEPYS alludes to this circumstance in his *Memoirs*, under Feb. 31, 1666.

THE ACTORS' SYMPOSIUM
The Green Room Bar

© Ronald Searle

PLAYERS PLEASE

The John Player centenary, to be celebrated next month at London's Festival Hall, will (according to press reports) include the presentation of a new play by Tom Stoppard. Other playwrights have of course travelled the tobacco road before him, and SHERIDAN MORLEY now proudly presents extracts from some of their lesser-known work.

A balcony. South of France, circa 1930. Enter Elyot. Sees Amanda.

ELYOT: What are you doing here?
AMANDA: Smoking, silly, what does it look like?
ELYOT: Smoke can be cruelly deceptive.
AMANDA: Very thick, smoke.
ELYOT: Or very thin. Depends how you puff.
AMANDA: Can you blow smoke rings?
ELYOT: Naturally.
AMANDA: But how terribly, terribly seductive. Through your teeth?
ELYOT: No, through my ears, actually, A trick I learnt once from a circus dwarf in Rangoon.
AMANDA: Very big, China.
ELYOT: Or very small. Japan was very small. Mind if I smoke too?
AMANDA: Not at all.
ELYOT: Thank you.
AMANDA: Somehow, suddenly, here in the moonlight, with that damned orchestra, and all those memories of Norfolk and the soldiers, somehow, suddenly, I'd expected a pipe.
ELYOT: Pipes should be played, not smoked.
AMANDA: Simon always smoked a

pipe.
ELYOT: How very typical of Simon.
AMANDA: He said it soothed his nerves.
ELYOT: With nerves like Simon's, he'd have needed a blast furnace.
AMANDA: How terribly witty you are, Elyot.
ELYOT: Yes.
AMANDA: But what happens to the ash?
ELYOT: Ash?
AMANDA: You know, silly, off the end of the cigarette?
ELYOT: I flick it off. Very, very quickly and very, very well.
AMANDA: I love you terribly.
ELYOT: Then I expect somebody comes along to clean it up. Or else it just lies there on the balcony all winter.
AMANDA: How terribly tragic.
ELYOT: What do you like best? Apart from me, of course.
AMANDA: Du Maurier. They come in those terribly, terribly pretty little red boxes and Mama says they remind her of that nice man who used to play Raffles.
ELYOT: He was the one they named them after. I'm not altogether sure, though, that it was awfully, well, awfully right

somehow to give one's name to a lot of cigarettes. Not unless they're Egyptian.
AMANDA: Oh, Elyot, you're always so terribly knowledgeable about abroad and things like that. Perhaps that's why I love you so much.
ELYOT: Jolly good.
AMANDA: Would you smoke always, if you could?
ELYOT: Yes I think so: at least until I couldn't get a grip on the holder any more. Then I think I'd have it clamped to my teeth. God knows, one needs to look elegant at the end of one's life.
AMANDA: Do you find you cough a lot?
ELYOT: Coughing can be terribly attractive. I do it very deep in the throat, always, and terribly, terribly intelligently.
AMANDA: Oh good. I would so hate to be married to a man who had choking fits.
ELYOT: I always thought that was why you divorced Simon.
AMANDA: That was Terence. Simon had the yellow fingers.
ELYOT: Chinese blood?
AMANDA: No, no, his family came from Leatherhead.
ELYOT: Very big, Leatherhead.

The drawing room at the Rectory. Enter the Inspector.

INSPECTOR: I expect you're all wondering why I've gathered you together like this. As you know, the body was found by the butler at seven-thirty this morning. Since then, nobody has been allowed to enter or leave this house.

CYNTHIA: But what about you, Inspector?

INSPECTOR: Good question. I allowed myself to enter at about nine-thirty. Since then I have asked you all individually where you were last night, and I must say some of your answers have been thoroughly satisfactory.

CYRIL: But surely, Inspector, you can't seriously imagine that any of me, I mean, that any of us could have perpetrated this foul deed?

INSPECTOR: Can't be too careful, Sir; not since that breakout over at the prison last week.

CYNTHIA: But he had a moustache and they said he smoked like a chimney. Mainly filter tips.

CYRIL (coughing): There's no one here answering that description, Inspector. I myself am, as you can see, clean-shaven, and these cigarettes have no filter tips left on them, er, that is, they are the non-tipped variety.

INSPECTOR: Very true, Sir: I wonder, though, if you'd be so good as to show me that packet?

CYRIL: Of course, Inspector: an innocent man has nothing to hide, what?

INSPECTOR: Purvis, take a look at this; anything strike you as, well, interesting?

PURVIS: No Sir, nothing special. Like me to take him down to the Yard with the dogs, though, Sir? Just a few questions and a nip or two?

INSPECTOR: No, Purvis, I don't think that will be altogether necessary, not once we have his confession.

CYRIL: Confession? What confession?

INSPECTOR: Perhaps you'd care to tell me, Sir, in your own words of course, just when this packet of cigarettes was acquired by you?

CYRIL: Why, certainly, Inspector: it was just after I drove Cynthia down here on Friday night. I

popped out to the pub and bought them.

INSPECTOR: Examine that packet carefully, Purvis: anything strike you as, well, unusual, about it?

PURVIS: What, you mean this writing on the side where it says "Contains only three plus 10p change of a £?" That means a vending machine, doesn't it, Sir? Ha, so we've caught him: and he said he went to the pub!

INSPECTOR: No, Purvis, they have vending machines in pubs these days. Look again.

PURVIS: Nothing else that I can see, Sir.

INSPECTOR: It's what you can't see that counts in this kind of investigation, Purvis. Look, here on this side: no government health warning. What does that suggest?

PURVIS: That they're safe to smoke, Sir?

INSPECTOR: No, Purvis. It means these cigarettes were bought and paid for in or before 1972. And what does that suggest?

PURVIS: That they'll be getting a little stale by now?

INSPECTOR: No, Purvis. It means that whoever bought these cigarettes must have been away somewhere for a long time. For a very long time.

PURVIS: But you can't mean…

INSPECTOR: I think Mr Trentham knows exactly what I mean.

CYRIL: Now look, Inspector, I never meant to kill him, that is, er, the gun went off in my…..

INSPECTOR: Quite so. You know what they say, Purvis: smoking can damage your health. Well, not smoking can, too.

PURVIS: Oh, Sir…

CYNTHIA: Oh, Inspector, I never knew the police could be so wonderful.

INSPECTOR: All part of the service, Madam: I'd never have guessed if it hadn't been for your casual remark about the van-driver you saw restocking the cigarette machine last week. Shall we go in to lunch? The rest of us, I mean; Purvis and Mr Trentham will unfortunately have to be leaving. They have another engagement.

A factory near Nottingham. Time: the present.

SORTER: Small cigars.

PACKER: What?

SORTER: Small cigars. That's what it means. Cigar-ettes. Ettes from the French. Means small. Like usherettes.

PACKER: Usherettes aren't small. Not always.

SORTER: They were at the Odeon in Sidcup, when I went to collect my papers. Smallest usherettes I'd ever seen. Probably the smoking that did it. That or the ice creams.

PACKER: I don't have to do this, you know.

SORTER: Do what?

PACKER: This: stood here putting twenty tubes of tobacco into packets every twelve seconds. I was going to be a nuclear physicist before the war.

SORTER: What war? I never had no war.

PACKER: The war. Then there was the accident, then my teeth and now I'm here forever.

SORTER: Not necessarily: they could move you over to pipe tobacco. Then you'd be on tins.

PACKER: I like tins. Solid. Know where you are with tins. Bloody crush-proof packets, all you need do is stamp on them with both feet ten or twelve times and there you are.

SORTER: I had an aunt, once.

PACKER: Stamp on her much, did you?

SORTER: No, but she was a real smoker. Benson and Hedges, Dunhills, Sobranie Tipped, Virginia Slims, she wasn't proud.

PACKER: I remember Virginia Slims: had a juggling act up the Holborn Empire, 1922. Next year she won Wimbledon.

SORTER: Anyway, this aunt, she said it's not what you smoke, or how many, it's where. Smoking anywhere away from home was all right, see, even if it was on a bus or in someone else's house. Long as you were away from home, she said, the smoke couldn't get you: no coughing, no cancer, nothing. But smoke at home, and that's it — drop dead within forty years or so. That's what she said, anyway. Then she died. Hasn't been the same at home, somehow. No one could wheeze like she could in the mornings. Not that we haven't tried.

PACKER: It's the writing on the outsides I can't follow. Not any more. Full of warnings and addresses and recipes for tar, but never says "open here" or "stick fingers in this end if you want to grab hold of a fag" or anything like that. Not like the old days. They had proper instructions then. "This end up" it used to say, or "Unwrap cellophane before trying to open box". Now you have to bloody guess how to get inside. Need a bloody technology degree before you can buy a packet of cigarettes. They don't even tell you which bloody end you're supposed to be smoking, let alone how to work the matches.

SORTER: Never worried my Mum: she'd just tear them in half and stick the tobacco up her nose. Said it made her feel sort of light-headed, and if she stood very still with her eyes closed and tobacco up her nostrils she could see wonderful colours dancing in front of her eyelids.

PACKER: She were like Arthur's friend Terry: he could take a packet of twenty, King-size mind you, and within twelve minutes he'd have chewed through the whole lot, filter tips and all. That was just his breakfast. Lunch, he used to gnaw pipes. Then of course he wanted to be the first human cigarette in Margate, and that was the end of him. Bloody stupid, I called it, and the coroner said it didn't show signs of superhuman intelligence either.

A cherry orchard near Moscow, 1891.

VARYA: Oh, Anya! To Moscow! If only we could?

ANYA: Our lives, my dearest sister, are not to be lived in the same city as our dreams.

NATASHA: But if only they were! And it was! And they would! Now that the regiment has left, and Chebutykin's duel has ended so sadly, and Vaskilikov without his leg, if only we could leave it all behind and take the train at last!

ANYA: But for Moscow? What is there in Moscow that we have not here, here in our own wonderful orchard with Ravnetska and the samovar and the peasants so happily employed dredging the lake — what has Moscow for us beyond all that?

VARYA: But have you not heard, my sisters? Why, when Hildebrayakov returned last summer he told Lopahaykin who told Rashkolnikov who told his mother that by the post office in the big square there he'd seen a man take a roll of black paper from a box under his armpit and insert it in his lips and suddenly smoke billowed out through the gaps in his yellow teeth — oh, it must have been wonderful!

NATASHA: And we would be allowed to witness such an event?

VARYA: Moscow has many wonders. Why, Sokolyakov told Barsnitsikov that the flames from his beard could be seen as far away as St Petersburg, and many men, yes and ladies too, had come to watch. Oh, Anya, my dearest Anya, I tell you times are changing! Russia is no longer the healthy mother that once she was: soon they'll be coughing all around the estate, and you won't be able to see the cherries for ash. I tell you we live in stirring times! Why, in Moscow today there is a man selling upturned samovar lids with dents in either side for the nobility to rest their fingers on while smoking. I tell you, the world is never going to be … *(night falls)*.

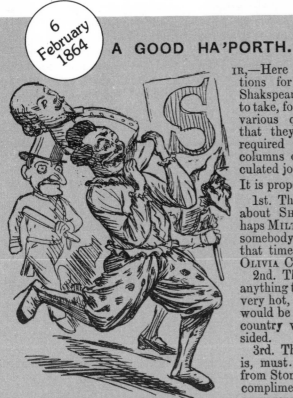

6 February 1864

A GOOD HA'PORTH.

IR,—Here are a few suggestions for the form that a Shakspearian Memorial ought to take, forwarded to me from various quarters, in order that they may obtain the required publicity in the columns of your widely-circulated journal.

It is proposed—

1st. That it ought to be about SHAKSPEARE, or perhaps MILTON, but at all events somebody who lived about that time, always excluding OLIVIA CROMWELL.

2nd. That it must not be anything to eat, or if it is, not very hot, like a salad, which would be emblematical of the country where the poet resided.

3rd. That it, whatever it is, must be made of stones from Stoney Stratford, out of compliment to the district-surveyors of England as a body.

4th. That it shall be portable, with pockets inside.

5th. That it shall be a Shakspeare Scholarship, to be holden on the following conditions; viz. :—

That the candidate shall be able to repeat by heart and sing all COLLIER'S emendations to MALONE'S notes.

That the holder shall be required to read aloud the entire plays of SHAKSPEARE every morning before breakfast, for the space of one year.

That in his second year of holding, he shall repeat the performance with the addition of dressing himself in the costumes of *all* SHAKSPEARE'S characters, including the *Witches* in *Macbeth* and the greasy citizen in the Roman crowd.

That on the 23rd of every successive April, he shall hunt samphire gatherers on the Cliffs of Dover.

That in honour of *Falstaff's* ragged army he shall go to Coventry for the remainder of the year.

Hoping, dear *Punch*, that the Members of the Shakspeare Committee will give their serious attention to these propositions.

I remain, yours, energetically,

A RETIRED HAMLET.

THEATRE
Jeremy Kingston

There is no doubt in my mind that Laurence Olivier's production of Arthur Miller's **The Crucible** *(National Theatre, Old Vic)* contains the best ensemble acting to be seen in London at the present time. The play was written in 1953 during the McCarthy era of American politics when the Un-American Activities Committee (a title not even George Orwell could have bettered) was hunting Red witches in and out the State Department and all round the land. The play is set in the year 1692 in the Massachusetts town of Salem, where the sexual hysterics of some precocious girls provided the excuse for almost an entire community to relieve itself of its festering envies by accusing one another of witchcraft.

Witches were the perfect scapegoats for calamities like bad crops and infant mortality. They also provided convenient objects for a projection of sexual fantasies, and a belief in devils and witches would seem to be associated inevitably with the repressive, Puritan type of religion. If an accused person did not confess, this was taken as proof she was a hardened witch. The only way she could save her life was by confessing she had indeed trafficked with the Devil, danced with Lucifer, supped with Satan, lain with succubi and incubi and all the rest of the superstitious nonsense. The hero of Mr. Miller's play is John Proctor, a farmer who refuses to sign a false confession. By no means a saint—indeed, an admitted sinner, unfaithful (once) to his wife—he yet knows that his life will mean nothing to him once he has signed away his name. He is hanged.

Mr. Miller has constructed his play with marvellous skill, steadily tightening the screw on our indignation and our pity, and chief among the actors who serve him so well are Colin Blakely and Joyce Redman in the parts of Proctor and his wife. I commend particularly the playing of their difficult first scene together, Miss Redman reproachfully unforthcoming, Mr. Blakely embarrassed and uneasy. The previous act has ended with the shrieking of possessed girls, and this following scene has to be quietly spoken and spread with silences. They manage it superbly. Robert Lang gives a performance of considerable subtlety as the visiting witch-tracker who increasingly doubts the truth of the grisly proceedings. Through the doubts of such men and through the stubborn resolution of such as John Proctor those periods of terror and mass mania into which mankind passes are at last followed by periods of enlightenment.

This production is certain to be a sell-out and it deserves to be.

"We start auditioning audiences next week."

CHRISTMAS-TIME WITH OUR STAGE CELEBRITIES.

MISS URSULA JEANS, MISS TALLULAH BANKHEAD AND MISS OLGA LINDO WAITING AT THE CASTLE GATE FOR A GIFT OF FLANNEL PETTICOATS.

MR. DAVY BURNABY AS A HEAVY-WAIT.

MISS ELSA LANCHESTER HAS A CHRISTMAS-TREE ALL TO HERSELF.

MR. ROY BYFORD PLAYS AT FATHER CHRISTMAS.

MISS SYBIL THORNDIKE TELLS A BLOOD-CURDLING GHOST STORY.

MR. NORMAN McKINNEL AND MR. BROMLEY-DAVENPORT, HAVING BOTH CONCEIVED THE IDEA OF DRESSING UP AS SPECTRES, MEET IN THE CORRIDOR.

MISS POTIPHAR CASALIS CATCHES MR. PAUL CAVANAGH UNDER THE MISTLETOE.

MR. ALLAN AYNESWORTH LEADS MISS MARIE TEMPEST OUT FOR SIR ROGER DE COVERLEY.

MR. ERNEST THESIGER PRESIDES OVER THE WASSAIL BOWL WITH GENIAL ACIDITY.

123

STANDING ROOM AT THE TOP by Philip Oakes

ACT I SCENE I

Night. A street in South Kensington. The lamps are lit. Framed in each window sits a young may pounding the typewriter. Barrow boys on the corner are selling the "Daily Express"-ed version of "Room at the Top," the Colin Wilson diaries, and horsewhips for outraged fathers. Just lately trade has been slack. Several publishers nip in and out of doorways. Mr. Gerald Hamilton asks one of them for change to make a telephone call.

HARRY FLITCH, a struggling young writer from Dunmow, enters in search of a night's lodging. He sees the "No Vacancies" signs and starts to sing.

HARRY:
My father made boots and my mother cured bacon,
  But Social Reality caused me to think
That the way to the top could only be taken
  By pinning my faith to the old kitchen sink.

I want a Lagonda, a Rolex Gold Oyster,
  A suite at the Dorchester, money to burn;
I'll get them, I know, but I'll get them much faster
  By playing the provincial with plenty to learn.

Outsiders have had it, the Beatniks are boring,
  The Angries are looking back hard for the rent;
But down in the provinces something is stirring
  For sex is remarkable north of the Trent.

CHORUS:
It's Social Reality that we're all seeking,
  Mud on the boots, and a win on the Pools.
In Kensington West the perspective is lacking.
  But we'll do the job if you'll give us the tools.

Two publishers rush forward waving their cheque books. Paul Tricky, a gossip writer on the "Daily Slant," takes HARRY to one side to explain about an agent's ten per cent. Christopher Logue enters from the direction of the Royal Court Theatre reciting an extempore ballad, composed three months earlier, entitled "It's Holy to be Poor, but it's Nicer to be Rich."

ANGELA BLOODSTOCK, a refugee from the Aldermaston Defaulters Purge, falls over HARRY'S sleeping bag, and as he helps her to her feet, love blooms in South Kensington. Factory hooters play their theme as they trudge off in search of a soup kitchen.

ACT I SCENE II

Later the same night. A camp on Hampstead Heath. Still without a place to sleep, HARRY and ANGELA have applied for a bed space in the Gollancz Talent Sanctuary. There is no charge, but squatters have to attend nightly readings from the works of Stuart Holroyd and the Camden Town Mystics. Meal tickets are awarded to all those who can shout "Genius" six times without being lynched.

Squads of campers carrying banners march in from both sides of the stage, and a fight breaks out between the Redbrick contingent and the Zenmen. Trying to restore order, HARRY is trampled into the mud. ANGELA tries to help his to his feet while a camera team from the British Film Institute order him to stay put.

HARRY remains flat on his back while the squatters parade round a bonfire piled high with manuscripts rejected by Theatre Workshop and George Devine. In solemn march-time the evening liturgy begins.

CHORUS: Shades of night are falling fast,
              Noël Coward will not last:
              Grant us some financial blessing
              In the name of Doris Lessing.

              Patron saints look to our good,
              Osborne, Wesker, Littlewood:
              Teach us that a taste of honey
              Isn't all there is to money.

              Give us shelter when we go
              From rain and hail and C.P. Snow:
              And grant us that the house to come
              Is not a William Douglas-Home.

Christopher Logue leaps through the flames, slightly singed and reciting a ballad inspired by the tourist who trod on the toe of a Buckingham Palace sentry, entitled "Feet are what the Workers stand on." The Redbricks and the Zenmen set light to effigies of Julian Slade and Dame Edith Sitwell. Kenneth Tynan watches the whole thing from the wings, and rushes off to catch the first 'plane back to New York.

ACT I SCENE III

A week later. The waiting room of the MacGibbon and Kee Foot Clinic. HARRY and ANGELA have been expelled from the Talent Sanctuary after confessing that they once wrote a fan letter to John Lehmann. For the past 24 hours they have been tramping the streets in search of a room, but before they are issued with free corn-plasters they have to fill in a questionnaire asking:

(1) Do you believe in (a) Fairies, or (b) The Establishment?

(2) Does Benn Levy sleep with his whiskers (a)

Time and the Censor Pass Away.

WHEN I was of a tender age
I had a passion for the stage.
My parents, who were rather prim,
Essayed with true parental vim
To put an end to "all that rot"
And place the Drama on the spot;
But, notwithstanding what they said,
I used to sing each night in bed—

    "Oh, I could write a dashing play,
    A flashing and a smashing play.
    Its plot would be on every tongue,
    Both near and far its praises sung
    By elevated brows and low,
    Who'd flock to see this *outré* show—
    But
        It wouldn't pass the Censor.

Oh, I could write a stunning play,
A cunning and long-running play.
I'd have a Ruritanian queen,
A most abandoned bedroom scene,
An abdicating Balkan prince
Who'd make poor Mrs. Grundy wince—
    But
        It wouldn't pass the Censor.

Oh, I could write a masterpiece,
A vaster and faster piece,
With dialogue so full of pep
That SHAW would have to mind his step,
And situations so acute
That soon I'd be of world repute—
    But
        It wouldn't pass the Censor.

Oh, I could write a porty play,
A sporty and a naughty play.
In each pulsating poignant Act
I'd state a most surprising fact...
And then, when it had run and run,
I'd built a castle in the sun—
    But
        It wouldn't pass the Censor.

Now many years have passed away
And I at last have penned a play
Containing all the daring bits
Of those oft-dreamt unwritten hits.
I stuck it up and sent it to
A well-known West End magnate, who,
On reading it, was filled with joy.
He rang me up and said, "My boy,
You've seen your last financial care
And soon you'll be a millionaire.
For years this play will ease the lives
Of dowagers and vicars' wives."
I reeled. And then I said aghast,
"There is a Censor to be passed!"
The great man clearly pitied me.
"It's nineteen-thirty-six, A.D.
I mean to advertise this piece
With: 'BRING YOUR NEPHEW AND YOUR NIECE.''
    And
        It cantered past the Censor.

—————————————————— (1936)

over or (b) under the sheet?
(3) Where does the rain mainly fall on Nancy Spain?

Two chiropodists trip lightly on stage to collect the answers, followed by Dan Farson and a camera crew. Farson asks HARRY and ANGELA what they understand by the word "Love," and 24 gossip writers, headed by Paul Tricky, crowd into the room as they start to reply.

HARRY:
Love is what will get me to the top
    Without even trying.
Love is human, a feature in *Woman*
    That people are buying.
It's a one-way ticket to success,
It's the chairman's opening address,
    And one morning you'll wake up
    In Bradford or Bacup,
To see my picture in the *Daily Express*.

HARRY hands round excerpts from "Make Room for Me," his novel about tripe dressers in Nottingham. Paul Tricky recognizes ANGELA as the daughter of Lord Bloodstock, the gutta-percha king, and as she sings he scribbles the words down.

ANGELA:
Top people don't know about love,
    Our parents would never approve;
For tips on finesse we
Read James Pope-Hennessy,
    But royal romances are out of the groove.

It's hip to drink gin on a train,
Though passengers often complain;
    But contemporary kicks
    Now come straight from the sticks,
Delaney's in Salford, and Bradford's got Braine.

The gossip writers break into a clog dance. Christopher Logue bursts through the window reciting a poem called "Only Hit a Critic when the Customers are Watching." HARRY reels off his ten tips for success, beginning with "Try to be born where there's whippet racing on Fridays." And ANGELA, seeing that fame has already started to corrupt our hero, runs into the street pursued by the two chiropodists.
THE CURTAIN FALLS, *but the clog dance goes on all through the interval.*

ACT II SCENE I
A month later. The offices of Social Reality Ltd. Deserted by ANGELA, HARRY has engaged Paul Tricky as his agent. "Make Room for Me" is big business. Tricky has sold the book rights to Hutchinson; the stage rights to Wolf Mankowitz; a serial, based on the script, to "Marilyn"; and a picture-strip, based on the serial, to the "New Statesman." As the curtain rises someone suggests asking Richard Hoggart to write the captions.
HARRY *is wearing a suit by Daks, shoes by Lobb, and a small neon badge that flashes the word "Integrity" at five-second intervals. But he is not*

happy. *Totting up his bank balance on the back of* ANGELA'S *photograph, he sings.*

HARRY:
My coat is vicuna, my tie's something special
    That Turnbull and Asser made up for a duke;
The critics are starting to call me commercial
    But Beaverbrook warned you can't trust to luck.

My notebooks are crowded with social adventures,
    Next week I'm to speak at a banquet by Foyles;
But love is still lacking, despite my debentures,
    While Social Reality rings up the sales.

Tricky interrupts to say that Lord Bloodstock is on his way up, followed by Marjorie Proops, Logan Gourlay, and Eve Perrick. Pocketing his souvenir horsewhip, HARRY leaves by the back stairs, and heads for St. Pancras. On the way out he passes Mr. Gerald Hamilton, who advises him where to change trains. Christopher Logue arrives too late to recite anything. He is furious.

THE SAVOYARDS.

MESSRS. GILBERT AND SULLIVAN'S *Gondoliers* deserves to r immediately after *The Mikado* and *Pinafore* bracketed. The m
en-scène is
every way ab
as perfect as
is possible to
Every writer
libretti, ev
dramatist
every compo
must envy
Two Savoyar
their rare
portunities
putting th
own work
their own sta
and being l
the two Kin
in this pie
jointly a
equally mo
archs of all th
survey, thoug
unlike these t
potentates, th
are not th
subjects' se
vants, and ha
only to consid
what is best
the success
their piece, a
to have it carr
out, whatever
is, literal
regardless
expense. A
what does the
work amount t
Simply a Tw

"Once upon a time there were two Kings."

Act Opera, to play two-hours-and-a-half, for the production of whi they have practically a whole year at their disposal. They can as near commanding success as is given to mortal dramatist a

ACT II SCENE III

An hour later. St. Pancras station. The platform is crowded with emigrant writers from South Kensington, all heading north. Paul Tricky is doing a brisk trade in "Integrity" badges, assorted views of the Wedgwood factory, and a short history of provincial customs entitled "Where there's Muck there's Money." A man from the Special Branch reads a sample page and seizes the lot as pornographic.

Lord Bloodstock and ANGELA drag HARRY away from the ticket barrier. The train pulls out, and a massed choir of critics, led by Alan Pryce-Jones and Sir Harold Nicolson, sing a madrigal entitled "Prithee, But the Prestige Papers." Christopher Logue arrives in time to deny authorship.

HARRY and ANGELA embrace. The clog-dancers, the Redbricks, and the Zenmen join hands and sing.

CHORUS:
You can keep your *Lolita*
And *Finnegan's Wake*,
We like Reality for its own sake.

Ambiguous authors

Can stay on the shelves,
We want something we can do ourselves.

Mr. John Gordon awards HARRY a testimonial from the Fleet Street Watch Committee; invitations to address the Primrose League shower from the roof, and Lady Lewisham complains about the litter.

The lights slowly dim, and the entire cast regroups so that their badges form a huge, illuminated INTEGRITY across the stage. In unison, they sing.

CHORUS:
Just give us the facts and don't leave the sex out,
A true blue Briton can do better than the French;
The readers are waiting, their tongues and their cheques out,
So don't give a thought about the Swindon Bench.

Several "Integrity" badges start to fuse. Lord Bloodstock presses a button illuminating a tableau (symbolizing Social Reality) of five authors, a shop steward, and a strike committee paying homage to an Irving Theatre nude. And with dignity.

THE CURTAIN FALLS

---

mposer, and for any comparative failure they can have no one to ame but themselves, the pair of them.

Whatever the piece may be, it is always a pleasure to see how oroughly the old hands at the Savoy enter into "the fun of the ing," and, as in the case of Miss JESSIE BOND and Mr. RUTLAND ARRINGTON, absolutely carry the audience with them by sheer uberance of spirits.

Mr. RUTLAND BARRINGTON possesses a ready wit and keen appre- tion of humour; and, as this is true also of Miss JESSIE BOND, e couple, being thoroughly in their element with such parts as e *Gondoliers* provide for them, legitimately graft their own fun the plentiful stock already supplied by the author, and are literally e life and soul of the piece.

On the night I was there a Miss NORAH PHYLLIS took Miss .MAR's part of *Gianetta*, and played it, at short notice, admirably. e struck me as bearing a marked facial resemblance to Miss RTESQUE, and is a decided acquisition. Mr. DENNY, as the Grand quisitor (a part that recalls the Lord High Chancellor of the ex- voyard, GEORGE GROSSMITH, now entertaining "on his own hook"), esn't seem to be a born Savoyard, *non nascitur* and *non fit* at present. od he is, of course, but there's no spontaneity about him. How- er, for an eccentric comedian merely to do exactly what he is told, d nothing more, yet to do that, little or much, well, is a perform- ce that would meet with *Hamlet's* approbation, and Mr. GILBERT'S. r. FRANK WYATT, as "the new boy" at the Savoy School, doesn't,

as yet, seem quite happy; but it cannot be expected that he should feel "quite at home," when he has only recently arrived at a new school.

Miss BRANDRAM is a thorough Savoyard; *nihil tetigit quod non ornavit*, and her embroidery of a part which it is fair to suppose was done in her own quaint and quiet fashion.

A fantastically and hu- morous peculiarly Gilbertian idea is the comparison between a visit to the den- tist's, and an interview with the questioners by the rack, suggested by the Grand Inquisitor Don AL- HAMBRA, who says that the nurse is waiting in the

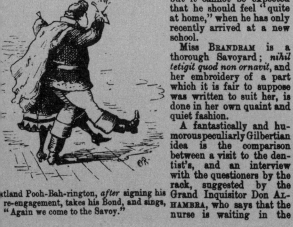

atland Pooh-Bah-rington, *after* signing his re-engagement, takes his Bond, and sings, "Again we come to the Savoy."

torture-chamber, but that there is no hurry for him to go and examine her, as she is all right and "has all the illustrated papers."

There are ever so many good things in the Opera, but the best of all, for genuinely humorous inspiration of words, music and acting, is the quartette in the Second Act, "In a contemplative fashion." It is excellent. Thank goodness, *encores* are disen- couraged, except where there can be "No possible sort of doubt, No possible doubt whatever" (also a capital song in this piece) as to the unanimity of the enthu- siasm. There is nothing in the music that catches the ear on a first hearing as did "*The Three Little Maids*," or "*I've got a Song to Sing O!*" but it is all charming, and the masterly orchestration in its fulness and variety is something that the least technically educated can appreciate and enjoy. The piece is so brilliant to eye and ear, that there is never a dull moment on the stage or off it. It is just one of those simple *Bab-Ballady* stories

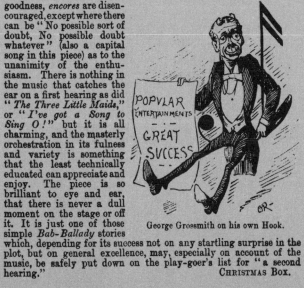

George Grossmith on his own Hook.

which, depending for its success not on any startling surprise in the plot, but on general excellence, may, especially on account of the music, be safely put down on the play-goer's list for "a second hearing."
CHRISTMAS BOX.

4 January 1890

AT THE PLAY

PEER GYNT
(Old Vic)

The Old Vic Theatre Company has hurtled into London with Ibsen's wild north-easter. There is a grand buffeting here for any playgoer who does not mind being tempest-tossed. Even in a cut text—the full play is longer than *Hamlet*— the philosophic fantasy of *Peer Gynt* lasts for more than three hours. Apart from its sudden lull in the desert (we can hardly cherish Ibsen's version of "Africa and golden joys") much of it has a stinging exhilaration: Mr. Ralph Richardson, as its monarch of egoists, now survives the test like an Olympic athlete.

Details of *Peer's* progress from the interrupted wedding to the play's dying fall, the reunion with *Solveig* forty years on, may sometimes baffle. ("Interesting but tough," as Huck Finn said on another occasion.) Still, it is a virtue of this revival that the argument is made as clear as possible: we are disturbed less than we used to be by a clashing of symbols. As in the last major production at the Old Vic, so in this: nothing impresses more than the scene in which *Peer* plays at coachman to his dying mother and, lit by the wayward flame of his imagination, sees himself galloping with her towards the halls of heaven and Saint Peter's challenge. Mr. Richardson renders the speech with a fine impetus and conviction, and Dame Sybil Thorndike's *Aase* compels tears. A twin peak in this revival is the Asylum scene, savagely ironical and directed with inspiration by Mr. Guthrie. Here the play rises steeply from *Peer's* desert hours as a minor prophet and his dalliance with the gold-digging *Anitra* (Miss Vida Hope)—later a heavy item on his prophet-and-loss account.

Mr. Richardson shoulders the piece. Whether as flying Norseman, as the middle-aged *Peer*

pavilioned among the sands, or as the racked elder, his performance lacks nothing in variety, pace, and acute intelligence. Others in the Old Vic Company follow their leader. Thus Mr. Nicholas Hannen makes a sharp grotesque of the *King of the Trolls* who rules his green court in a green shade; Miss Joyce Redman preserves *Solveig's* simplicity without edging into the sentimental; Mr. Harcourt Williams gustily embodies the amiable lunatic who crowns *Peer* in the asylum; and Miss Margaret Leighton's troll temptress comes straight from the pine-forests, crags and haunted caverns of folk-tale. When the play is approaching its end Mr. Laurence Olivier brings an uncanny radiance to the *Button Moulder.* This teasing part demands, but seldom gets, an actor of Mr. Olivier's quality.

Mr. Tyrone Guthrie's production enriches the London stage. Its rout of trolls, its shadow-show in the Boyg scene, the bare cottage of the dying *Aase*, the Asylum's frenzy, the benighted ship, *Solveig's* hut seen mistily through the last dropping veils of lawn—for these we are in Mr. Guthrie's debt. (Possibly the third act might benefit a little from more

"I hate being an actress really — but it's the only way I can get to sleep with the producer."

kindly light amid the encircling gloom).

Mr. Norman Ginsbury's new translation is lively and apt; Mr. Herbert Menges conducts an orchestra which does justice to Greig's music; and the production as a whole—the first of a repertory season—gives much honor to the new "Old Vic."

ARMS AND THE MAN
(New)

After the Scandinavian the Shavian, as Dame Sybil Thorndike says in the rhyming address (by another hand) with which this revival unexpectedly ends. The first of Shaw's Plays Pleasant, now produced by Mr. John Burrell, enters the Old Vic repertory as a gay interlude between the stormy night of *Peer Gynt* and the red morning of *Richard the Third*. The G.B.S. of fifty years ago, guying fancy-dress heroics and the romantic view of war, remains irresistible. We are grateful for the sight of Mr. Laurence Olivier cutting a dash as the sabre-rattler-in-chief, the happily ridiculous *Major Sergius Saranoff*—a Ouidaesque warrior in his sugar-stick uniform and clearly a delight for any languishing girl fed on Byron, Pushkin, and the opera season at Bucharest. Mr. Olivier has the nicest possible sense of burlesque: at every turn he swiftly pinks his operatic paladin, and *Arms and the Man* should be seen if only to hear him declare: "This hand is more accustomed to the sword than to the pen."

Mr. Ralph Richardson's quiet method admirably serves that professional man *Bluntschli*, the "chocolate-cream soldier": the performance, like Mr. Olivier's, is wittily-timed. Miss Joyce Redman finds the right degree of defiance for *Louka*, the maid with ideas above her station, who pairs off with *Sergius;* Mr. Nicholas Hannen illumines *Major Petkoff*, obviously a foundation-stone of the local club; Dame Sybil Thorndike enjoys *Catherine's* pride in her home, her electric bell, and her family descent; and Miss Margaret Leighton is a good *Raina*.

The settings and costumes which so brightly restore a vanished world are the work of Miss Doris Zinkeisen.   J.C.T.

PUNCH'S ALMANACK FOR 1866.

PRIVATE THEATRICALS.—JONES'S DRESSING-ROOM.

(The Costumier has forgotten to send Jones's Jack Boots). Jones. "CALLED AM I? I CAN'T PLAY Charles XII. IN PATENT LEATHER BOOTS WITH GREEN TOPS! I MUST HAVE YOURS!" *[Brown, who plays 2nd Officer, don't see it.*

Norman Mansbridge

After "King Cophetua and the Beggar Maid," by Sir Edward Burne-Jones, R.A.

Her First Audition

AMATEUR DRAMATICS

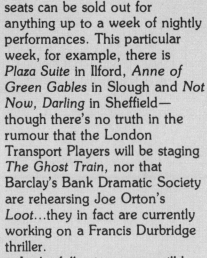

THE professional theatre may be in the midst of an economic crisis, but for amateur dramatics the box-office has never been healthier. This year an estimated five thousand local societies up and down the land will be staging at least one production each, and given the undying loyalty of families and friends seats can be sold out for anything up to a week of nightly performances. This particular week, for example, there is *Plaza Suite* in Ilford, *Anne of Green Gables* in Slough and *Not Now, Darling* in Sheffield—though there's no truth in the rumour that the London Transport Players will be staging *The Ghost Train,* nor that Barclay's Bank Dramatic Society are rehearsing Joe Orton's *Loot*...they in fact are currently working on a Francis Durbridge thriller.

In the following pages will be found the recollections of those who escaped from the world of amateur dramatics and lived to tell their tales, but ever mindful of those still actively involved in rehearsals and those even more gallantly preparing to be part of their audience,
Punch Productions proudly present an all-purpose script, compiled in the knowledge that two of the most popular plays in the amateur theatre are still Noël Coward's *Private Lives* and Agatha Christie's *The Hollow.*

The script comes complete with its own review (which should be filled in and sent to local papers at least one week before the first night) and is respectfully dedicated to Samuel French, the source of all amateur play texts and the publisher who once described *The Importance of Being Earnest* as "Comedy. Oscar Wilde. 5 Male 4 Female. 2 Morning Rooms. One Garden. No Fee Required"...

SAMUEL FRENCH WITHOUT TEARS

A dramatic comedy in two acts or possibly just one, depending on the licensing situation in your village hall. One set, comfortably furnished (NB the Vicarage furniture would be most suitable and, being Christian, the Vicar's wife can scarcely complain; if however she turns nasty or has been asked in previous years, try nearest and dearest neighbours but do leave them a chair or two for mealtimes). Six characters, 4m 2f plus 1d (dog). No fee required...

DRAMATIS PERSONAE:

Cynthia Harcourt-Brace-Jovanovich: Elegant, middle forties, well-dressed, sun-tanned—try lady in the Big House; failing her, Vicar's wife might just be all right, especially if it *is* her furniture.

Reggie Colman-Prentice-Varley: Ex-RAF, moustache, also middle 40s. Bit of a rotter. Try publican or station-master.

Inspector Gorringe: Pipe-smoking, tweed-suited, thoughtful policeman. Not too quick on the uptake, also somewhat churlish with strangers. Try Bank Manager or local Dentist.

Phyllis: Comical cleaning lady, bad legs, doubtful teeth. BE VERY CAREFUL WHEN CASTING THIS PART. DO NOT APPROACH VICAR'S WIFE: IF NECESSARY, PRODUCER SHOULD PLAY IT HIMSELF IN DRAG TO AVOID LOCAL DISHARMONY.

Mr Trumper: Middle 60s: somewhat sinister, carries black bag throughout. Try for local doctor, or traffic warden if male. Maybe even if female.

Mr Trumper's Friend: Younger, somewhat gay. Try local ballet school. AGAIN, BE VERY CAREFUL NOT TO OFFER THIS ROLE INDISCRIMINATELY. DRAMATIC SOCITIES HAVE BEEN DISBANDED FOR LESS.

The curtain rises. (Well, it could actually be drawn open from side to side on a wire. Or you could have two of the stronger members of the society pulling it back from the centre. In this latter case have them start from behind the curtain and walk backwards in opposite directions, otherwise you'll still have half the stage invisible. Since 1956 there have been one or two revolutionary directors who've done away with curtains altogether but this is not recommended here as the audience may then be inclined to sit on the stage especially if the seating arrangement there looks more comfortable.)

Enter Cynthia. Do not let her start speaking until she gets on the stage. Have her face the audience at all times and remind her to speak up—we're none of us getting any younger.

CYNTHIA: Alone at last. If only Reggie were alive.

The French Windows burst open. It is Reggie. Warn him to undo the latch on the windows before bursting through them. Loss of blood could otherwise result.

REGGIE: It is me.
CYNTHIA: No! I ...
REGGIE: Oh very well, then. It is I. I have come back. The Legion is disbanded. We are together at last.
CYNTHIA: So I'll see you again?
REGGIE: Whenever Spring breaks through again.
CYNTHIA: Time may lie heavy between ...
REGGIE: But what has been is past forgetting. Did they ever find the body?
CYNTHIA: Yes. In the study. It was father's.
REGGIE: Well, the whole house was, really.
CYNTHIA: No, no, the body was father's. Inspector Gorringe is still here, making notes.

Inspector Gorringe enters, with notebook and his faithful dog, Sleuth. NB Dog should not be pekingese or poodle as these are apt to produce ribald comments from the audience.

INSPECTOR: Mr Colman-Prentice-Varley, I presume? Perhaps you'd be good enough to answer a few questions. On the night of the 23rd, where were you?
REGGIE: Africa. Very big, Africa, and very flat.
CYNTHIA: That was Norfolk. Very flat, Norfolk.
REGGIE: And Japan?
CYNTHIA: Very small.
INSPECTOR: As I thought. The Taj Mahal is nowhere near Africa! And nor, Sir, were you! I wonder therefore if you'd mind coming down to the station with me and

the dog. Just a few routine questions and perhaps a nip or two.

REGGIE: Oh my God!

CYNTHIA: It's like a terrible nightmare. But wait! Look! Coming up the garden! Who can it be?

At this point it is preferable to have all three characters looking in the same direction, ideally that from which TRUMPER and his FRIEND are about to appear. Enter PHYLLIS, doing funny walk

PHYLLIS: Excuse me Sir, Madam, Sir ... ooh my feet are killing me. There's a couple of gentlemen outside ... seems they're just good friends.

CYNTHIA: Show them in.

Enter TRUMPER and FRIEND. Try not to have them collide with PHYLLIS who will be leaving through the same doorway. Practice makes perfect.

MR TRUMPER: Evening all. We heard a noise. Thought we should investigate, seeing as how we've come to live next door. I'm Trumper, this is my friend.

CYNTHIA: Drink?

MR TRUMPER: If you insist.

Cynthia pours him a glass of sherry. If real sherry unavailable, any brown liquid will do. Well, almost any brown liquid.

MR TRUMPER'S FRIEND: Hello everybody! My, what a lovely room. And what lovely furniture. Especially the chairs. And the table. And what a beautiful lampshade!

These lines should ON NO ACCOUNT be cut. They may not add much to the plot but they will make the Vicar's wife very happy, assuming of course that it is her furniture that has been borrowed for the occasion.

INSPECTOR: Well, now, if you don't mind, Sir, perhaps you'd just come along quietly with me.

MR TRUMPER: Oh very well, but I must say I'd expected a few questions first. I mean, it's not as though I was anywhere near the library on the night of the 23rd and as for the body, I ...

INSPECTOR: Did anyone mention a body in the library?

MR TRUMPER: Oh my God! You mean, Inspector, if I hadn't come in just now ...

He breaks down. This can be achieved by turning the back to the audience, bending down and heaving your shoulders, much after the fashion of Mr Heath doing up a shoelace.

The curtain falls ... or (see above) the two strong members of the Society could be asked to pull it slowly back along the wire, being careful to stop when they get to the middle.

The producer should then make the speech outlined in our "Helpful Dramatic Hints" pamphlet, the one starting "I know you won't want to hear too many words from me after all that excitement" and ending twenty minutes later with "and Mrs Wilkins for the lovely flowers".

Review

At the ... Hall last week the ... Amateur Dramatic Society (or Thesps as we've affectionately known them for so many years now) presented an admirable production of that very witty thriller "Samuel French Without Tears". Mrs ... was enchanting/ splendid/very audible as Cynthia and Mr ... was equally dashing/impressive/well-dressed/tall as Reggie. In the smaller (but no less important) roles dear Mrs ... was most amusing/lifelike/punctual as the maid and Mr ... offered a very striking/interesting/ novel/clean performance as the wily policeman—no Sergeant Dixon he! As for the two strangers who bring about a most unexpected and exciting finish, Mr ... and Mr ... did very well/all that could be expected of them/their best. The furniture look very nice indeed and the lighting effects by Mr ... were very clever/successful/bright. As for the production, Mr.... reached his usual standard and the interval tea/coffee/ biscuits/itself was especially good. Next year/month/season/Christmas the Thesps will be organising their usual pantomime/ Gilbert and Sullivan operetta/fund-raising barbecue and it is hoped that as many as possible will attend/contribute/take part/stay awake.

...And all the men and women nearly players

Five who escaped from the dressing-rooms tell all

Eamonn Andrews

To be asked, as I am, if there is much in the way of amateur theatre in Ireland, gives me the jaw-dropping feeling that someone wants to know if there are fish in the sea.

The green isle is awash with amateur dramatics. I remember Micheál-Oscar-Wilde-MacLiammóir trying to make an honest penny in the Gate Theatre, Dublin, lifting his hands and eyebrows as if they were tethered to the same ligament.

"Dear boy, the competition for audiences is not from the Abbey or the Gaiety or the Olympia but from some three hundred audience-swallowing amateur productions—God bless them—going on this very minute within a twenty mile radius of Nelson's Pillar".

A touch of statistical hyperbole, perhaps, but quite a grain of commercial and artistic truth.

For me, it didn't take too long to lose my boyhood blushes at seeing my real-life chisel-and-plane-carrying dad in toga plus sword saving the Christians from the lions at St. Teresa's Temperance Society (Amateur Drama) Hall. A fingers of years later, I was High King at school (amateur drama) on a mighty but shaky throne. Even then— vital to all dramatics—I was wormed by the feeling that Charlie Fitzsimons, who had the more mobile and loquacious part, didn't have it because he could walk better and talk better and look better (at least two of which he could) but because his sister was Maureen O'Hara, the Film Star.

(I never did discover why she changed her name from Fitzsimons to O'Hara. To protect the innocent? The family? Convent-backed amateur drama forsaken for the perils of paid professionalism?)

At any rate, the happy disease (amateur dramatics) pursued me beyond the school—as it does thousands of Celtic thespians to this very day. There isn't a bank in Ireland that hasn't been raided for at least the assistant manager, or an insurance company, or a co-operative dairy, or a national school not distracted by a touch of the number nines—a greasepaint of popular but vital importance in almost any production outside sunnier climes.

Those who are not acting in plays are writing them. Being one of the greedy ones, I did both in Dublin's Peacock theatre—rent £10 a week, Capacity 105.

One review went something like this: "This play is like the measles. Now that he's had it he may do something better."

I never did. I turned pro and forgot to change my name.

Joan Bakewell

Viewed from childhood, life is one huge amateur theatricals and I spent mine vainly casting myself in different parts and waiting for the applause. Only occasionally did reality meet fantasy in the sharp focus of a school performance—with real tickets, coloured lights and flowers afterwards. Then, in however fantastic a part, I felt sure who I was.

It all began with the dressing-up things: a rag-bag of discarded nighties, lengths of curtain and feathered evening dresses of my aunts—les plumes de ma tante, in fact—in which I perpetually attended meals, did my homework and practised at the piano-forte. My appalled parents feared I might go on the stage...or on the streets. Nowadays dressing up is all very healthy and progressive play-groups call it role playing. And I've noticed amateur theatricals to be similarly preoccupied by details of costume and make-up: solicitors and teachers in the back row of the chorus fretting about five and nine, while stars at the RSC go on as they are.

When theatrical roles eventually came my way they offered no clue as to where I was heading. All I can make of Michael in *Peter Pan*, the Dormouse in *Alice* and Malvolio in *Twelfth Night* is a clear case of adolescent identity crisis. Things shaped up a bit as I shaped out. Hermia, Natasha and Cecily are all wilful young women lucklessly in love. And at the time I was beginning to find myself distinctly at home with their emotions.

But by then I was into the big time. Not church halls or scout huts any more but the Cambridge ADC theatre. I thought my moment had come when I was cast as one of the prostitutes (my mother's heart sank) in *Point of Departure*. The director was an energetic young student beginning to show promise. He recognized my potential at once and never gave me another part. Still if you're going to have a career stopped in its tracks, it might as well be by the future director of the National Theatre.

"It's gone to his head - he was a spear-holder in the last act..."

Ned Sherrin

The good cause being supported, I can't remember; but the first Amateur Theatricals I saw, called *Brought Home by Broadcast*, took place in a large room in the Squire's house, and told the moving story of how an old lady (the Squire, *en travestie*) tricks her erring daughter (the Squire's daughter) into returning home by means of an S.O.S. broadcast over the wireless (Alvar Liddell = the Squire's wife.) In fact the old lady was well and in the interest of the Dramatic Unities the daughter was staying just up the road anyway. In due course the broadcast brought her home. I was bowled over by

the style, subtlety and verisimilitude of the whole enterprise. Some people may have been inspired by first sights of Marie Lloyd or Henry Irving. For me it was an elderly gentleman in drag. My enthusiasm was soon confirmed by the efforts of the ladies of the Somerton W.I. in a piece by Mr Novello and the W.I. of Glastonbury in *Ladies in Retirement*.

In the Royal Corps of Signals at Catterick there was the very sophisticated Carey Theatre presenting a standard of theatricals to which we in 4 Training Regiment did not aspire; but we had our production of *Someone At The Door* by Dorothy and Campbell Christie which we felt was almost as good. About now I became aware of that phrase beloved of amateurs "Better than the professionals". That is the splendid thing about Amateur Theatricals—the aura of success that always attends them. It sustained me through *The Sport of Kings* (British Troops in Austria Amateur Dramatic Society) and through a radio production by the

same society of Maugham's *The Circle* recorded on some sort of wire recorder which gave the convincing effect of having been recorded in a biscuit box. ("Better than the BBC"!)

By the time I arrived at Oxford doubts had begun to set in. These represented the first glimmerings of professionalism. John Wood cast me as a Bishop in *Tis A Pity She's a Whore,* and sacked me one day later. Nearly cast as Sir Toby Belch for the OUDS, I was pipped at the post by Patrick Dromgoole. The ETC summer revue was the only alternative and so I embarked on a career of frivolity, variously supported by the Editor of *Esquire* (ambitious at that time to be a choreographer), a past Editor of the *Spectator* and now MP (a plumpish, charming, rather static, chorus boy), a Vice-President of Twentieth-Century-Fox (Romantic Juvenile), someone senior at J. Walter Thompson (who wrote everything—"I've fallen in love with myself, and it's working out frightfully well."), a promising playwright (knock-about comedy), a National Theatre Director (Co-Director) and Miss Maggie Smith (already a professional actress).

But Miss Smith apart, we were still true amateurs. We must have been. When the BBC televised "Oxford Accents" the notices still said, "Better than the professionals."

Esther Rantzen

Looking back I really feel sorry for my parents. When my recorder had finally squeaked to a standstill in the last school concert, mother put away her petal hat, father dumped his ear plugs, and they both settled down to shouting at the telly and other adult amusements. Not for long. When I went from school to university, my family had many gruelling hours ahead of them.

The only student performance they enjoyed was an open-air production of *The Importance of Being Earnest*. They enjoyed it because the weather was fine, and the wind wafted our words away so that father fell asleep at once. They quite enjoyed my clothes, too. They were provided by the college. It was a man's college—in fact, it was Balliol. Balliol have a dressing-up box, and in that box I found a slinky black taffeta number. It may have belonged to a gentleman don's aunt. I suppose it may, at a pinch, have belonged to a gentleman don. Either way, it was fringed from knee to ankle, and when I sat down and crossed by ankles the fronds knotted themselves round my heels. On cue, I stood and hobbled towards the audience, bent over backwards like a croquet hoop. The knots tightened. I delivered my best line. "Do you allude to me, Miss Cardew, as an entanglement?" It had never gone as well at rehearsal.

Of course, we had much more fun than our stoic audience did. But then we didn't do it for them. We did it for the glory of our names printed splodgily in the programme. For the romance of unrequited love—all the girls fell for the director, all the boys fell for the leading lady. But most of all, for the chance of a free trip. College productions were invited to all sorts of interesting places, some went to Germany, some went to the States. Even I got as far as Henley. We slept in a farmer's barn. I remember, on bales of straw. Those summer nights were tickly, companionable, and moving. Literally moving, all night long, because the tickling companions were fleas, and fleas don't need much sleep. We doused the straw with Dettol. That only did for them what honey does for Miss Cartland, it jollied them up enormously. After our second week in the barn I slunk into the local hotel, and locked myself in the bathroom. I still remember the luxury of that wonderful bath, with the manager rattling the handle and shouting through the keyhole "Don't think you'll get away with this, Miss. It'll cost you half a crown."

I hope I didn't get him into hot water.

The Fringe of the Edinburgh Festival is the Olympics of student drama—in church halls all over the city they compete for the gold medal, a mention by Harold Hobson. My year at the festival, the actors decided to improvise. In the heat of the moment, one picked up a chair and hurled it into the audience, striking Mr Hobson a painful blow. Afterwards he said he was carried away. The actor, I mean, not Mr Hobson. But even physical danger didn't discourage the audience. The revues played to full houses, not because they were brilliantly performed, but because the writing was original and the direction was fresher than professional sketches. "Why didn't you walk out, Mother?" I asked her once. "We didn't dare," she said. "You outnumbered us fourteen to one." And I suppose that is the one weapon all amateur theatricals know—and use. Fear.

"And I'll double that order if you can guarantee delivery of a bus-load of your society at our Mikado on Wednesday."

Lord Mancroft

I have not appeared in many theatrical performances—2½ to be exact. But I think I acquitted myself with courage in all of them.

My first appearance was at my Prep School, where we mounted a play about Boadicea. Matron played Boadicea, and I played third halbardier from the right. Every so often we halbardiers had to rush out through the locker-room, and come back through the Fifth Form library wearing different helmets. (They play the same trick in *Aida*, but more lavishly.)

Originally, I was first halbardier, which was a speaking part. My duty was to march on and exclaim anxiously, "My lord, the Queen has swooned".

Unfortunately I have a poor verbal memory, and my piece often came out at rehearsals as the Queen has sweened, or even the Sween has quooned. I was demoted.

My next appearance was also in a non-speaking part. I played William Caxton in the *Pageant of Parliament* at the Albert Hall in July 1934. For twenty minutes I stood looking calm and printy, which isn't easy in a heat wave when you're wearing about five tons of Renaissance robing. My next door neighbour was Chaucer who used to tuck a whisky flask under his doublet to help strengthen his nerves. On the last night he strengthened them to such effect that he fell head-long down the emergency exit, whence he lay bellowing Chaucerian obscenities.

Edward IV and I, not caring to see our old friend in such disarray, nipped down the stairs (in as much as one can nip anywhere in five tons of Renaissance robing)

and bore our stricken poet back on stage, thus ruining (so the Producer maintained) the entire Grand Finale. I didn't see it this way.

My ½ performance was in a one-act play called *Sargeant Peter,* which I wrote at Oxford for the OUDS. The curtain rose on the waiting-room of a criminal court where four men (old, middle-aged, youthful and young) were arguing with the turnkey. Symbolism, you realise; the four ages of the same man waiting for St. Peter to let them in for trial. I wrote the part of St. Peter for myself (cheeky!) but I could never remember the words even though I had written them myself, and this, said the *Oxford Mail,* was hardly surprising, as the words were very unmemorable. The Producer sacked me, and took over himself.

The *Isis* review was kinder. "Poignant," it said, "eloquent, tidily constructed." Happily, not everyone knew that, under a nom-de-plume, I was myself the dramatic critic of the *Isis*.

semé.

The Hell of the Greasepaint, The Bore of the Crowd

Basil Boothroyd looks back on his days as a part-time strolling player

Taxed with it, I'd have said I'd never trod the boards of the Scala Theatre in *Night Must Fall*, as one of the Thalian Repertory Players, under the patronage of Baroness de Goldsmid da Palmeira, all proceeds to the Polish refugees. You forget these things.

But here's the programme, and there am I. Twice. Lord Chief Justice in the prologue and Inspector Belsize in the play. More, I have an asterisk and a footnote: "By permission of St. Pancras People's Theatre". So my career on the amateur stage was well beyond its budding.

Further down the cast list, playing Mrs Bramson's comical cook, was Daisy Nichols. She's changed it to Dandy now, and you'd know her better as Mrs Alf Garnett. There's a picture of us. Her in her fur tippet, me in my cascading inspector's moustache, in case the audience thought I was still the Lord Chief, doing a bit of ultra vires and heading the police enquiries.

All proceeds didn't, in fact, go the the luckless Poles. My watch, cigarette case and wallet went to persons unknown, nipping in from Charlotte Street while I was on stage passing sentence of death. Portraying, as I was, both executive and judicial arms of the Law, I now remember being narked at this. Cheeky. I ran about backstage in full-bottomed wig and underpants threatening to sue the manager. He might have said, and possibly did, that my inspector, so astute in bringing Mr Emlyn Williams's anti-hero to the gallows, should strictly have made short work of a pretty pilferer working the make-up tables.

It was a lesson in distinguishing Theatre from Life, something I was having difficulty with at the time.

To have forgotten the engagement is pardonable. The run was short, occurring on February 6, 1939. It was not my London début as a man of the theatre. That had been in the previous September, at the Phoenix, Charing Cross Road. I suppose Munich was happening around then, but I took no notice. When you're young, and writing the music for a Chinese play (under the patronage of H.E. the Chinese Ambassador) you need all your concentration for what matters. So I was only in the orchestra pit for that one, and conducted from the piano, much relied on for clever chords representing gongs. Gwen Ffrangcon-Davies did most of the singing, in a surprisingly sweet soprano which was a great relief to me on the opening, i.e., the closing night. I wasn't used to the self-conserving professional approach, and she had rehearsed in a husky mutter, through billowing cigarette smoke and powerful pince-nez.

There was a further piece of professionalism from another member of the cast, who liked the score so much that he took it to America and lost it. I shrugged. It was tough on the world of the arts, deprived of a second *Chu Chin Chow* like that, but for me, what of it? Plenty more where that came from. I was already at grips with my 1938 *Dick Whittington*. Again the orchestra pit. The piano pit, rather. John Furness played the other piano. Now a TV producer. Hi, John, any jobs going? As for the cast, I fancy Margery Mason was in it, and probably Cecile Chevreaux. I know that Princess April Shower was in the capable hands of a Miss Joy Adamson, only later to ask such pointed questions as 'Can you eat it?'

This was at the St. Pancras People's Theatre, a rum, rum, repertory set-up that was ruling my life around then, until Hitler's voice, with its harsh insistence on costly blackout materials, penetrated even there, and closed us down for good. Resources were bound to be slender, with unreserved seats curiously fixed at sevenpence, and the best in the house at half-a-crown. The wardrobe was sparse, but infinitely adjustable under ingenious needles. A few feet of gold piping on Dad's suit from *Love on the Dole*, and you'd got General Robert E. Lee shooting up Harper's Ferry in *Gallows Glorious*. Trollope crinolines from *The Small House at Allington* were next week's full-sleeved Russian pyjamas for *Tovarich*. Wigs were a desperate scramble. You could get lumbered with the least favourite, known to us all as Little Nitty.

I often wondered, myself, stuck with it, whether it had once been worn by Maurice Evans, André Morell, Michael Hordern and others who got their first heady whiff of grease-paint at St. P. and went on to lose their amateur status. The grail of professionalism danced before us all, but out of a company of about a hundred I don't suppose more than a dozen got their hands on it. My own exit was somewhat blocked by fond parents having put me into a bank, thus realising their proudest hopes. Clean, safe, reputable work. Pension at sixty. A postcard saying that I'd quit, and was doing ASM at Horsham Rep for two quid a week would have been brutal. True, it was a bank recently quitted by T.S. Eliot. Did he knock off *The Waste Land* on some ledger desk, as I did *Dick Whittington*? Wodehouse had been a banker, and got out. I lacked his stern resolution.

Most part-time Thespians, or Thalians if you prefer, manage one production a year: perhaps two, in rare organisations free of the temperamental in-fighting that folds up most amateur groups like deck chairs and has whole villages not speaking to each other. At St. Pancras we did one a week. Temperaments were frowned on. Discipline was fierce. Miss a rehearsal and you were out. When the cast-lists went up in the green room there were cries of agony and bliss. The agonised, unselected this week, were fit to take their lives. The blissful left at a run for French's, in Southampton Street, to get a copy of the play, and avidly count their lines at the bus-stop, standing the while in the actor's stance, weight on the right leg, the left a half pace forward and bent, surprising the rest of the queue with sudden, outflung gestures, or tentative mouthings of telling repartee.

Don't think, by the way, that I walked straight into the London theatre, drawing the sevenpenny audience, without distinguished provincial successes behind me. My *Our Miss Gibbs* ran for three nights at Brigg, and toured for another at Sleaford. The *Horncastle News* described my performance in *Are You a Mason?* as 'effective', and noted that the Act II curtain rose on my solo rendering of 'I Love the Moon' for alto saxophone. By hindsight, I worry about that. We weren't much concerned with interpreting the author's intention in those days. He didn't see the production, being luckily dead. How, I wonder, did I dispose of the instrument and slip smoothly back into the character, a man whose musicianship wasn't even hinted at in the text?

Actor's biographies tend to

leap from the years 1939-1945. 'After seeing service in North Africa...' In my case, this would be to conceal a significant period of my career. I saw my own service in North Lancashire, at a remote RAF station with no aeroplanes, where time hung heavy and no bomb fell. Morale could have sagged dangerously, even despite the dedication of a few bold spirits among us who did our best for it with an unremitting stream of cabaret and variety. I hadn't been up there long before it was accepted that the gymnasium was used for nothing else. My monologue on the state of the East Camp ablutions, which got two sergeants posted to Iceland, is still, I think, remembered, especially by them. This was fearless stuff, for an acting corporal. Was it enough? We knew about the war from the radio. It seemed remote. What was needed to bring it home was our production of *Journey's End*, which ran for years, off and on, and was toured round the bomber and fighter stations to show the crews what the real thing was like.

I went through hell as Captain Stanhope, and never had a qualm about pinning up his MC ribbon for the second act. To endure the offstage explosions—we must have shot off more ordnance than the whole Eighth Army—

called for nerves of steel. Realism was all. We bashed dents into our mint-fresh tin hats with revolver butts, and wondered, every time the sensational dugout collapse came round, if we hadn't overdone it and enfeebled their protective standards.

My finest hour, though, had come in the early days of the project. With only non-commissioned status, but fired with artistic integrity, I pulled my stage captain's rank on a genuine flight-lieutenant in the cast, playing Mason, a mere private, who thought himself entitled to the best breeches in the costume basket. It meant going over his head to the CO, but I got them, all right.

It was a long time, back again in the palmy days of peace and village dramatics, before I had to give anyone a piece of my mind on that scale. That was when my own bank manager—I'd at last graduated to the customer's side of the counter—crouched over the sound-effects tape of *Love From a Stranger*, brought up the national anthem loud and clear in the middle of Act One. I was alone on stage at the time. It takes skilled ad-libbing to get round a thing like that, especially when some other fool, triggered like a Pavlov dog, drops the curtain on you just as you're getting the situation mastered. I told him, I remember, that I had a damned good mind to take my account elsewhere. If he'd had the figures handy he wouldn't have paled and trembled as he did.

One thing about the amateur drama, it makes you "feel it here, dear", as a lady producer at St. P., rumoured to have been three years in *The Garden of Allah*, used to say.

And what you feel, inanely, childishly enough, is that nothing else matters. If for that reason alone, I'm sorry to have quit the amateur boards (though I was offered a Second Wise Man in a nativity play last year—didn't they realise I'd once played no less than Herod?).

Just now, what with one thing and another, it might be restful to slip back into something more real than real life.

"We're in luck, the press is here."

The Art of Coarse Acting

Michael Green reviews some unforgettable first and only nights

Amateur drama provides the most fruitful field for that strange off-shoot of genuine art, Coarse Acting. I define a Coarse Actor as one who can remember the pauses but not the lines, and my first encounter with Coarse Acting occurred when I had a small part with a local group. Four of us merely had to sit playing cards upstage, while the main action continued in front of us. One man did have a speech to say but he didn't bother to learn it, he wrote it on the back of a playing-card (together with such useful annotations as "sneer here" and "shake fist"). Unfortunately, we played a genuine game of whist, the card the the lines on was trumped, and it was shuffled into the pack just before his cue came.

Playing-cards flew in all directions as we frantically sought the vital card, until we were all on hands and knees with the pack spread on the floor while the cue came closer and closer. It arrived just as we found the card and the wretched actor bellowed his lines while kneeling under the table. Later we discovered he'd found the wrong card, and said the speech from the next act.

It seems there is a deep-rooted Coarse Acting streak in most amateurs, including the one who during *Henry V* found himself in the wrong army and spent Agincourt fighting against his own side.

But Coarse Acting is not only a matter of being bad, or experiencing a disaster, although these form part of it. It is an attitude to the part, a determination to *shine* at all costs which makes a Coarse Actor.

This is partly because of the dreary, small parts he has to play. While the others are grappling with the terrible soul-weariness of Chekhov, the Coarse Actor merely clumps in and says, "Shall I put some more logs on the stove?" In Shakespeare he will probably play at least five parts, one of which will be a direly unfunny assistant clown, with incomprehensible lines about horns and French tailors.

Thus Coarse Actors take refuge in grotesquerie to stand out. Cast a Coarse Actor as an 18th century innkeeper and he will automatically assume a patch over one eye and a limp. Any part over the age of 40 is played with positive senility. I have seen entire stages covered with gibbering Shakespearian lords, mowing, sawing and making those meaningless gestures beloved of the Coarse Actor.

There are no subtle shades in a Coarse Actor's approach to his part. All characters not young must be immensely old, and preferably deformed. Thus a friend covered his face in false warts and boils in an effort to stand out. Alas, one night he sneezed and the whole disguise simply exploded in a cloud of powder. Boils and warts flew in all directions and his false nose landed in the stalls. When the dust settled a young man was standing there.

In this way the Coarse Actor hopes to avoid merging into the background. He refuses to be submerged and can frequently be seen marching about the stage for no reason at all, to the distress of other actors.

But we all have a streak of Coarse Acting in us. Take the time when I was playing a smuggler, circa 1810. I slipped on-stage, broke my leg, and was taken to hospital. My arrival caused consternation in Casualty. To start with I was in ragged seaman's costume. I had a patch on one eye and a beard of two feet long. I appeared to have only one leg (the broken one), the other being

"I have in mind here a sweeping panorama of Venice and the beautiful Ponte Di Rialto."

strapped up inside my breeches. Instead of a right hand I had a large hook. Finally, there was a sword sticking out of my chest, which was covered in stage blood.

The nurse hardly knew where to begin, but decided to start by trying to pull out the sword (which was stuck in a block of wood strapped to my body). I pawed at her with my hook to attract attention and she gasped and fled for the doctor, who after glancing at my deformities muttered, "They really shouldn't send these orthopaedic cases here."

Now, Coarse Acting has reached the status of an art form. Several festivals have been held in recent years. At Ealing, a team from the Royal Shakespeare Company performed a version of Julius Caesar in which the dying Caesar, knives sticking from all parts of his anatomy, was pursued round the auditorium by Brutus, administered the final stab by the emergency exit, through which Caesar fell with a faint cry of "Et tu, Brute".

At Salisbury Playhouse, the National Theatre entered a side which performed a murder mystery, noteworthy for a masterly performance by the butler, who actually aged with each entrance, until by the end he was so old he had to be helped through the door by a maid. It has even been discovered that the French have a word for it—Cabotinage.

Yet it is the genuine article which always proves stranger than the fictitious. It would be difficult to invent anything as bizarre as the occasion when I was playing in King John and the Archduke of Austria fell off the stage during a black-out. Dazed and bewildered, he groped blindly round the audience looking for a way out, until he came to the aisle, up which he began to crawl on his knees. At this point he was halted by an attendant, who asked if he wanted the gents' toilet.

Meanwhile, backstage, there was panic as we discovered we were a Duke short. Luckily, the stage manager had seen the accident, and sent out the English army as a search party. We poured

"...your loins ache with desire...your very soul is in torment."

into the hall through an emergency exit, and dragged the grateful Duke away.

As the local paper said: "The director's use of the auditorium as part of the acting area was sheer inspiration. It reached its climax when the treacherous Duke of Austria, pursued by the English army, took refuge at the very feet of the audience—superb symbolism, this—from where he was mercilessly dragged to his doom."

Although often one feels one has now seen it all, new facets of Coarse Acting are constantly being revealed.

Recently I saw a village group perform a rather dated

drama in which an officer, injured on some expedition, decides to commit suicide to avoid "being a burden on the other chaps".

He crawled out of his blankets and painstakingly dragged himself to the tent pole, where his revolver hung. After a journey of excruciating slowness, he got to the pole and with trembling hands reached up for the revolver.

At that moment he loudly broke wind.

There was a short silence, and then a great shout of laughter. The audience were still laughing when he shot himself, which was just as well, as the noise drowned the fact that the gun didn't go off.

DRAMATIS AMATEURPERSONAE

William Hewison draws up a cast list

Melvyn Tripp *Drama critic* Reviews the annual play for the school mag. At the moment he writes in the verbosely ornamental style ringing with words like *resonance* and *roman à clef.* He has yet to learn that all that is required of him is to mention everyone in the cast by name and say how good they were.

Harry Buckton *Driving force* Every amateur dramatic group must have a Harry Buckton if it is to survive longer than a twelve-month. He is the power pack, the fanatical enthusiast, the whipper-up of flagging interest. He organises, directs, acts, paints scenery, soothes nerves, sells tickets. Yet he needs the Group more than it needs him.

Dame Sarah Grinham-Phelps, JP *Magistrate and character actress* Once off the bench and on the boards she's a real scream, a perfect hoot. Comical Irish maids, tipsy Cockney charwomen, garrulous Scotch landladies—these are her speciality—delivered in the broad regional accents you hear nowhere but on the stage. Her brazen scene-stealing is the kind of theft that gets three months from her when she's in court.

Dorothy and Isabelle *Ardent supporters* attend all first-nights in the West End; they clutter up the foyer and ogle the resting professionals who are on display and touting for work. Occasionally Dot and Belle buy seats for the upper circle where they spend the whole performance whispering how much better their own Carshalton Thespians did it. Sometimes they are not far wrong.

Simon Fotherington *Lecher*
A real Anyone-for-tennis? man.
Joined the Group for the extra-
mural activities and all those
unscheduled rehearsals he tells his
wife about. Is currently the male
lead in *Private Lives* and is having it
off with his co-star, an upper-class
scrubber who believes that
actresses should be naturally
promiscuous.

Robin Selkirk *Method actor* Has soaked himself in
Stanislavsky and Lee Strasberg so has no difficulties in
the Group's work sessions when he is called upon to
be a typewriter or a broken gate or an infertile egg.
Unfortunately he has never actually appeared in a play
yet—what he can't do is remember his lines.

Jason Gore *Playwright* It's his first play and he has
entered it in the College drama competition. It has a
small cast: The Man, The Woman, The Tramp, and a
simple set: one table, three chairs, a wind-up
gramophone. The script is short on words but long on
silences. The Tramp represents God, or Death, or
Conscience, or something. The play will win the
competition because fourteen plays exactly like it won
it in previous years.

g *Props man* The only
rking-class member of
e Group and the one who
t only doesn't want to grab
e meatiest role but doesn't
nt to act at all. Instead, he is
e knocker-up of sets and props, the
at fixer; what he does with chicken
re and old newspapers is wondrous
behold. The one time he was given
redit in the programme they got his
me wrong.

AT THE PLAY

3
June
1925

THE CHERRY ORCHARD
(Lyric, Hammersmith)

As I sat gazing expectantly on the darkened scene which Mr. NIGEL PLAYFAIR, ignoring his author's stage directions, had provided for the opening of ANTON TCHEHOV'S *The Cherry Orchard,* I tried to put myself in the position of one who had never heard of this comedy as an established classic, and to face it as I conceive an ordinary phlegmatic middle-class Briton would do, entirely refusing to be overawed by my intellectual friends, all soulful and agog with excitement around me.

What extraordinary people! (my thoughts ran). Why does everybody pay no attention to what any other body has just said, but go vaguely off at a tangent of his own? Why does an eccentric old gentleman with a complex about billiards always imagine himself chipping the red into the middle pocket? What does the corpulent land-owner with a frock-coat over his white smock and a face like a horse do in life besides borrowing twenty-five pounds? Has darling old *Firs,* the man-servant, wandered with his top-hat out of the Bank of England courtyard? Why does everybody say, "It is late; let us go to bed," without making the faintest attempt to do so, so that they fall asleep in their tracks and are carried off and dumped into the adjoining bedrooms?

Is this a picture of a Russian lunatic asylum, or a skit on the futility of Russian folk, or a piece of ultra-realism or ultra-symbolism or dadaism, or what? Is it a desperately sad comedy or an amusingly gay tragedy? Aren't the intellectual ladies and gentlemen by whom I am surrounded occasionally laughing at points which don't exist by way of showing their intelligence—a phenomenon I have observed before in this admirable little theatre?

Thus I kept my defences through the whole of the First Act and a part of the Second, feeling a little as if I ought to write to *The Times* about it, as those infuriated omniscient gentlemen rush in and write about Mr. EPSTEIN'S Memorial. "Call this art?" they say. "well, I'm—!"—or words to that hysterical effect.

And then insensibly I found myself falling under the soft spell. These people are very odd, but they are very lovable, very real. There is *Madame Ranevsky* (Miss MARY GREY), sentimental humbug at bottom, passionately happy, it would seem, to get back from Paris to her Cherry Orchard and discreetly glad to get back to Paris and her invalid lover when the beautiful place is sold over her head; *Leonid* (Mr. ALAN NAPIER), her brother, the billiard maniac, with his incredible fecklessness and hopefulness and genuine deep affection and kindliness; the "mouldy gentleman *Peter"* (Mr. JOHN GIELGUD), the student, a free man, above love, above money, and desperately concerned, at the height of the tragi-comedy, with the loss of his goloshes, the adorable *Firs* (Mr. O. B. CLARENCE), the old man-servant, who looked upon the great liberation of the serfs as the one disastrous thing which had happened to Russia, kissing the hem of his fundamentally indifferent mistress's garment, over-anxious lest his master should have gone off with the wrong coat to catch his death of cold, dying forgotten and uncomplaining in the locked-up house.

There is *Lopakhin* (Mr. FRED O'DONOVAN), the one man with the idea of work as an anodyne and a livelihood, son and grandson of a serf, and finally (a little less than half-ashamed and a little more than half-triumphant) buying the Orchard over the heads of the family after repeated attempts to warn them of the impending calamity—a man fine in grain, vulgarised by the muddy traffic of life, practical in an utterly and fantastically unpractical environment; *Yasha* (Mr. BYAM SHAW), the sophisticated man-

THE CHERRY ORCHARD SCARECROWS; OR, WILD LIFE IN HAMMERSMITH.
(From left to right). MESSRS. JOHN GIELGUD, BYAM SHAW, ALAN NAPIER, FRED O'DONOVAN, R. S. SMITH, MISS MARY GREY AND MR. O. B. CLARENCE.

servant from Paris, taking his pleasure as he finds it with *Dunyasha,* the housemaid, and thoroughly content to follow his mistress back to Paris and escape the dull and inadequate fare made necessary by her persistent habit of giving to beggars and tramps all the money she happens to have in her purse, which incidentally she has borrowed; *Barbara* (Miss VIRGINIA ISHAM), the virginal, in love yet utterly ignorant of the arts of love, cumbered with much serving; and *Anya* (Miss GWENDOLEN EVANS), the "mouldy gentleman's" friend, unawakened and unspoiled. All these move before us alive, pathetic, memorable.

It is a charming assembly of incomponents, whose life is regulated more by the rules of the Sermon on the Mount than by those of the Trades Union Congress or the Federation of British Industries; feckless, irrelevant, lifelike and completely delightful—a lovely thing.

The production seemed to me to be admirable. I assume that it owes much to that of the Moscow Art Theatre, as much as can have been gathered from report by an intelligent producer like Mr. NIGEL PLAYFAIR, who knows his Europe. The scenery, painted by the Brothers HEMBROW, and owing not a little to the late CLAUD LOVAT FRASER, was entirely satisfactory; and the costumes served to remind us of what a drab, impracticable and essentially idiotic fashion we maintain in our enlightened country and century.

I thought the translation by the late Mr. GEORGE CALDERON a little stiff and unemotional, but the playing was beyond praise. A well-drilled group of actors, among whom only Mr. FRED O'DONOVAN *(Lopakhin)* and Mr. O. B. CLARENCE *(Firs)* have a considerable reputation, presented this beautiful piece of work in the most persuasive and moving manner.

I candidly do not think the Town folk will flock in great numbers—but it will be the Town's loss.   T.

"Come on, everybody — time to audition for this year's 'Peter Pan.' "

OUTDOOR DRESS REHEARSAL

Scene Two; we'll start from there.
    (This is Illyria, lady.)
Remember, Viola, project your voice—
    It doesn't carry in the open air.
(Art thou good at these kickshawses, knight!)
    Those cedar trees are perfect; dark and shady,
An ideal setting—yes, the Vicar's choice...
    The colonnade? Just plywood, painted white...
Bring up your limes!—Lend me a Number Eight—
    (Make me a willow cabin at your gate.)

Floodlight on leaves and grass...
    (The spinsters and the knitters in the sun.)
Enter the courtiers!... Against black trees
    Bright silhouettes and dancing shadows pass.
(Daylight and champain discovers not more.)
    Into the spotlight—run, Maria, run!
Behind the bushes, murmurous as bees,
    They wait their cues in darkness. Now, Scene Four—
Ambers and cypress; foolery and sadness...
    (Why, this is very midsummer madness.)

Oh, dear, Sir Toby's beard has come unstuck.
    (More matter for a May morning.)
No earthly use in looking at the script—
    It's too late now for words; rely on luck!
(Now, as thou lovest me, let me see his letter.)
    Electrics, kill that spot!—you've had the warning!
Remind me I must get that box-hedge clipped...
    Let's hope to-morrow night it will go better...
I wonder what the weather forecasts say...
    (The rain, sings Feste, raineth every day.)

(1950)

The Theatre Guide

"OH, YES, I'VE SEEN THIS PLAY BEFORE—VERY THRILL-ING; YOU NEVER KNOW WHAT'S GOING TO HAPPEN NEXT—

THAT'S THE VILLAIN—THE ONE WITH A BEARD—THOUGH NO ONE SPOTS HIM. AND ERIC HASN'T REALLY STOLEN THE DIAMONDS—HE'S ONLY SHIELDING DORIS; AND SHE'S NOT REALLY THE MAID, BUT WE DON'T KNOW THAT YET—AND SMITH ISN'T REALLY THE BUTLER; HE'S A DETECTIVE, AND NOBODY GUESSES IT UNTIL THE END—

NOW SIR JAMES IS GOING TO BE SHOT IN A MINUTE, THROUGH THAT WINDOW ON THE RIGHT, AND NO ONE SEES IT DONE—IT'S REALLY DR. ROBINSON, BUT EVERYONE THINKS IT'S ERIC—

AND NOW MRS. ARKWRIGHT IS GOING TO FIND THE WILL BEHIND THE CLOCK ON THE MANTELPIECE, BUT IT ISN'T THE WILL REALLY, IT'S A FORGERY; THAT WE DON'T FIND OUT TILL THE LAST ACT—

NOW CAPTAIN HOLDSWORTH IS GOING TO DRINK A WHISKY-AND-SODA THAT'S BEEN SECRETLY POISONED BY THE CON-TESSA—BUT HE ISN'T REALLY GOING TO DIE; HE KNEW ABOUT IT ALL THE TIME."

AND NOW VERY SHORTLY A MAN IN THE STALLS, WHO'S BEEN SPOILING EVERYONE'S ENJOYMENT—

IS GOING TO HAVE HIS SILLY MOUTH SHUT WITH HIS OWN OVERCOAT—

AND THE BODY IS GOING TO BE DISPOSED OF UNDERNEATH THE SEAT.

OEDIPUS BRUCE

Alan Coren

In Australia a recommendation was made recently that incest between a mother and son should no longer be illegal.

ACT ONE

Enter Chorus. They are citizens of Adelaide. They have corks dangling from their hats. They are all dead drunk.

CHORUS   Our mouths are like the inside of an abbo's trousers. We have all been walking through yesterday's lunch. We are as much use as an earwig's tit. What happened to last Wednesday?

Enter Barry, King of Adelaide, on all fours.

CHORUS   Hallo, Bazza, you look like two ton of old fish-heads.

BARRY   I've just been out in the fly box, saying goodbye to breakfast.

CHORUS   It's not like old Bazza to honk the bacon down the pipes after a night on the frosty tubes. Old Bazza has a gut like a ship's boiler. We have seen old Bazza sink ten gallons of Mrs Foster's Finest without threatening the drainage. Old Bazza must be upset about something.

BARRY   Too right! I was reading my horoscope in *Beer Weekly*, and it says where it's bad dos on the family scene this year, my flaming son is gonna flaming kill me, also beer could go up by as much as ten flaming cents a tube!

CHORUS   Stone the crows, Bazza! Ten cents a *tube?* This could spell the end of flaming civilisation as we flaming know it!

BARRY   Next thing you know, the supermarkets'll be charging corkage on flaming Parozone! I blame the Japs.

CHORUS   Too right. What's this about your son? We didn't know you had a son. We didn't realise you ever went near your old lady. Isn't she the sheila who looks like a '37 Holden pick-up, sounds like a drag-saw, and smells like a dead dingo?

BARRY   Time was. She's past her best now. Still, when a bloke's tied a few on of a Saturday night, it's no worse than cleaning the chimney in your bare feet. That's how we ended up with young Bruce. He's a bright little bastard, can't be more'n ten months old, and he's already been done twice for being in charge of a push-chair while unfit. I'll be sorry to see him go, straight up.

CHORUS   Go? What are you gonna do with him, Bazza?

147

BARRY   I'm not risking some flaming kid growing up and doing his
             daddy with a lead sock. I'm gonna drive him out to
             Broken Hill and nail him to the floor.
CHORUS   Good on yer, Bazza! Trouble with kids today, they need a
             firm hand. No flaming authority left. No sense of family.
             Good luck, Bazza, got to rush now or they'll be picking
             bits of bladder off the ceiling.

Exeunt.

ACT TWO

*The outback, near Broken Hill. Enter King Barry, carrying Bruce, and
Wayne, a shepherd. They are all drunk.*

BARRY   There you go, Wayne, I've tied his flaming feet together,
             all you have to do is drop him in the sheep dip. Watch
             how you handle him, he can go off like a flaming mortar

PYGMALION

BOB HOSKINS as Alfred Doolittle
ALEC McCOWEN as Professor Higgins
DIANA RIGG as Eliza Doolittle

when he's had a few, we had to redecorate the entire bungalow once.

WAYNE   Count on me, Bazza. I'll pop him in the dippo when I go to fill up me bottles. I'm expecting a few blokes over this evening for a bit of a blast.

Exit Bazza. Wayne stands holding the baby for a moment or two, then falls down and begins snoring.

BRUCE   Burp.

Exit Bruce, crawling.

ACT THREE

Twenty years later. During this period, Bruce has been brought up as a sheep by an elderly man and ewe who found him as a baby. He walks on two legs, but neither he nor his adoptive parents think this in any way odd. This is Australia. Bruce's diet has been grass and sheep dip. He is tall, strong, and permanently drunk, and has picked up a little English from the labels of the beer cans with which the outback is strewn.

It is a hot morning. Bruce is staggering along a dusty track, when he meets another man staggering towards him. The man is Craig, a brewing representative. He is drunk.

CRAIG   Stone the flaming crows, it's Bruce.

BRUCE   You got the wrong bloke, blue. My name's Sixteen Fluid Ounces. It was Pull Ring Here for a time, I'll give yer that, but it's never been flaming Bruce.

CRAIG   Well take it from me, cobber, it's Bruce now all right, they had your picture in *The Daily Beer*, and if you want my advice you'll keep away from your folk. It says in the paper that as sure as flies lay eggs in a wombat's trademark, you're gonna fill in your old man and marry your old lady!

BRUCE   Yeah, well, the bloke who wrote that never saw my old lady. She's got four black hooves and twelve nipples, not to mention some bloody peculiar personal habits. You'd think twice before jumping on a mattress with that.

CRAIG   Don't argue, mate, *The Daily Beer* never lies!

He falls down. Bruce hesitates for a time, then shrugs, sets his shoulders, turns his back resolutely on Broken Hill and takes instead the opposite direction, towards Adelaide.

J H DOWD. 24

"PARDON ME, MADAM, BUT DO YOU MIND REPLACING YOUR HAT? I CAN'T SEE."

"THANK YOU!"

ACT FOUR

The road near Adelaide. A battered truck is rattling along it, with King Barry at the wheel, lurching in every pot-hole and spilling old beer-cans at every yard. At the top of a little rise stands Bruce, albeit unsteadily. As the truck approaches, he thumbs it down. Barry looks out of the window.

BRUCE   Afternoon, Sport. You wouldn't have a tube of Foster's aboard by any chance? I haven't eaten for six weeks.

BARRY   Well, now, blue, that's a very interesting question! A very interesting question indeed. Why not have it engraved on brass and shove it where the moon never shines, har, har, har!

At this, Bruce tears the door off, drags Barry out onto the road, and batters him lifeless with it. He removes eight cans of lager from the body, drains them, belches happily, climbs into the truck, and sets off on a zig-zag course, back towards Adelaide.

ACT FIVE: Scene One

A month later. Adelaide, before the royal palace. It is an attractive wooden bungalow with a pleasing neo-Georgian room-extension in primrose mock-stucco nailed to the front. There are five carriage lamps on the front door, and a gnome holding a sign that reads '38 to 38A Alopecia Avenue'. Enter Bruce, who pushes open the wrought-iron gate and rings a doorbell. The chimes of Viva Espana die away, the door opens.

BRUCE	Queen Glenda?
GLENDA	That's right. Sorry about the Marigold gloves, sport. I was jut worming the cat. What can I do for you?
BRUCE	Promise you won't laugh, Glenda, only I met this sphinx up the road.
GLENDA	I know how it gets sometimes, blue. I usually get pink spiders running over the flaming sideboard.
BRUCE	No, straight up, Glenda. I met this sphinx and it said if I got three riddles right I could come round here and marry you. I didn't have anything else on this morning, so I

SHACON AND BAKESPEARE.

Homer. "LOOK HERE, WHAT *DOES* IT MATTER WHICH OF YOU CHAPS WROTE THE OTHER FELLOW'S BOOKS? GOODNESS ONLY KNOWS *HOW MANY* WROTE MINE!"
[*Nods, as usual, and exit.*

thought, what the hell, it's better than a poke in the eye with a sharp stick!

Enter Chorus, supporting one another.

CHORUS   He'll be flaming sorry he said that!

Exeunt, one hands and knees.

GLENDA   So you answered the riddle all right, then?

BRUCE   I don't know. The sphinx was legless. It was all he could do to give me your address before he fell over.

GLENDA   I swear they put something in it up the factory. When I was a girl, you could drink thirty-one pints before breakfast.

They marry. The wedding reception goes on for nine weeks. At the end of it, the bungalow has disappeared beneath a pyramid of beer cans. A number of guests are dead.

        Scene Two

Some of the cans clatter to the ground. Bruce emerges from the gap, obviously distressed. He has a stick up his nose. Enter Norman, a neighbour. He is drunk.

NORMAN   Stone the flaming crows, Bruce, what's that stick doing up your conk?

BRUCE   I've been trying to poke me flaming eyes out, Norm. I can't seem to get the flaming range. I guess I'll have to wait till I'm flaming sober.

NORMAN   You don't want to go poking yer eyes out, mate. They'll rob you blind up the off-licence. It could cost a flaming bomb! What made you think of it?

BRUCE   I found out Glenda's me mum, Norm. I've only gone and married me flaming mummy!

NORMAN   No cause to pop yer headlights, blue! Mind, I can see it could be a bit awkward. Been a few naughties, have there?

BRUCE   Nothing like that, Norm. Nothing of that order. I haven't been capable, for one thing. Glenda says they put something in it up the factory. No, it's giving up the bungalow, Norm. You spend twenty years as a flaming sheep, suddenly you got gas central heating and three flaming low-flush pastel suites, it's not easy to give it all up just like that.

NORMAN   Strikes me you're being a bit previous, cobber. I can't see why you and Glenda can't make a go of it. She's a very nice woman when she's drunk and no beard to speak of.

BRUCE   But it's against the flaming law, Norm!

NORMAN   Then they'll have to flaming change it, mate!

BRUCE   Would they do that, Norm?

NORMAN   Would they...? You just come down the pub with me, cobber, we'll wake up the Home Secretary and put it to him straight!

Exeunt. Enter Chorus, dragging one another.

CHORUS   In Australia, all is flaming possible! In Australia, a new world is flaming born! In Australia, I flaming will! In Australia...

They collapse. They lie there. They snore.

        CURTAIN

Sir Alec Guinness

Sir Alec Guinness
Thinks that the Eighth Deadly Sin is
Inaudibility to the bods
Sitting in the Gods.

SITUATIONS WANTED.

WANTED, by several Dramatic Authors, Situations of Thrilling and Sensational Interest. Must be Novelties, with as much Reality as possible, capable of introduction into any part of any piece: dialogue and plot no object. Here they are:—

SCENE—*At the end of some Act or other, the bottom of the Sea, anywhere. The entire width of the Stage will be occupied by a large Aquarium, reaching up to within eight feet of the "Flies." This will contain real Sharks, young Whales, Porpoises, and other smaller fish, all alive, alive oh! There will also be real Rocks, and real Submarine Vegetation. The Submarine Telegraph wires will be seen passing across the Stage. Music: tremelo and mysterious, just like what* WOULD *be heard in the depths of the Ocean.*

On the opening of the Scene, real sand-burrowing Bicalves discovered amusing themselves: real Grey Mullets, real Madrepores, and genuine Actiniadae flitting about in the distance. Wild Periwinkles, Chitons, and Scallops seen clinging to the rocks: and, in the foreground, a Goby is discovered feeding on a Codium tomentosum; while other really happy Zoophytes disport themselves in their native element. Music: "The Sea! the Sea!"

Enter above, that is, on the surface of the water, a small boat, containing RICHARD GRADGRASS, *the villain of the piece, and young* WHESTLEY, *the rightful heir to the property, whatever it is.* MARIAN, *the heroine, in love with* WHESTLEY—*with a song—is steering the boat while* RICHARD *is rowing.*

Marian (speaking through the music). What is this mysterious place? *(Looking first at the "flies" then at the real water.)*

Richard (darkly). The Ocean!

Young Whestley. I have heard of it in childhood. Well do I remember how my old nurse—

Richard. She told you right. In these depths lie the only legal proofs of your inheritance.

Marian. Ha! *(Nearly upsets the boat in her emotion. Sensation.)* I beg pardon.

Richard. 'Tis so—the will—

Marian and Whestley. Ay! the will—is—

Richard. At the bottom of the sea.

Whestley. Then will I plunge in, and drag it from its coral hiding-place! *(Is about to prepare for bathing, but remembers that* MARIAN *is present.* MARIAN *hides her face in her hands.)*

Richard. Nay, not so. Behold! *(Produces a diver's dress, air-pump, ropes, and lines, &c., &c.)*

Whestley. How can I ever sufficiently thank you! *(Adjusts the air-tube, puts on the helmet, and looks lovingly at* MARIAN *through the glass eyes, then gets out of the boat, and is seen slowly descending to the bottom of the sea.)*

Richard (seizing MARIAN). Now you are mine!

Marian. Never!

(Struggle, during which MARIAN *works the air-pump, and* WHESTLEY *is below, attempting to rescue the will from a fierce Shark, who will be trained for the purpose.* MARIAN *is becoming exhausted, when a shot, from somewhere or other, is fired, and* RICHARD *falls, capsising, however, the boat.* RICHARD *sinks to the bottom, the Shark leaves the will, and attacks him;* WHESTLEY *clutches the document,* MARIAN *clings with one hand to the boat, now topsy-turvey, and an air-pump, which she works. Her arm gets weaker and weaker.*

Marian, I faint! I die! Help!

*(*WHESTLEY *having received no air for the few seconds, rashes madly to and fro. The Shark, diving off with* RICHARD *in his mouth, is caught by Submarine Telegraph wires.* WHESTLEY *in pantomime, expresses that a good idea has just struck him. He seizes the wires, and swings himself up, so as to grip the boat with his legs, then, with another effort, he gains the surface, putting his arms round* MARIAN *just as she is sinking, sits on the boat, keel uppermost, supporting* MARIAN'S *senseless form with his right arm, and with the hand waving aloft, in triumph, the important will. Two Sharks and a whale dispute for* RICHARD GRADGRASS *as the Act-drop descends.*

We present this, as a novelty, to the consideration of the Sensationalist School. If nothing else will draw, the boat ought to: say, about a foot of water.

17 December 1864

"I have great difficulty learning lines," says Lord Olivier. "Sometimes I can get away with making it all up, of course…I ad-libbed for 20 minutes once in Shakespearean blank verse. Absolute gibberish. But the audience never knew the difference."

MACBETH

(starring Lord, um, Olivier)

Act III scene iv
Banquet. Enter Banquo's Ghost.

Macbeth: Avaunt, and quit my sight! Let the earth hide thee!
Thy bones are marrowless, thy blood is cold;
Thou hast no speculation in those eyes
Which thou dost glare with.
Lady Macbeth: Think of this, good peers,
But as a thing of custom, 'tis no other,
Only it spoils the pleasure of the time.
Macbeth: What man dare, I dare.
Approach thou like the rugged Russian bear,
The arm'd rhinoceros, or the…of the other beast,
That beast which yet though fierce of teeth, does slip
So easy through the net of memory.
Ha! I'll have it yet, or be undone!
Once more I say to thee, accursed vision,
What man dare, I dare.
Approach thou like the Russian rugged rhinoceros…
Ragged Russian bear…This roaring reptile…
Round and round the rugged bears the Russian ran…
Or sells, perchance, her seashells on the seashore.
Thou seest that I can twist my tongue as well
As any man, can float along in verse
And strut the stage with gestures proud and bold,
Hamming the while as if it all made sense,
Yet what I cannot strain my aging brain to do
Is bring to mind what follows "rhinoceros."
Banquo's Ghost: *(whispering)* "Or the Hyrcan tiger!"
Macbeth: Those lips did move, methinks, and made a noise
So soft, so faint, the very breeze itself
Could never bring it hither to my ears,
These ears which even now are strained to hear
What syllables are missing from my speech.
Banquo's Ghost: *(louder)* "Hyrcan tiger!"
Macbeth: I seem to hear thee saying "Impetigo",
Which must be wrong. That illness never struck
The denizens of Elizabethan Stratford,
Or, if it did, was not called impetigo
But something crude like "crop" or "lumpy skin."
Good wife, may I a tiny favour ask?
That which you said just now, say it again,
So that perchance it may release my tongue.
Lady Macbeth: Think of this good peers,
But a thing of custom, 'tis no other,
Only it spoils the pleasure of the…

Macbeth: …Hyrcan tiger!
I have it now! Thanks, wife and gentle ghost,
for stirring up my memory like a bonfire.
What comes next?
Prompt: Take any shape but that…
Macbeth: Take any shape but that, and my firm nerves
(How fast the words come back when given help!)
Shall never tremble. Or be alive again,
And dare me to the desert with thy sword;
If trembling I inhabit then, protest me
The baby of a girl. Hence, horrible…what?
I know it's horrible, but not what 'tis.
Lady Macbeth: To lose your place in Shakespeare *once*,
Can be accounted accident. To lose it twice my lord,
Comes precious near to being carelessness.
Macbeth: Touché. This piece of Oscar's wit, being fit,
Shall win thee nomination for an Oscar,
And I, forgetting lines, have driven thee wild,
The which has driven thee to Wilde. Where were we?
Lady Macbeth: Hence, horrible…
Macbeth: Ah yes! But what? That is
The question. Whether 'tis nobler—hang on a moment.
I seem to find myself in the wrong play.
Messenger: *(Running in)* My Lord and King, I bring this urgent
Scroll from one without.
Macbeth: From the producer?
Messenger: No less.
Macbeth: Hot dog. Let's see what tidings he thinks fit to write
(reads) "This farce has gone on long enough, my Lord.
Now say your lines and let the curtain down.
P.S. It's horrible *shadow*." Of course! Hence, horrible shadow
Unreal mockery hence! *(Exit Ghost.)* Why, so. Being gone,
I am a man again. Pray you, sit still.
Lady Macbeth: You have displaced the mirth, broke the good
Meeting with most admir'd disorder. *(Exeunt all but Macbeth.)*
Macbeth: She's right, you know.
This time I went a little far. But if
A man forgets his lines, mayn't he ad-lib?
(To the audience) Good folk, I pray, a little longer tarry;
It isn't *them* you've come to see—it's Larry!
(Exit. Cheers, ovations, whistles, excursions to the bar, etc.)

MILES KINGTON

CHORUS TO CORONET

S. McMURTRY

"Only 52 actresses have married into the peerage since 1722." — Daily Mail. R.G.G. PRICE presents the best of the fifty-two...

LITTLE McGUIRE (1690-1774).
She became famous for her tambourine solo in Nahum Tate's *Romeo and Cleopatra*. She was under the protection of a dissolute ensign of the 9th when the debauchee Lord Maux saw her as Kitty in the opera *Jael and Sisera*. Pretending to invite her to a supper-party to play the tambourine to his guests, he abducted her and married her at night in his family charnel-house.

Worn out by his excesses, Lord Maux soon died and his widow took possession of some of the broadest acres in the land. She then wed in turn the Viscount Luffham, the Earl of Holtchester and the Marquess of Trent; but her pursuit of the Duke of Vectis was estopped by the Queen, who wished the order of nobility nearest to the throne to remain unsullied.

Her Ladyship, a noted termagant, spent four fat fortunes on building Castle McGuire, said to be three times the size of Blenheim. Her son, Peregrine, fell in with a company of players at Oxford and travelled with them. It was believed

that her rage at him slew her, though some said it was a surfeit of batter.

MRS PLANTAGENET (1784-1860).
Born Nellie Sprock of Ratcliff Highway, she acted with Mrs Siddons's company and later became famous for her frenzied playing, especially in Goldsmith.

The Honble, Hosea Prayle was lured into a playhouse by fellow collegians, despite his promises to his Mother. Watching Mrs Plantagenet as she raged her way through a dramatic version of *The Vicar of Wakefield*, he feared for her soul and, to lure her from the primrose path, offered her his hand.

Under the influence of her godly spouse, soon to become Lord Woolstoke, the ex-Thespian threw herself into the duties of her station. Sunday Schools, Orphanages and Bible Reading Circles called forth her vehemence. She eschewed the popish practice of fasting and died of gout in the stomach.

MILLIE LUPTON (1860-1927).
She began on the halls but her Cockney verve caught the eye of "The Guvnor" and George Edwards introduced her at Daly's in such musical comedies as *The Girl From Tokyo* and *The Tea-Shop Girl*.

One assiduous stage-door johnny persuaded her to dine with him in a private room at the *Monico,* from which she emerged as the future Countess of Welvaux. Unfortunately the Earl had a roving eye and, solaced with an alimony, the Countess returned to the stage, this time legit.

Millie Lupton's success in Pinero's *His Excellency's Widow* and in plays by Henry Arthur Jones and Somerset Maugham was followed by, what many of her friends considered beneath her, a part in a play by G. B. Shaw which Clement Scott denounced as "A foul exhalation from the sewer". It dealt with trapping for furs.

In later years, she was the constant companion of the Marquess of Lerwick, whom she married on the death of his wife. Her only child, Prue Cade Cade, joined the Russian mystic Ordmirov's Theatre Without Audience and died in mysterious circumstances at the Gare St. Lazare.

PATTY WILSON (1927—).
A New York talent-spotter heard her singing in a Dallas hairdressing salon. She came, via New York, to sing for the American forces in Britain and starred in several London productions of Broadway musical comedies, including one based on Hemingway's *Fiesta* but

called *A Farewell to Arms*.

There was press speculation on which of Patty's noble dates would marry her. Lord Woolstoke won. It was a stormy marriage. She stayed the tops in Britain and the States while he failed as a framing consultant, a nectarine-farmer and a monologuist—*An Evening with Norman Douglas*. After the divorce she married the Earl of Seign, owner of several stately homes, a private yet with George & Gilbert as a mural and a flourishing theatrical management. She persuaded him to star her in a rock *Parsifal*.

BRENDA HOPE TANTRIX (1947—).

After Heathfield and RADA and Rep at Oswestry and Windsor, she joined the Royal Shakespeare Company, transferring in a couple of years to the National Theatre. She also acted from time to time in films and won an Oscar for her alcoholic nymphomaniac in Ken Russell's *Haworth Blues*.

She married Viscount Chevy, the crime novelist Rupert Chace, her cousin. She is living at present with "Honey-chile" Mary-Lou Baker, the octopus wrestler.

VICTORIA STREET (1958—).

Born Madge Grzek, she was discovered at Butlin's and produced her first album when she was fourteen. Her world tours broke every record and at seventeen she bought Castle McGuire, installed stereo in every bedroom and built a disco under the principal lake. She married a boy from the local garage, Lord Luffham, but remains the shared girlfriend of the Earl of Holtchester, the Marquess of Trent, Lord Woolstoke, the Earl of Welvaux, the Marquess of Lerwick and the Earl of Seign, who form the pop group called *The Dregs*.

NO MAN'S LAND

MICHAEL FEAST as Foster
RALPH RICHARDSON as Hirst
JOHN GIELGUD as Spooner
TERENCE RIGBY as Briggs

How a Receptive One visited the Spectacles of the City
To Wit:

The Music-Hall.   A screaming farcical Comedy.   Another.   A patriotic Drama at the "National Theatre."

The Opera.   The Lyceum.   A Melodrama at the Surrey.   A pathetic "Comedy-Drama."

...And   3 Acts   of Henrik Ibsen.   The deplorable issue.

THE SLANG OF THE STAGE.

5 January 1861

E think for curiosities of advertising literature, next to the second column in the first page of the *Times*, the best column is the last in the first page of the *Era*. To readers who are not versed in the slang of the Green-room the following may appear a curious requirement :—

NEW THEATRE ROYAL, CORN EXCHANGE, SHORTHORN-FORD.

WANTED, immediately, a Good WALKING GENTLE-MAN, and a Walking Lady (one who can sing preferred); also, a Steady Property man and Bill Deliverer. Other Theatres.—Address the Manager.

From the wording of this notice, the ignorant might fancy that pedestrianism belonged to the theatrical profession, and that theatres were sometimes the scene of walking feats. But we fear that were the ignorant to inquire of any "call boy" if such really were the case, an answer more or less impertinent (and rather more than less) would be immediately returned, the reply perhaps consisting of the mere word "Walker!" It will be noticed that the male walker is wanted to be "good," whereas this quality is not thought an essential for the female. But without dwelling on this, we pass on to another puzzle in the same day's sheet :—

FOOLWICH.—THEATRE ROYAL.

WANTED, a good Juvenile Lady; also, Juvenile Gent, Heavy Man, and one or two good Utility People. A fair salary given for talent. Apply.

Here we find the lady is required to be "good" and likewise to be "juvenile;" to which latter qualification every lady under sixty would of course consider herself entitled to lay claim. How far the coming census will be allowed to throw the light of truth on ladies' ages, it is not our pleasure just now to inquire. But we think that to apply for a "juvenile lady," is almost as superfluous as to require a "female woman;" and just as needless was it to ask during the Cattle Show for a "heavy man," seeing there were none else to be seen then in the streets.

The next announcement introduces to our notice a Stage personage whom we have no desire to know in real life :—

THEATRE LOYAL, SCREAMINGTON.

WANTED, a first class SINGING CHAMBERMAID.

Waits are bad enough, and so are cats and sweeps. But of all the most unmusical, most melancholy nuisances wherewith the ears of sleepy sufferer could be nocturnally afflicted, commend us—or, no, *don't* commend us—to a "Singing Chambermaid." We can conceive no greater torment that to hear the "*Power of Love*" squalled nightly on the staircase as we turned into bed, while "*Sally Come Up!*" squealed through the keyhole would wake us out of our first sleep. Banjoed, bonesed, and barrel-organed as we are throughout the day, we should go stark staring mad—*fanatico per la musica* in pitiable truth—if when we retired at night we were conducted to our room by a Singing Chambermaid, whose lullaby would most effectually prevent our going to rest. As it is, we often spend a night at an hotel (say the Star and Garter, Richmond, or the Bedford by the Sea) merely for the purpose of escaping the sleep-murderers, who with trombones in their hands infest the London streets. But we could no more hope to take our ease at our inn, if the dramatic "Singing Chambermaid" had a place in real life.

All these specimens of Stage slang we take from the same sheet, and we copy them verbatim merely altering the names, as we have not been paid to print them in our paper. With one more startling sample we must conclude our list :—

HALL OF HARMONY, BAWLBOROUGH.

WANTED, to open on Monday, Dec. the 24th, Two good NIGGERS that can dance well, a Lady Character Singer, and a Lady Sentimental ; also, a Pianist that can read well.—Address.

To inquire in this way for a Pianist "who can read well" seems like asking for a gardener who is a dab at painting, or begging for a butcher who can play the flute. If reading be the thing required, why not seek an elocutionist? But this is not half so strange a request as the preceding one ; that for the good niggers and the brace of ladies who are "wanted to open" on the day which is there mentioned. Wanted to open! In the name of LINDLEY MURRAY, wanted to open what? Is it oysters, or box-doors, or "Wonderful Cabinets" that these fair ladies and dark gentlemen are "wanted to open?" Is it—stay—a horrid thought springs in our frightened brain. "To open" is a neuter verb as well as active. Can it be that these four persons are wanted to be passive actors in the opening, and that for the sake of producing a sensation, some tragedy is going to be played "with real stabs!!" There is no saying what dodge next will be tried to fill our theatres, and for aught we know, there may be a good opening for persons who would every other night, say, undergo that operation; the salary of course varying according as the opening were made with a bare bodkin or with a *Shylock's* knife.

Verses for Every Day
(At the Theatre)
TO THE LADY BEHIND ME

DEAR Madam, you have seen this play;
I never saw it till to-day.
You know the details of the plot,
But, let me tell you, I do not.
The author seeks to keep from me
The murderer's identity.
And you are not a friend of his
If you keep shouting who it is.
The actors in their funny way
Have several funny things to say.
But they do not amuse me more
If you have said them just before;
The merit of the drama lies,
I understand, in some surprise;
But the surprise must now be small
Since you have just foretold it all.
The lady you have brought with you
Is, I infer, a half-wit too,
But I can understand the piece
Without assistance from a niece.
In short, foul woman, it would suit
Me just as well if you were mute;
In fact, to make my meaning plain,
I trust you will not speak again.
And—may I add one human touch?—
Don't breathe upon my neck so much.

THEATRE RHYMES

TO RUTH DRAPER, EXHILARATOR

"BABE RUTH," the Pitcher, leaves me
    cold,
    Though featured in my picture-paper;
Another RUTH takes stronger hold,
        RUTH DRAPER.

Most entertainers who unbend
    Distress or make me hot all over;
But you can keep me hours on end
        In clover.

Mistress of many tongues, you shine
    In satire, pathos, wit and *bonhomie,*
Yet practise in your "words" a fine
        Economy.

Your going casts us into gloom,
    And yet we feel less sad and sober
Since you were able to illume
        October.

So *Punch*, though loth from you to part,
    Cuts this admiring doggered caper
In homage to your perfect art,
        RUTH DRAPER!

---

16 October 1929

MR. PUNCH PEEPING.
A FIRST NIGHT

(Encouraged by the success of his young contemporary, the B.B.C., Mr. Punch begins to-day a series of experimental descriptive broadcasts of scenes of interest in London life. To-day he will take you to a First Night at the New Imperial Theatre, which will be described by Mr. Mervyn Flute.)

"This is Mr. Mervyn Flute speaking. I am at the microphone in the foyer of the New Imperial Theatre, London. This is the New Imperial Theatre, London, and I am Mr. Mervyn Flute. I am in the foyer of the New Imperial Theatre on this occasion, which is the occasion of the First Night of the musical comedy, *Say When!* Those listeners who have never attended a First Night would perhaps like me to explain that a First Night means the first performance of a new play, and naturally that is an occasion with a great deal of interest by all those concerned and which even some of those who are not— Well, here I am, Mr. Mervyn Flute, in the foyer of the New Imperial Theatre; and I am going to try to describe to listeners some of the things I can see on this most interesting occasion, which, as I have said, is the first performance of *Say When!* at the New Imperial Theatre, and which—

"Perhaps, however, before I begin describing this scene, which is really very interesting and full of interest—and really I feel very doubtful indeed whether I shall be able to convey to listeners any real idea of this interesting scene, because, as you all know, it is one thing to see a thing and another thing to put that thing into words; however I mean to do my best— but perhaps for the benefit of listeners who have only just oozed in I had better explain that I am Mr. Mervyn Flute and I am at the microphone which has been placed in the foyer of the New Imperial Theatre on the occasion of the first performance of the Musical Comedy, *Say When!*

"When I say 'first performance,' I mean, of course, the 'first *public* performance,' because no doubt the play has been performed in private before, and as a matter of fact one can see at once that it must have been rehearsed several times.

"Well, the first two Acts of this play have passed off without civil war, and the audience are stretching their legs, if I may use such an expression of such distinguished ladies and gentlemen, in the interval before the Third and last Act. I daresay listeners can hear the animated conversation of the gentlemen as they rush past into the bar and the curious shuffle of the dramatic critics. Some of the dresses are really very beautiful, and I wish you could see Lady COLEFAX'S dazzling silver dress, which I am sorry to say I cannot tell you what it is made of. I can see a number of well-known men and women. Mr. ST. JOHN ERVINE and Mr. AGATE are chatting merrily together about the play. I can see LORD MELCHETT. I can see Mr. EDWARD MARSH, who is a distinguished civil servant, enjoying one of his rare evenings off duty at the theatre. I can see Mr. JOHN DRINKWATER exchanging quips with Mr. GALSWORTHY, whose name by the way is also John. I can see Mr. HUBERT GRIFFITH, who is being ejected by the management. Lady ASTOR and Mr. BERNARD SHAW are standing silently in a corner, reluctant to attract attention. Now Mr. SWAFFER is passing by. I don't know whether listeners heard that—a rather peculiar sound, a sort of explosive snort. That was Mr. SWAFFER'S opinion of the play. I am told by a bystander that the management put on this play without consulting him, which, as some of you may know, is a very unusual step. I can see Mr. ALBERT HADDOCK, the well-known publicist. He is earnestly supporting his favourite thesis, that women are an over-rated sex. Lady ASTOR is listening attentively.

"Now MR. EDWARD MARSH is knocking out his pipe. Mr. ERVINE has thrown away his cheroot. The Bishop of LONDON has just come out of the refreshment-room. Most people are going back to their seats. The rest are stealing out with their hats and coats. Here comes Mr. Albert Haddock, arm-in-arm with the Mayor of EASTBOURNE. Mr. Haddock is in trouble with his stud, which looks like falling out. There are some of the SITWELLS, I do not know which. Now I am going back to my box, where a microphone has been installed, and I hope to be able to give you some idea of the conclusion of this most interesting evening, which is the first performance of the musical comedy, *Say When!* at the New Imperial Theatre. It is Mr. Mervyn Flute speaking, and I am now going to my box at the New Imperial Theatre, where, if you will wait a few minutes, I hope to give you some idea of the Third Act of *Say When!* the new and musical comedy which is being performed to-night for the first time at the New Imperial Theatre, and which—Two minutes, please.

"Now the hero and the heroine of this play are singing a duet. I am Mr. Mervyn Flute and I am speaking from a box at the New Imperial Theatre on the occasion of the first performance of the musical comedy, *Say When!* during the Third Act of which play the hero and heroine are now singing a duet. Miss Star Bright, who plays the heroine, is wearing a bathing dress; the hero, Mr. Mollop, is in flying costume. Mr. PETER PAGE has come in. Probably listeners will not be able to hear Miss Bright's voice, but the song is called 'I am Blue for You.' This is a duet call-ed, 'I am Blue for You' which is now being sung by Miss Star Bright and Mr. Mollop in the Third Act of *Say When!* Mr. E.V. LUCAS has gone out. Mr. ER-VINE is still in. Mr. SWAFFER has carried out his hat. Many peo-ple have contracted bad coughs since the interval. The gallery are becoming what is called 'restless.' That is to say, they are standing up and shouting angrily. I expect listeners can hear them. A bowler-hat has just fallen from the dress-circle. Mr. EDWARD MARSH seems to be enjoying the play. Mr. Haddock has lost his dress-stud and is crawling about the stalls on his hands and knees. Three of the authors have gone out. On the other hand a party of well-dressed young men have just taken their seats.

"Now the unfortunate misunderstanding between the hero and the heroine has been cleared up and the chorus are coming on to the stage for the finale. Mr. Haddock has found his stud and is writing a note—I expect about supper. I am afraid it may be difficult for listeners to hear me owing to the coughing and the restlessness in the gallery, but this is the Third Act of *Say When!* in which the hero has just explained to the heroine that the lady with whom he was dancing at midnight was his twin-sister. Dean INGE has woken up. The chorus are now singing; perhaps listeners can hear them. The ladies are dressed like tropical birds. The gentlemen are in polo costume. Now the curtain is falling, and perhaps listeners can hear the storm of applause. No,

that is the gallery. The authors' box is empty—no, there is still one gentleman cowering behind the parapet. Now the curtain is up again. Miss Bright is being presented with great masses of flowers and is smiling her thanks. The gallery are throwing onions and other vegetable tributes. More and more flowers. The stalls are putting on their coats. The surviving critics are rushing away. The stage looks like a herbaceous border. Miss Bright is almost crying with happiness. The stage-manager has just brought on to the stage a complete greenhouse, in which are growing a number of superb orchids and hothouse fruits. The generous donor has thrown in a gardener as well, whom I can see smiling in the wings. Miss Bright's many relations are calling 'Speech!' She is pointing modestly to the hero. He is pointing at the chorus. The chorus are pointing at the conductor. The conductor is pointing at the orchestra. The orchestra with modest shrugs are disclaiming any connection with the performance. The stage-manager is pointing up at the 'flies.' Silence has just fallen and Miss Bright is just stepping forward. She is very shy at facing so large an audience, not used to appearing in public. She has just said, 'From the bottom of my heart I thank you for this wonderful reception—'

"What you heard then was the gallery's reply. The curtain has fallen. That is the National Anthem, the first four bars. That is 'I am Blue for You'; perhaps you recognise the tune. And that is the end of the first night of *Say When!* Good-night, everybody—*good*-night."

That was Mr. Mervyn Flute describing the first performance of 'Say When!' at the New Imperial Theatre. Now we are going over to Kew Gardens for the experimental transmission of smells. Good-night, everybody—cheerio, all!"

A.P.H.

"PRIVATE LIVES" (PHŒNIX).

THE rosy glow that greets one on entering this handsome new theatre is a happy augury. The interior decoration by KOMISARJEVSKY and the enlarged old master (SELLAIO'S "Triumph of Love"), painted by VLADIMIR POLUNIN on the safety-curtain that masks the gold-and-crimson curtain proper, pleasantly quicken expectation. The entertainment itself, a little impudent comedy by Mr. NOEL COWARD, is so impenitently theatrical, so slight in substance and insular in spirit, that the impressions it makes last scarcely longer than do the echoes of the actors' voices and the quick responsive laughter it provokes.

Its recipe may be stated thus: Think of a quarrel and double it; add the better (because more amusing) halves of two newly-married couples; place them on a pretty balcony in France lit by the fading sunset and coloured candelabra; shift the scene to Paris and throw in a sketchy meal or two and much illicit love-making between cocktails and innumerable cigarettes: then take away the quarrel you first thought of and substitute spontaneous rough-and-tumble, and the result is an iridescent bubble of a play, a series of bubbles light as air kept dancing through three Acts by that blend of wit and impudence that is Mr. COWARD'S *forte*.

The First Act states, the Second Act confirms and the Third Act does its best to redeem the mistake made by *Elyot* and *Amanda* in divorcing each other five years ago. The three Acts together persuade them (and us) that, impossible as each finds the other to live with, the alternative to which they have just committed themselves is unthinkable now that they have met again.

Their new partners, *Sybil* and *Victor*, no sooner married than deserted by them, serve to point this grim dilemma at the beginning of the play and reappear at the end of it to rub the dilemma in. Though less fully charged with wit than the two principals, they are drawn with the same

light touch: and they only concern us in so far as they act as foils to *Elyot* and *Amanda* and justify their decision, quickly arrived at, to make the worst of a bad job.

Act I. having encouraged these hy-

BREAKING THE RECORD (GRAMOPHONE).

Amanda Prynne . . . MISS GERTRUDE LAWRENCE.
Elyot Chase . . . . MR. NOEL COWARD.

meneal defaulters to elope together to Paris on the night of their new honeymoons, leaving their lawful spouses behind, Act II. shows them illicitly at home, provoking love as only they can provoke it and keeping satiety at bay

HALF-COUPLES.

Sybil Chase . . . . . MISS ADRIANNE ALLEN.
Victor Prynne . . . . MR. LAWRENCE OLIVIER.

with repetitions of those sharp spontaneous squabbles that parted them five years ago. The intensive kissing and kicking, the provoking and provoked witticisms, the heart-to-heart confessions, rapturous surrenders and stand-up fights that constitute their only occupation are such as human beings might support only in heroic and lonely daydreams and will hardly be taken for a model.

Amanda lags not at all behind *Elyot* in "jagged sophistication." Indeed their only trouble is to coin the perfect phrase to shame satiety and keep their passion burning. All that in real life helps to safeguard love and render marriage tolerable goes into the fire to feed that passion; and when, as it frequently does, their explosive affinity for one another goes up, up goes the furniture too. The gramophone record that *Elyot* hates is smashed over his head, the electric-lights are torn out by their roots, and every chivalrous and womanly restraint is abandoned, to end in that horrible débâcle on which their deserted and dumbfounded spouses enter as the second curtain falls.

But it is less with the idea of pointing a moral than to amuse us with his skill in keeping the bubble dancing that Mr. COWARD brings the injured and injuring parties together at breakfast next morning, and completes as grim a demonstration of incompatibility as ever convulsed an audience by throwing the new-made marriages back into the melting-pot. The patterns his bubble traces grow thin at times while the wit that animates them renews itself in fresh felicities of phrase and further audacity. Our response is all but continuous laughter, charged with delight in the art with which he himself and delicious Miss GERTRUDE LAWRENCE sustain such fragile *rôles* without faltering or offence.

Yet, brilliant as are these two major displays of acting, welcome relief is provided by Miss ADRIANNE ALLEN'S amusingly shrewd and tearful *Sybil* and Mr. LAURENCE OLIVIER'S honest *Victor*. The loveborn squabbles that agitate the play are not so much storms

"In it's day it was probably thought quite impressive."

Detective-Inspector
Howard Jones
MR BARRY
JONES...

Detective
Inspector
Callon
MR PHILIP
PEARMAN

'Mrs. Inspector
Jones"
Savoy
Theatre
*

"POINT OF
DEPARTURE"
*

Monsieur
Henri ...
MR STEPHEN
MURRAY

..Ronnie Tearle
MR SYDNEY KING

Maria Jones...
MISS JESSIE
ROYCE LANDIS

Orpheus
MR DIRK
BOGARDE..

MR JOHN
MOFFATT......
Hotel Waiter

MR HUGH
GRIFFITH
as the father

"Point of
Departure"
lyric Theatre
Hammersmith
*

Eurydice...
MISS MAI
ZETTERLING

Ronald Searle

Theatre Sketchbook

IF THE FACE FITS
Robert Morley

Lady Lucan's complaint that the actor engaged to play her husband in a forthcoming documentary on the BBC doesn't add up in her book to a nobleman, and in any case lacks the necessary Slav blood, drew a sharp reply from Mr Tony Matthews. "I do not think," he is quoted as saying, "that 'yob' is a fair description. After all, I was head prefect of an English public school." The mother of the murdered nanny is similarly dissatisfied with the choice of the actress to play her daughter and suggested that although filming is almost completed, the BBC would be wise to switch the two leading ladies in the documentary reconstruction of the crime, thereby at least ensuring accuracy of hair colouring. The whole controversy pin-points the difficulties experienced by members of my profession when called upon to portray real-life characters in the historical or contemporary context.

I remember the comment of the playwright's mother when viewing my own interpretation of Oscar Wilde: "A walking stick is not going to help in the leading role." Like most actors of my girth, I have been asked from time to time to impersonate Winston Churchill. Mr. Timothy West recently succumbed to the temptation and succeeded where others (with the possible exception of Mike Yarwood) have failed. He wasn't Churchill, but he was very like Churchill might have been if he had been Mr. West. Compromise is the secret. In my time I collected my share of regal roles, usually from MGM and usually French about whom the public knows little; but I did once essay the mad father of the Prince Regent and got the mad bit so right that the present monarch, who had been forced to watch me in my nightshirt setting fire to the Windsor Castle organ, decided that thereafter her appearances at Royal Command film performances was by no means to be taken for granted.

Actors engaged to play Landru, Wilberforce, Paton or Hugh Gaitskell always profess themselves (at the outset, at any rate) delighted with the task ahead. Often they go to extreme lengths, carrying photographs of the character with them to prop up on the make-up table, prior to assuming the necessary disguise.

Traditional roles are often the easiest; Napoleon's method of resting his elbow, King Richard's rounded shoulder, Nelson's eye-patch and missing arm are cake walks compared to the problems confronting actors engaged to depict Shakespeare or John D. Rockerfeller the Third. In earlier times the late George Arliss and Anna Neagle triumphed by the simple expedient of being themselves and daring the public to argue. Of course Queen Victoria, Nurse Cavell and Odette looked and spoke like Anna, and Disraeli, Rothschild and Wellington were the spitting image of George, although it was rumoured that Miss Neagle in her portrayal of the Queen Empress chewed cotton wool in the final scenes.

My own most successful historical interpretation was that of the Duke of Manchester in the film *Cromwell*; by the time I had got round to securing for myself a role in this epic all the plums seemed to have fallen or been gathered by other actors who subscribed to the *Film Weekly*. I came late on the scene, and having discovered that the film was casting one morning, found myself by tea-time interviewing Irving Allen the producer. He leafed through the available vacancies and offered Manchester. I was surprised to find that there was such a city in those days, even more that it should have possessed a Duke. However, as he was still on the tree I picked him with alacrity, and

was relieved to discover that the researcher had not got round to deciding what His Grace would have looked like, and that there was therefore no necessity for me to disguise my features. Nothing is more conducive to comfort on film locations than not having to arrive at daybreak to affix a beard or stick on a wig.

In point of fact, I seem to remember that Manchester did wear the latter, but under a hat and it was the hat which saved the day as far as I was concerned: a wide-brimmed felt affair with feathers, supplying the necessary resemblance to *Puss-in-Boots*. I took enormous pains to keep the feathers dry, enclosing them in Cellophane, often in shot and on the battlefields provided the enemy and camera were not too close. For the first few days I mounted a horse, but whereas the other Dukes rode at full gallop I proceeded at a nervous walk. Spanish film horses (and the film was shot mostly in Spain) are trained not only to stop at a tug of the rein but then to gently keel over backwards, and it was to avoid this hazardous display of equine sagacity that I let the reins hang loose and hoped the creature understood he must stop before actually knocking down the director. Life became easier when I was transferred to a coach after my horse had once literally sunk from under me in a bog during a prolonged close-up.

There were not many close-ups available to Manchester; my role consisted chiefly of pinpointing the location for the various battlefields.

"Where are we?" I would bellow as I alighted nervously from my carriage.

"Edgbaston, Sire" or "Marston Moor" came the helpful reply and I and the public were thus able to catch up with history.

I was equally fortunate in my portrayal of The Emperor of China in the film of *Ghengis Khan*, perhaps even more than I deserved. Arriving on the second evening of the night location in Yugoslavia, and somewhat behind time, I dispensed with the Chinese Pallor and elaborate eye-shading and took my place among the hordes confident that my Caucasian characteristics would be undetected in the general scrum. Alas, the rain started, the cameras moved in, and I waited for the inevitable storm to break and the displeasure of all concerned to be manifested during an hour's delay while my features were corrected. Nothing of the kind occurred, and I almost completed my role in the picture as the first all-white Chinese Emperor with the occasional addition of elongated fingernails. On the very last day, however, and by this time in Berlin, the management engaged a crowd of genuine Chinese concubines with which to surround me and I successfully persuaded the director to allow me to stand at some distance from such implied debauchery.

So my advice to the cast of *Carry On Up The Zambesi*, or whatever this particular Lucan BBC epic is titled, is not to visit Madame Tussaud's, supposing the noble Earl and his entourage have already arrived there, but to play the roles as to the manner born, insisting that the film credits make it perfectly clear which character they are sustaining. Years and years ago, led out to the scaffold as Louis XIV on the vast set constructed by MGM for the filming of *Marie Antoinette*, I remember the proceedings being momentarily halted by the last desperate efforts of the historical researcher to draw the director's attention to the more blatant anomalies in the sets. Glancing at the historical engravings of the scene clutched in the hand of the elderly researcher, the great director Woody Van Dyke remarked sagely: "Kid! That's how it was, but this is how it's going to be!"

There's no Old Folk like Show-biz Old Folk

"Mr Stromboli! I've warned you before about practising on the other residents' pension books...!"

"Stop him! He keeps turning Mr Delaney's walking-stick into a bunch of crêpe flowers."

"...and I just can't stand it any longer, so I am taking the only way out that I know... Yours sincerely, The Great Illuso."

165

AT THE PLAY

RICHARD III
(Old Vic)

There has been an attempt in some quarters to whitewash Richard the Third, to call him a good king and a man gravely misjudged. Non-specialists remain incredulous. It will take much argument, we feel, to convince them that Richard, in spite of his intellect, was anything at heart but a tough Sir Guy, a babes-in-the-wood murderer, a mediaeval Nazi about whom too many people lost their heads. Shakespeare's chronicle is the Gloucester faction's woe. Here is a Richard brilliantly evil, a villain self-accused, one rais'd in blood and one in blood establish'd. At various times in this glorious Saturday-night melodrama his enemies describe him as a boar—an easy choice when we remember that two boars "rampant argent" supported his shield—as a cacodemon, a dog, a rooting hog, a bottled spider, a bunch-back'd toad, a hedgehog, a tiger, and a cockatrice.

Now, to join this fair assembly, MR. LAURENCE OLIVIER presents him as a limping panther. The actor rejects the idea of a Richard set wholly in the "ceremonies and traditional" mould as a fee-fi-fo-fum ogre, a child of Giant Despair. His newer reading, so warmly cheered, loses nothing of the familiar excitement. Here are the theatrical flourishes, the relish, the entry "in pomp, crowned," the spurning of *Buckingham*, the fury—like Horatius "a wild cat mad with wounds"—on the lost field of Bosworth. MR. OLIVIER grants us these effects. He catches the king red-handed, but he also manages to impress us, as many *Richards* in the past have failed to do, with the usurper's dominant brain. This is a subtle *Richard*, swift in thought and action. His ambition (if we may add to the party) mounts on eagle's wings. He can make persuasive the wooing of Miss JOYCE REDMAN'S *Lady Anne*. He masters the realm by power of intellect and in unholy magnetism as well as by physical violence. No one in recent years has fixed the complete character so surely: the actor is at once knave, king, and ace.

In the past MR. OLIVIER has given us much to remember—notably his speaking of *Hamlet's* "How all occasions," the farewell of *Coriolanus* to Rome and the coming to Antium, and *Henry the Fifth's* night thoughts from abroad. Now to these memories we can add *Richard's* coldly glittering overture, the sudden assumption of majesty at the phrase "Farewell, good cousin," which ends the king-making charade at Baynard's Castle, the thunder-and-lightning on the throne, the bravado and growing fear in the messengers' scene, and, not least, the anguish of the close.

MR. JOHN BURRELL'S Old Vic production leaves us too often in the twilight. Otherwise, it is a worthy frame for such a *Richard* as this. The grouping is unobtrusively right: Mr. BURRELL

MRS. LANGTRY AS "LADY MACBETH"
(Anticipatory of the notice which would probably appear in a Morning Paper.)

31 December 1881

MACBETH is at best but a dreary, tragic play, full of inconsistencies, which only the greatest dramatic genius can gloss over or explain away. *Lady Macbeth* is a woman at once cold, yet burning with an inextinguishable fire, scheming yet noble withal, delicate yet robust, arch yet statuesque, feminine yet unwomanly, fierce yet lamb-like. That all these qualities should be united in one woman appears, at first sight, as paradoxical as this old-fashioned play itself. Yet when MRS. LANGTRY tripped on to the stage the other afternoon, with a curtsey which cannot be acquired without an intimate knowledge of court etiquette, everyone felt instinctively, that there stood the human embodiment of these opposing elements.

MRS. LANGTRY did not walk in the conventional manner—she did not even glide—she *floated* before *foot-lights*. The one hand holding the letter, the other toying carelessly with the pale blue Indian scarf she wore round her neck, she reminded one forcibly of the Venus of Milo started into life by the spark of genius. The opening words:—

"They met me in the day of success,"

were rendered with a modesty which at once went home to every heart, and the following words directed with a sweet and meaning smile straight at the critical element in the stalls—

"And I have learned by the perfectest report, *they have more in them than mortal knowledge,*"

—was at once felt to gain an application hitherto unexplained by Shakspearian commentators. By the time these first few words were uttered, MRS. LANGTRY'S success in the character were beyond dispute, and the piece was saved.

As *Miss Hardcastle* she was *surprising,* as *Lady Macbeth* she was *overwhelming.*

That brilliant undefinable something which surrounds this lady, and which, for want of a better simile, we may describe as a Dado of Royalty,* accomplished at one stroke what years of patient toil would have failed to produce with others less favoured. Her beautiful form combines the willowy suppleness of a KATE VAUGHAN with the plump pertness of a MARIA WILTON, the fresh innocence of a achieves tension in the impeachment of that other Hastings—how well-judged are the silences here!—and succeeds also in marshalling the phantoms of the night before Bosworth, a desperately difficult business. For once we cannot mistake the line for a dispirited queue: the ghosts come like shadows and like shadows fade. Elsewhere Mr. BURRELL has wisely cut most of the invective, the ravens' revel. *Margaret* is confined to her earliest frolic, and Dame SYBIL THORNDIKE pours the acid so generously that we are sorry to miss a second draught. Miss

REDMAN animates her *Snow Queen*, and Mr. NICHOLAS HANNEN, playing *Buckingham* against his temperament, glows into life when the kingmaker realizes his doom. (Again Mr. HANNEN's make-up is a small triumph.) *Richmond* is honoured by Mr. RALPH RICHARDSON, who has every excuse for letting the part stream like a banner; this is a Saint George triumphing over the dragon. Incidentally the first-night programme told us, to our mild surprise, that Richmond became "King Edward the Seventh." Mr. GEORGE RELPH makes no fuss

about *Clarence's* aria, and later he has a good minute or two as a single-speech Archbishop.

Like all the histories, the play bristles with small parts. Not all are well done in this production; we expect more from *Catesby*, who is *Gloucester's* faithful follower to the last ("Withdraw, my lord; I'll help you to a horse"), and from *Tyrrell*, with whom this *Richard* so forcibly rehearses the murder of the Princes. On the other hand, Mr. HARCOURT WILLIAMS gives his burning-glass intensity to *Edward the Fourth's* single scene and final collapse, though here it will be long before we can forget the late Ion Swinley's silver-point at the Old Vic. Mr. MICHAEL WARRE fights gallantly as the loser in the second battle of Hastings—his severed head is not to prominent or so incarnadined as usual—and, unexpectedly, the cast includes the name of "Jane Shore, the mistress to the King," decorative but dumb.

Finally, nothing at the New Theatre causes us to echo Hazlitt's loathing of the "fantoccini exhibition of the young Prince Edward and York bandying childish wit with their uncle." The scene, often alarming for both the audience and the children's fellow-players, is now a quiet success.

J.C.T.

CONNIE GILCHRIST, with the mature thoughtfulness of a GENEVIÈVE WARD. There was, above all, a Society tone about this *Lady Macbeth* with which the part had never heretofore been invested.

The fair lady's dresses (marvels of the milliner's art) were voted charming. The pale pink satin, trimmed with yellow roses, and *décolleté* with daring delicacy, sent a thrill of excitement through the audience, and evoked an impromptu sonnet from the trembling lips of Mr. OSCAR WILDE, who fainted with ecstasy, and was carried out by the attendants.

SHAKSPEARE has been applauded by Fashion, and Art is satisfied!

Of the remainder of the cast, suffice it to say that the Actors did their best to render the support worthy of the occasion, and that no special apology for their efforts is needed to the fair *débutante*. Mr. COGHLAN made a gentleman-like *Macbeth*, Mr. VEZIN an intelligent *Macduff*, Mr. IRVING was a respectable *Witch*. Other characters were entrusted to Messrs. TOOLE, BROUGH, FARREN, KENDAL, CLAYTON, Mrs. KENDAL, and Miss ELLEN TERRY; the acting of these Ladies proving an excellent foil to that of the heroine of the day.

We trust, however, that Mrs. LANGTRY will shortly have an opportunity of appearing in a part more worthy of the high social position which she has held by the Divine right of Fashion, and from which she has been pleased to descend to extend a not ungracious hand to Art, Fashion's poor relation and *protégée*, in whose humble dwelling she will be received with a blush which, it is to be hoped will not be misconstrued, and which has hitherto baffled photography.

*We fancy the writer must have meant "halo". But of course the experienced Dramatic Critic on a morning paper, who evidently writes only in the true interests of Art, must know best.—ED.

(The London Correspondent of the Paris *Figaro* says:—"Ceux de mes contemporains qui ont vu les débuts de CORA PEARL aux Bouffes, se rendront compte de la valeur de ce que vient de faire Mme. LANGTRY au Haymarket Théatre. Comme jolie femme, Mme. LANGTRY, qui a été une *professional beauty*, est digue de tous les hommages; mais comme actice, elle a rudement besoin de travailler." And this is the truth, and nothing but the truth, in a nutshell. But if it be true that this fortunate novice is already engaged by the BANCROFTS, at a salary as handsome as the Lady herself, to appear in a Robertsonian Revival and in Mrs. KENDAL'S part in *Diplomacy*, why talk about starting a school for the encouragement of Dramatic Art?—ED.)

"No, this is the queue for the busker."

Little
Willies

STAGE LAWYERS.

Reader, constant or inconstant reader, have you ever noticed how the lawyers are maligned and maltreated by the dramatists. As a rule, one never sees a honest lawyer on the stage. Indeed, the part would be so novel that an actor would require to be paid extra for performing it. We should as soon expect a dramatist to write a part for a Gorilla as introduce so strange an animal as a honest lawyer. No. A lawyer on the stage is invariably a bad one. In Comedy he is the evil genius of the piece, and though he triumphs for an act or two, before the curtain falls he always gets the worst of it. In Melodrama he is, if not the villain of the piece, at least the villain's bosom friend and illegal adviser. In a National drama he is always found consorting with the smugglers and the pirates. The Jack Tars call him "land-shark," and threaten to harpoon him or to "darken his skylights." They nickname him a "lubber," and bid him "sheer off, or they'll scuttle him." They shiver their timbers when he heaves in sight, and swear they'll make lobscouse of him if he comes athwart their hawse.

In Farce, too you may be sure, a lawyer's never introduced excepting to be laughed at. His make up is always the signal for a roar. His lean lanthorn-jaws are as yellow as old parchment, and he dresses in a seedy shiny swallow-tailed black coat, buttoned tight across his chest to make him look still thinner by being cased in tights; and his hands are enveloped in a mass of woollen fabric, which appears to be supposed to do duty for gloves.

Then, the treatment he receives is of as bad a fashion nearly as his dress. He rarely comes upon the stage excepting to be kicked off it. Like the dog upon the racecourse, everybody boots at him. In fact, the part which lawyers have to play upon the stage, is to get the kicks and cuffs but not the six-and-eightpences. Like Pantaloons in pantomimes, they get knocked about and jeered at, and are continually touched up with the red end of the hot poker.

It must have been a bitter disappointment for Mr. Terence Rattigan when his musical "Joie de Vivre" only ran for four performances. By way of compensation, B.A. Young offers this suggestion for a musical adaptation of his current success "Ross." It is appropriately re-entitled

SHUFTI BINT!

SCENE I

The Orderly Room in "B" Flight. FLIGHT-LIEUTENANT STOKER *sits behind his desk.* AIRCRAFTMAN ROSS, *alias* T. E. LAWRENCE, *stands before him under escort.*

STOKER:
> Your conduct's prejudicial to good order
> And to Royal Air Force discipline too,
> So if you've no excuse I must award a
> Salutary punishment to you.
>> But you're a man with some education—
>> Can't you offer an explanation?

ROSS:
> O-O-O-O, I went out to dine with some friends,
> A gay intellectual pack.
>> We had whisky and wine
>> Where I went out to dine,
> And I fell off my bike coming back.
> They're respectable folk, are my friends,
>> And we'd hours of intense conversation.
>> But I cannot produce
>> This as my excuse
> For being back late on the station.

STOKER:
> So-o-o-o you went out to dine with some friends!
> Well, airmen get up to some games.

You insolent chap,
Take that smile off your map
And just tell me some of their names.

ROSS:
I doubt if the names of my friends
  May be asked under R.A.F. law,
    But there were the Astors,
    The Leicesters, the Worcesters,
Archbishops and Dukes by the score—
    Yes, I'm ready to bet
    We'd the whole Cliveden Set,
To say nothing of George Bernard Shaw.

Black-out. The lights fade up on a dream-ballet, choreography by Agnes DeMille, in which GENERAL ALLENBY, RONALD STORRS, COLONEL BARRINGTON, AUDA ABU TAYI and the Turkish Military Governor remove ROSS'S uniform and dress him up as an Arab sheikh.

"*Fancy bringing kids.*"

SCENE 2

A tent in the desert. LAWRENCE is putting on his Arab clothes, watched by STORRS and BARRINGTON in their dress uniforms.

BARRINGTON: I say, it's a bit thick, old chap, what? You're as much like an Arab as my old Aunt Beulah.

LAWRENCE: Ah, but I'm a Circassian. They have fairer skins than the other sort.

STORRS: As long as they have whole skins, eh, Lawrence?

BARRINGTON: Well, frankly I think the whole thing's a lot of dashed nonsense.

LAWRENCE: Perhaps… Who knows?… At any rate it will be a great test of the will.

BARRINGTON: Come on then, Storrs, we'd better be toddlin'.

STORRS: Good luck, Lawrence. (*He tries to shake his hand, but LAWRENCE ducks it.*) Oh, I forgot you don't like shaking hands. (*Raises his hat.*)

STORRS and BARRINGTON go back to Cairo. LAWRENCE sits cross-legged on the sand.

LAWRENCE (*sings*):
    Where shall I at last find peace?
      Does it come from Ancient Greece?
   Here, enfolded by solitude's wings,
  Or in some deep dig in the Valley of Kings
    Shall I at last find peace?
    I seek it like the Golden Fleece,
  And it may be my projection of an Arab insurrection
    Will bring me in the end to peace.

Enter HAMED, a young tribesman with a rifle and a scowl.
Ah, my bodyguard.

HAMED: *Aiwa.* (*Spits.*)

LAWRENCE: Allah will forgive you if you refrain from spitting until the end of the present emergency, I'm sure.

HAMED: It helps to keep the sand down. (*Spits.*) Besides, I have to spit now so that I can stop spitting when I get to like you. (*Spits.*)

LAWRENCE: May it be soon. Meanwhile, saddle the camels, Hamed, and let us make haste to join Prince Feisal.

HAMED: *Kuwais qetir, effendi.* (*Spits.*)

SCENE 3

Headquarters, Deraa District. The TURKISH MILITARY GOVERNOR *sits (on an ottoman, of course) drinking French wine and dictating into his Dictaphone. A Turkish* CAPTAIN *watches him coldly.*

GOVERNOR:
> I love cruelty, I love lechery,
> I love victory, I love Beaune;
> I love subtlety, I love treachery,
> But most of all I love my Dictaphone!
> I get passions for fair Circassians
> In curious fashions that I can't condone,
> But the loveliest slave, or a vintage St.Estephe,
> I never would crave like my Dictaphone!

(Dictates): To all troops in the District. Watch out for Lawrence, alias El Arauns, alias Emir Dynamite, believed to be heading north on Highway 69. A reward of ten thousand pounds will be paid to anyone who captures this man alive. That is all.

CAPTAIN: You make him sound too important.

GOVERNOR: He *is* important. He is a menace. A menace.

SCENE 4

Another part of the desert. LAWRENCE is talking with AUDA ABU TAYI and his troops are singing a ballad off-stage.

LAWRENCE: Anyone for menace?

AUDA and his men gallop off on camels to capture Akaba. Enter HAMED.

HAMED: El Arauns, before we attack Akaba there is something you must know.

LAWRENCE: Why, Hamed, you have stopped spitting.

HAMED: *(adjusting the folds of his robe):* You will see why. *Shufti.*

LAWRENCE: Why, *Hamed!*

HAMED: Yes, El Arauns, now you know my secret. I am no desert Beduin warrior. Once I danced at Madame Badia's. And now, El Arauns, I love you, and I will follow you to the end of the world.

> *(sings)* O'er the burning sands of the desert,
> 'Neath the pitiless skies above,
> Take me, kiss me, hold me,
> Your Oriental love.

(and so on—sixty-four bars altogether)

LAWRENCE: Hamed! And I—never guessed. But there is sterner work before us now. On to Akaba!

HAMED: To Paradise!

SCENE 5

Headquarters, Deraa District. The GOVERNOR switches his Dictaphone on and off a couple of times. Useless! It doesn't work.

GOVERNOR: Are they still flogging him?

CAPTAIN: It's inhuman! Tell them to stop!

GOVERNOR: Inhuman? Do you know what this man has done? Bridges blown; trains destroyed; hundreds of soldiers massacred.

CAPTAIN: I say it's inhuman.

GOVERNOR *(inexorably):* In Akaba there was a consignment of new cylinders for my Dictaphone. They destroyed them all. Every one. Without mercy. *(Calling.)* Bring them up here!

LAWRENCE is brought in, and collapses on the floor.

CAPTAIN: No, No! It's too much! *(He rushes off.)*

GOVERNOR: Now, I think we understand one another. You have the plans for General Allenby's offensive? **(**LAWRENCE *takes no notice.)* So you will not speak? Then we shall have to use other methods, shall we not? *(Flicks his fingers.* HAMED *(or* FIFI, *as she is really*

THE STAGE G.P.

I do not know the result of the deliberations of the learned society which met recently to consider the position of doctors on the stage, but I certainly think it is high time that some publicity was given to the case of the stage General Practitioner.

As every playgoer knows, the stage G.P. is invariably a very genial and jolly fellow and, to all appearances, as well qualified for his job as any G.P. in real life. What, I fear, often escapes the casual eye is the extreme difficulty the unfortunate man must have in making a living.

His lot is very diffe[rent] from that of the s[tage] specialist. Stage folk, w[ho are] extremely partial to obs[cure] and complicated disea[ses] which keep the stage speci[alist] in regular and profit[able] employment, appear to [be] miraculously immune f[rom] the majority of mi[nor] ailments. One rarely sees t[hem] in bed with influenza, prostrate with lumbago, making a nuisance [of] themselves with hay-fe[ver;] their delightfully precoci[ous] children never go ab[out] whooping with whoopi[ng] cough, nor do they go sp[otty] with measles or pallid w[ith]

"Apart from anyt[hing]

iousness.

When therefore the stage P. makes his appearance it pretty sure to be in the pacity of a family friend, d as such he is in fairly nstant employment. In urn for a good deal of sage sdom, embracing sometimes ite a few well-prepared igrams, we see him warded with a cup of tea, a hisky-and-soda, and metimes a very rapid meal. iis sort of thing may, as it re, keep him going, but it nnot conceivably support s wife and family.

What I, as an admirer of the ge G.P., am anxious to ow is whether he is entitled to a fee for his services, and, if so, does he ever get his money? After all, a man who labours, as he often does, to bring a husband and wife together or reconcile a daughter to her father is surely entitled to charge as much, if not more, for that as for feeling their pulses or looking at their tongues.

The dark mystery surrounding the remuneration of the stage G.P. distresses me a good deal, but I must confess that what seems to me to be even more mysterious is that the good fellow, having no visible qualifications, ever came to be a doctor at all.

D.C.

'se, of course, this is bound to revolutionize the whole ter-dinner cabaret and light entertainment field."

called) is dragged on in chains.) You see, Major Lawrence, that no harm has come to her—so far.

FIFI: For Prince Feisal and an independent Arabia—and for our love!

(sings) Whate'er misfortune befall us,
My faithfulness naught shall move.
I'll cling to you now and for ever,
Your Oriental love.

GOVERNOR: As I thought. He is lost, utterly lost. (To an orderly): You can release them both.

SCENE 6

GENERAL ALLENBY'S *Headquarters at Gaza.* ALLENBY *is in conference with* STORRS *and* BARRINGTON.

ALLENBY:
The gentlemen of the press
Are crawling all over the place.
They lurk in the Officers' Mess;
They keep photographing my face.

BARRINGTON:
How can we get rid of them all?
They fill me with deepest abhorrence.

STORRS:
Distract their attention
By chancing to mention
Another great hero.

BARRINGTON: Who?

STORRS: Lawrence.
Yes, Lawrence must rate as a hero—
They'll all want a story from him.

BARRINGTON:
For me his attraction is zero—
Conceited and cruel and dim.
But still, if you think it would do,
I s'pose we can send him a 'plane.

ALLENBY:
Forgive the rebuff,
But oddly enough
I need him to lead a campaign.
Incidentally, I wonder where he is?

LAWRENCE (entering dramatically): He is here. But General, don't send me back. I'm finished. Send me to GHQ. Send me to Abbassia Transit Camp. Send me anywhere. I'm a broken man.

STORRS (quietly): And how about that will we were so proud of?

LAWRENCE: I've made it and sent it to my solicitor.

ALLENBY: Very well, if that's how you feel, you shall stay here with me and bask in the limelight you have earned.

LAWRENCE: Will it be all right if I back into it?

ALLENBY: Certainly, if that's the way you like it. You can begin straight away by backing into a press conference in half an hour's time.

(sings) The gentlemen of the press
Are waiting to file their stories.
So give them the works
On your fights with the Turks.
And stand by for the cheers and the glories.

ORDERLY (entering hurriedly): Sir, there's a lady to see Major Lawrence.

ALLENBY: A *lady?*

ORDERLY: An Arab lady. If you will pardon the expression sir, a bint.

LAWRENCE: No, no! General, send me back to the desert!

The stage darkens. A spotlight picks out FLIGHT—LIEUTENANT STOKER *behind his desk and* AIRCRAFTMAN ROSS *at attention in front of it.*

ROSS. So you see, it was quite necessary for me to change my name and sink my identify in a serial number. Ross... Shaw... Guinness... Brando... somewhere, some day, in some metamorphosis, I may perhaps find peace.

> (*sings*)   Where shall I at last find peace?
> In the Palestine Police?
> I must bear life's banderillas till I've
>   done *The Seven Pillars,*
> And then I shall perhaps find peace.

30 June 1894

A SARA-SCENIC SHOW.

WELCOME to SARA as *Izeÿl,*—"with the dotlets on the *y,*"—and welcome to SARA generally, whatever she may play. She may not, perhaps, be quite so ethereal as heretofore, she may be a trifle more solidified, but "for a' that and a' that," SARA is SARA, the same incomparable SARA. There is nothing particularly new in *Izeÿl,* a poetical tragical drama in verse and four acts. Its first two scenes are as tranquilising as a scientific lecture, and as pretty as a pastoral dissolving view. Representing the converted courtesan, SARA is the same sweet, magnetising, purring person, with an occasional fit of tiger-cat just to enliven the otherwise drowsy proceedings.

It is not till we come to the Third Act that there is anything at all approaching a dramatic sensation. *Scyndia* (M. DENEUBOURG), the gay young spark, who, as his mother, the remarkably fine *Princess* (Madame MARTHOLD) thinks goes to bed at eight, and remains there, comes to *Izeÿl's* palatial residence, and brings with him a handsome present for her of all sorts of, apparently, Palais Royal jewellery, and imitation coins in large boxes. These gifts the still fascinating but recently converted courtesan at once hands over to the poor, whom she has always with her, in the shape of a crowd of invisible beggars waiting outside, all cheering loudly, and no wonder, at the distribution of this *largesse* by the hands of one *Yoghi,* a sort of Bogie-man, well played by M. DE MAX. But the young *Scyndia,* being on pleasure bent, and evidently not "of a frugal mind," like JOHNNIE GILPIN, has also ordered in, from the nearest Stores, a sumptious supper, consisting apparently of "pine-apples for one," and several dishes of more or less ripe fruit, with a few empty goblets—"No Bottles to-day,"—all placed on a portable table, which is brought in by handy attendants, also probably hired from the waiter-supplying greengrocer's.

But *Izeÿl,* having turned from the error of her ways, is, so to speak, "living with mother now," and refuses the proferred supper. Moreover, she rejects with scorn the amorous advances of the gay young *Prince,* who, becoming still gayer and more amorous every minute, exclaims in the language of ancient melodrama, "I must and will possess her!" or words to that effect, and

Sarah (of the Soothing-Syrup voice). "Me voilà encore une fois, mes enfants! Toujours le même vieux jeu!"

incontinently rushes to embrace his victim. But *Izeÿl* recalls a situation curiously like this in *La Tosca,* table and all included, and so snatching a queer sort of triangular dagger from *Scyndia's* belt, she poignards him sharply, fatally; and from being all life and energy down goes *Scyndia* dead as the proverbial door-nail. With dramatic prescience he falls close to the table, and in a few minutes the distracted *Izeÿl* on hearing, like *Lady Macbeth,* "a knocking at the door," partly drags him underneath the table, partly drags the table over him, and as a "happy thought," being a person of considerable resources, she, at the last moment, manages to hide his legs, which are sticking out awkwardly, under the tablecloth.

Enter the stout *Princess,* who, in the character of the mother unaware of her son being out, has a pleasant confidential chat with the interesting convert to Buddhism, during which poor *Scyndia* has to lie under the table, (rather trying this for an actor who would be "up and doing,") and then she suddenly discovers the truth. The infuriated *Princess* orders *Izeÿl* off to be tortured, and to have a lot of pleasant things done to her previous to being publicly exposed—which no adventuress likes—in the desert.

In the last Act, all we see is poor *Izeÿl* gone to the desert with her eye out—both eyes out; but as there is no trace of hot irons, nor any sign of any cruelty having been inflicted on her body, she seems to be none the worse for whatever may have happened to her—indeed, she is just a trifle more purring and fascinating than ever. There she sits, in a light and airy chemise, which, considering her fragile form, may be described as "next to nothing," or almost so, while a few rude persons—idlers, of course—stand by and jeer at her. Then the mad enthusiast, the cause of all this trouble, enters, and pats her on the head, but the Prince, suddenly appearing, dismisses Yoghi-Bogie, has a love scene with the unfortunate *Izeÿl,* who still seems to be more of the courtesan than the convert, and who finally dies in the Prince's arms; whereupon some of his followers, having palms ready in their hands, (which, of course, anatomically, is quite natural,) enter, and there's an end of *Izeÿl.* Not exhilarating, but memorable.

I'm Funny That Way

"I hope that's the orchestra!"

THE FIRE, AGAIN

30 January 1864

Another victim has been sacrificed to the grinning Moloch. Another young girl has been burned to death to make an evening's show. MARIA CHARLES, a dancer at the Pavilion Theatre, is the sacrifice. Her dress caught fire from some unprotected gas-lights used in the Pantomime, and she has since expired. A puff paragraph, in which it was stated that the means of extinguishing fire on such an occasion were ready at hand, has been contradicted by the poor child's sister. We shall of course read more puff paragraphs about the sorrow of the management, and how nothing could exceed the kindness of its inquiries, and the like. But why are not the lights protected, or if that cannot be, why is it not made impossible for a girl, in her eagerness to help a theatrical picture (and knowing what sort of gentle rebuke will reward her for being out of place) from approaching the flaring gas? A stage-manager will of course say that this is impossible. So said the factory people, when they were asked to screen their machinery, and prevent children from being torn to pieces; but the factory people found it easy enough when the alternative was a heavy fine, and the evidence was to be given by no sycophantish servant of the establishment, but by a Government inspector. Something of the same kind, enacted in reference to the theatre, would prevent these oft-recurring burnt sacrifices; and English mothers in the boxes, with their laughing children, would be spared the thought that when the scene is the most brilliant, the chance is greatest that a shriek will announce that someone else's child is in the agony of burning. If some remedial measures are taken, poor MARIA CHARLES will not have died entirely in vain. We may say, with almost literal justification, Peace to her ashes.

Younger and Younger

(Actresses, according to interviewers, are always younger)

We found that Miss Lilian Braithwaite had become so young she had been bowling a hoop in the garden.

Miss Edith Evans was practising scales and looking very flapperish.

Miss Laurie Cowie was playing with a toy engine.

Miss Celia Johnson was holding a conversation with her doll.

Miss Yvonne Arnaud having slipped back to her pre-English days was busy learning the rudiments of the language.

Miss Tallulah Bankhead regarded us with grave eyes from her pram.

Miss Eva Moore was dividing her attention between a ball and two butterflies.

Miss Connie Ediss was waiting with plump happiness for her dinner.

Miss Phyllis Neilson-Terry was in the hands of her nurse.

Miss Gertrude Lawrence was putting her doll's-house in order.

Miss Edna Best was asleep and her Nanny said she must not be disturbed.

"Did you see it on television?"

THIS ONE WILL RUN AND RUN AND RUN

The real-life drama of CHRISTOPHER MATTHEW, written, directed, performed and now reviewed by himself

Anyone who seriously believes that the Social Contract has put paid to the politics of confrontation shouldn't miss *An Ugly Scene Between Myself and the Caretaker*.

The plot has a classic simplicity: I buy a small motorscooter of the sort that could very well invite horseplay from passing local youth on its way home from the Black Eagle around 11 o'clock of an evening; the Caretaker, on his own initiative, agrees that I can leave it in the yard behind the flats; suddenly he receives a message from the landlord's agent that all vehicles are to be kept in the street. Yet beneath the surface of this deceptively straightforward story, strange undercurrents are at work; primitive passions are aroused, based on centuries of class warfare. My attempts to appeal to the Caretaker's better nature ("Come now, Mr. Smith, surely we can reach some sort of compromise? After all, it's no skin off your nose ...") are immediately misinterpreted, and his almost incoherent reply, "Look ... look ... how many more times ... either you get that fart-box out of here or I bleeding throw it out," has a tragic inevitability about it.

Mr. Smith, in the role of the Caretaker, gives a workmanlike, though at times somewhat unconvincing, performance as the simple, one might almost say stupid, man, buffeted between the Scylla of his heart which urges compassion and the Charybdis of his head which tells him that if he doesn't do as he's told and look sharp about it he's likely to find himself warming a bench down at the local Labour.

As the smooth-talking but in the end totally ineffectual sitting tenant who suddenly realises what it means to live in a constituency with a Labour majority of over 11,000, I give a pathetic performance, but one with which many sitting tenants up and down the country will readily identify.

And talking of sitting, I am frequently asked these days by friends if, as a bachelor of many years' standing, I can recommend a place to eat that has good food, first class service, a pleasant atmosphere, car parking facilities, and costs less than £8.50 a head without wine.

I can do no better than suggest an old favourite of mine: *At Home in front of the Telly* (3rd floor flat at the rear; Mon-Fri; hours vary according to programme times).

I have been eating here for many years now, ever since that evening of gastronomic magic in the late of autumn of 1967 when I discovered for the first time that boiling water does something for an egg.

The study cum spare room where, as regulars will know, one normally eats, looks very much the same today as it did then—the wallpaper, the furniture and piles of books on the floor in the corner all combining as they do to create an atmosphere of shabby-chic that takes one straight back to the middle fifties. The menu too has altered very little since those early days, despite the acquisition in 1971 of a new frying pan. One evening, for example, I started off with a really delicious pre-dinner *Cup of Instant Coffee* with *Nationwide,* which contrasted in a most interesting way with the *Heinz Cream of Tomato* (small) which accompanied the recorded highlights of the *State Opening of Parliament* shortly afterwards. (In one bachelor flat I know of, soup is spooned down straight from the saucepan as part of a drive to save washing-up; I am seriously thinking of introducing the habit in my own.)

As a main course, I toyed for a long while in Safeways with the possibility of *Three Haddock Portions* and *Four Faggots in Gravy,* but settled in the end for *Six Fish Fingers.* Not only are they a particular favourite of mine, but I see from the packet that they now "contain best quality cod." Unfortunately, on this occasion I did them less than justice, owing to a particularly gripping moment in *Mission Impossible,* as a result of which they ended up a little browner on the outside than they might have been. Fortunately, however, the *Tender Young Green Peas* ($1/4$ oz size) were perfect, despite my forgetting to add salt while they were cooking, and the last minute substitution of brown bread and butter for crinkle-cut chips (which I forgot to buy) was a brilliant touch—a most apt complement to Donald Burton's earthy performance as Commander Nialls in *Warship.*

Anything that followed was bound to be something of an anti-climax, and so it was with the

Show-biz folks at home

a LARRY documenta[...]
on Life after the Show[...]

Mild Farmyard Czechoslovakian Cheddar—a disappointment that was more than made up for, however, by the *Banana Yoghurt* with the *Nine O'Clock News*. The *Instant Coffee* was hot and plentiful. Drinking very acceptable house tap water, the whole meal came to 43½p, including B & B.

For sheer entertainment value I recommend *A Look-In at the Local Gas Show Room* (daily 9-5.30; early closing Weds and Sats).

From the moment I pushed open the door to the accompaniment of the familiar *per-ting* of the bell, I knew at once I was in for 20 minutesworth of non-stop warmth, good-hearted advice and high jinks at the hands of Mrs. Mavis Brynmaer. Her first entrance between the Rangette and the Mayflower Automatic was sheer nylon-coated magic (hair by Grace of Hairnette, just down the road; make-up by plaster-husband Cyril); while her opening number, "May I Help You?" reminded one that beneath the veneer of modern bloody-mindedness, old-fashioned Christianity is still alive. But willingness, however good-hearted, is not everything, even these days, and here South East Gas can count themselves fortunate indeed to have found in Mrs. Brynmaer a demonstrator of quite exceptional talent. Supported only by a pair of sensible suede Dolcis lace-ups, she moves from one cooker to another in a manner that reminds one irresistibly of Beriosova in *La Cuisine Enchantée*. And as for the long and difficult speech in which she extols the virtues of the self-cleaning oven ("You see, there are thousands of tiny holes, and the grease just evaporates through them,") she handles it with the warmth and humour one normally associates with Dulcie Gray.

And yet, we are reminded, all is not laughter in the world of gas cookery. "The Diana has the added attraction of a rotisserie," says Mrs. Brynmaer at one moment, then adds with meaningful poignancy, "and what they *call* a toastmaster;" while the cautionary epilogue in which she points out that half the models I have been looking at are not available in the North Thames area where I live, gives the whole event a sting in the tail that is not altogether unacceptable—especially when you see the prices.

Unfortunately South East Gas have fallen down once again on their décor which is as *vieux châpeau* as ever. "Order Your Split Level Cooker Here" does little for me, despite the bold red lettering, although the poster depicting Arthur Askey in a ballet dress, waving a wand, entitles "Save on Supercookers with your Fairy Gas Mother," seems to raise a titter or two from the odd passer-by.

On then to *Another Silly Row with My Girl-Friend* (twice nightly—outside the Chelsea Odeon and later in the San Frediano Restaurant, Fulham Road, SW7). An everyday saga of neurotic folk. The less said about this lamentable farce the better—except to add that I still say she's wrong. Not one of her better performances by any means.

I only wish the same could be said about *Taking the Dog out for a Widdle* (every night about 10.30-ish, but liable to be cancelled at very short notice in the event of rain or slight ground frost). Always a great performance in every sense of the word.

COMING ON: Friday 6.30 pm. *A Visit to the Lauderette.* A routine weekly event, enlivened only by the occasional outburst from Wanda (38-24-42), the chirpy, dark-eyed manageress, always a delight to the eye in her navy housecoat, pale blue woolly slippers with pom-poms, and matching hair-net. Her comments last week on Mrs. Davies from the paper shop's bundle of underwear, although they might offend some people (not least Mrs. Davies from the paper shop), were in the best Music Hall tradition.

Tuesday 9.30 am. *Having the Car Serviced* (every 3,000 miles, when I remember). Will the funny knocking noise turn out to be a big end going as the gloomy garage man predicts, or is it only the spare wheel coming loose in the boot again? And does that nasty burning smell mean a new head gasket and all that that entails or does the ashtray need emptying? A suspense drama that strikes at the hears, and wallets, of every middle class male in the country.

PASSING THROUGH

Elaine Stritch talks to David Taylor

Maybe it's the price that onions went, they're pushing martinis; the fact is, you order a dry one in The Savoy, it comes with all of this onion salad in it, almost there's no room for the liquor. Elaine doesn't need all of that garbage. And also, she's going to tell you something: you don't know anything about anybody inside forty-eight hours, right? We don't want any of that bullshit about How I Sleep In Chanel No. 5 and doesn't it sound smart? You know, she said to her husband, what am I going to tell these *Punch* guys? He said, tell them you ran away at fourteen to join the Spanish Civil War and then went into real estate. It's crazy. Matter of fact, she just had a little row with her husband. One of those "You're not making any sense, you know that?" affairs—nothing fundamental. It was about turning off the radiators in The Savoy. She figured Up, he said Down. You know what it was? He's left-handed. Say it again, it sure is a crazy life. Siddown and pull up a drink.

In the bulletins that The Savoy dishes out to people who are curious to know who's staying there: Elaine Stritch, American actress. Indefinitely. Story of her life, nearly, who needs detail: understudied Ethel Merman, years on the road in the US, Noel Coward plays in London (he was a pal, a real sweetie) who needs all of that? So we are going to talk about two things and the first thing is her home, The Savoy. All of twelve years ago, now, Noel suggested she move in, it was convenient for the Savoy Theatre. She had room 712. And that's not dollars-per-week, mind, even with the breakfast. You shouldn't take marmalade—that's the 12. OK, pull ourselves together. She's had so many apartments, but for what? You collect all of the stuff, antiques; flowers out of teapots, inlaid marble coffee tables, then you go on the road and you sub-let and the stuff gets spoiled. In any case, cost it out: a really nice flat in London, plus all of the service? It almost pays to settle for The Savoy. If she had her way, she'd live there the rest of her life. She might just. First off, if you have any personality, you make friends with the best people in the world—the chambermaids, the bartenders—it's just like having a staff of a thousand, all friends. Listen, you just blink in that place, there's five guys in tuxedos. You think it's your funeral. They're dressed for it. You can get a broiled lobster or a hot dog or whatever twenty-four hours a day. She doesn't do that, you know, but it's there. Was it Dean Martin (another close pal) who said he never drank after dinner? He ate at 1 a.m.

Topic two is Elaine. Boy, that's a tricky one, right? Let her tell you a story. In New York, two o'clock in the morning, acting career in Hollywood temporarily loused up. She says to a choreographer pal, let's take a walk and have a stinger, the way you do. The find this bar, called *Elaine's,* on 2nd Avenue and 89th. Big lady in charge, hitting the

beer. You should watch that. Bartender's off sick, so Miss Stritch mixes for herself and the choreographer (no, really, some of them are straight) because a Stinger's kind of tricky. So, after a while, the fat lady in charge wants to know who she is. Elaine? Why, for heaven's sakes, that's her name too, half an hour's boredom, you know? Anyhow, cut a long story short, she gets taken on at the bar, does six months through 5 a.m. and let her tell you it was one of the best times of her life. It's a wow and the columnists go crazy—*Thespian shakes martinis*—and pretty soon it's *the* place in town: Tennessee Williams and all. Still is. Norman Mailer's a regular. And you know what got them? She could mix the drinks the way they ought to be. Her grandfather, this is 1901, he used to walk out of the saloon, and he'd buy everybody left a nickel beer and he'd toast: "Here's how we lost the farm!'at's what counts. One day, she figures she'll do cabaret, only it has to be right. She's talked it over with Dean Martin and the plan is to step out there and shut everyone up because they're going to learn about a lot. Out of nowhere, this waiter walks up and he enquires, Mr. Wright? Elaine says no, she hasn't found him yet. You have to listen to it; and order another—without the onion salad, OK?—and to quit never, because life's crazy, you know? And always remember what Noel once said, that if humour does not have some basis in reality then it's not worth doing. He knew, that guy, he knew.

"Bad news - they want to go solo."

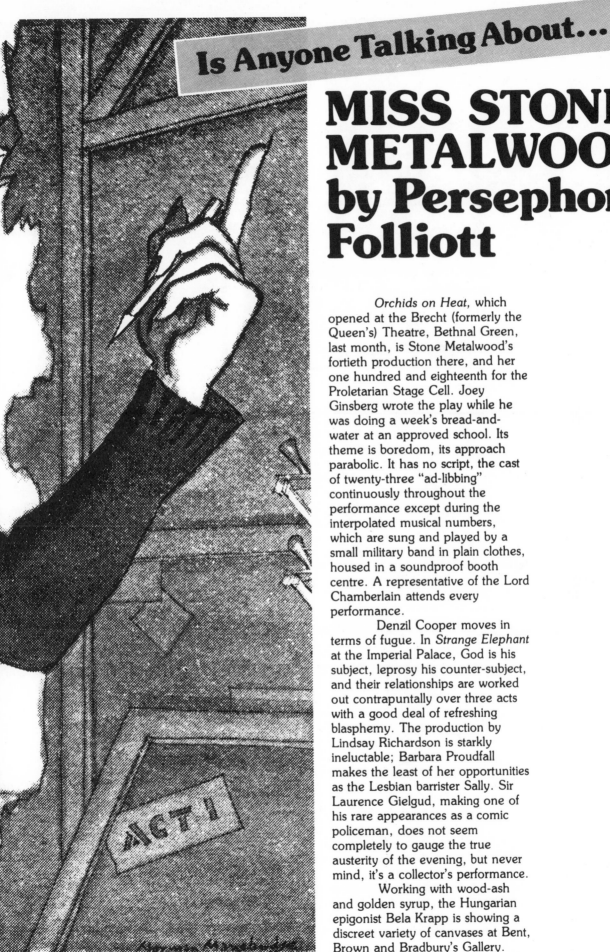

MISS STONE METALWOOD by Persephone Folliott

Orchids on Heat, which opened at the Brecht (formerly the Queen's) Theatre, Bethnal Green, last month, is Stone Metalwood's fortieth production there, and her one hundred and eighteenth for the Proletarian Stage Cell. Joey Ginsberg wrote the play while he was doing a week's bread-and-water at an approved school. Its theme is boredom, its approach parabolic. It has no script, the cast of twenty-three "ad-libbing" continuously throughout the performance except during the interpolated musical numbers, which are sung and played by a small military band in plain clothes, housed in a soundproof booth centre. A representative of the Lord Chamberlain attends every performance.

Denzil Cooper moves in terms of fugue. In *Strange Elephant* at the Imperial Palace, God is his subject, leprosy his counter-subject, and their relationships are worked out contrapuntally over three acts with a good deal of refreshing blasphemy. The production by Lindsay Richardson is starkly ineluctable; Barbara Proudfall makes the least of her opportunities as the Lesbian barrister Sally. Sir Laurence Gielgud, making one of his rare appearances as a comic policeman, does not seem completely to gauge the true austerity of the evening, but never mind, it's a collector's performance.

Working with wood-ash and golden syrup, the Hungarian epigonist Bela Krapp is showing a discreet variety of canvases at Bent, Brown and Bradbury's Gallery.

Hewison's PEOPLE

ALL
THE
WORLD'S
A STAGE
Alan
Coren

Playmates

Scene: The foyer of any London theatre. Time: Any First Night of a new production. Cast: An assortment of habitual First Nighters. There is much gush and a great deal of cheek-kissing and darlinging among the frilly dress shirts and off-the-breast gowns. There are also great batteries of dentistry flashing away at the press cameras. The group above is one small enclave within the throng. The man on the right is possibly an *angel* who is here to see what they've done with his money and clap like an idiot at every opportunity, but he is more likely to be an agent escorting one of his newly-acquired young actresses in order to show her off to anyone who might be instrumental in furthering her career. (At dinner after the show she will suddenly remember an urgent engagement at the moment her coffee is being poured, which will displease him not a little.) The other lady is the wife of an impresario, a lady remarkable for the cost and vulgarity of her clothes. And on the left are two critics. The shorter one will need to rush off at the first curtain call in order to bang out his

700 words of instant appraisal by the 10.30 deadline. His companion is a Sunday man so he has more time to ruminate and polish his prose and check up on what his daily colleagues have written. (These other reviews will have no effect on his own opinion, of course—he will be completely at odds with the rest as usual.) Their styles therefore tend to be different; the daily paper man crackles with puns and wordplay as he fillets historical detail from the lavish programmes (these are put out by the RSC and the National and many a critic's reputation for far-reaching erudition comes from this source); the Sunday man shows off his immaculate credentials by bringing in adroit references to the sister arts—the trouble is he confuses Debussy with Satie, Kandinsky with Klimt, Bruegel with Bosch, Palladio with Inigo Jones. He is also apt to miss vital moments of the action because he is scribbling away in the margins of his programme. Unlikely as it might seem to the playwrights, directors and actors on the other side of the proscenium, nearly all critics have great regard and love for the theatre; though individually they get a lot of it wrong, collectively they get much more of it right.

PAY POINT

KING RICHARD

Is not the king's name twenty thousand names?
Arm, arm, my name! A puny subject strikes
At thy great glory. Look not to the ground
Ye favourites of a king: are we not high?
High be our thoughts: I know my uncle York
Hath power enough to serve our turn.
But who comes here?
Enter W.H. SMITH
W.H. SMITH

Two floors below don't miss the wide display
Of novelties, board games, balls, clockwork toys
Plus all the latest paperbacks. Pens, cards,
And ringback binders, records, table mats;
I know I need not mention magazines.
KING RICHARD

Mine ear is open and my heart prepared:
The worst is worldly loss thou canst unfold.
Say, is my kingdom lost?
Alarums. Enter KNIGHT, FRANK, RUTLEY,
GIDDY *and* GIDDY
FRANK

I would point out to the clients in the stalls
Two flats remain, a penthouse and a nice
Four-bedroom maisonette, with ensuite baths,
South facing balconies, lift, porterage;
But stay—what would'st thou, Knight?
KNIGHT
You have not said

Both leases run till 1994;
The ground rents low, the heating underfloor,
With kitchens in which no expense—
W.H. SMITH
Hang on!

I have not pointed out that we now stock
Cake candles, Christmas crackers, shuttlecocks,
Donald Duck watches, and, unique to Smith's—
Fanfares. Sennets. Enter THE ANNUAL CON-
FERENCE OF SHOE SALESMEN
EXECUTIVE COMMITTEE UNDER THE
CHAIRMANSHIP OF HORACE WOL-
STENHOLME MBE
WOLSTENHOLME

Good evening! Unaccustomed as I am,
I feel it now behoves me, and I think,
I speak for all of us who are concerned
With boots, shoes, gaiters, wellingtons and socks,
And let us not forget—here, do you mind?
Enter HEAD WAITER
HEAD WAITER

Aftair ze show, may ah sugges' yu step
Into *Le Cochon Vert*, one flight below?

Tonight, we 'ave our speciality:
Noisettes de porc, avec des aubergines,
And, to commence, perhaps les moules farcies,
Served on a bed of—
KING RICHARD

Strives Bolingbroke to be as great as we?
Greater he shall not be; if he serve God,
We'll serve him too, and be his fellow so.
1st GIDDY

Who is this bloke? Is he from E.H.Brookes?
I know the face
2nd GIDDY
It might be John D.Wood;

I think they're handling the furnished rooms.
KING RICHARD

Revolt our subjects? That we cannot mend;
They break their faith to God as well as us;
Cry woe, destruction, ruin, loss, decay;
Enter CAR PARK ATTENDANT
CAR PARK ATTENDANT

The owner of RXV 135
Has stuck his car in front of Exit 4,
And gone off with the keys. It's bleeding chaos;
You can't get in or out.
W.H. SMITH
Not Exit 4?

But that's our loading bay! I've got twelve vans
Due in from Watford any minute now
With Harold Robbins' latest masterpiece—
A gift at sixty pee—and
TALL CITIZEN IN BOX
That one's mine!

Green Rover, wire wheels, twin foglamps?
CAR PARK ATTENDANT
Right!

You better come right down, and bloody quick!
Enter J.B. SMEDLEY *and* SON
J.B. SMEDLEY

Excuse me, sir, are you a smoker?
TALL CITIZEN IN BOX
Yes.

SON

May we suggest that on your way downstairs
You drop in at our kiosk, where you'll find
A range of smoker's needs second to none?
KING RICHARD

Where is the Earl of Wiltshire? Where is Bagot?
What is become of Bushy? Where is Green?
RUTLEY

Nothing in Bushey. Got a very nice
Semi in Stanmore, though: four up, two down,
Gas central heating, freehold, and a snip
At thirty-four.

FRANK
Or offer.
KNIGHT
Thirty-six

Might very well secure it; if you're quick.
Enter AUDIENCE. *Shouts, chequebooks, used
notes. Auctions without.* RICHARD *is borne off by*
MANAGEMENT.

CURTAIN

187

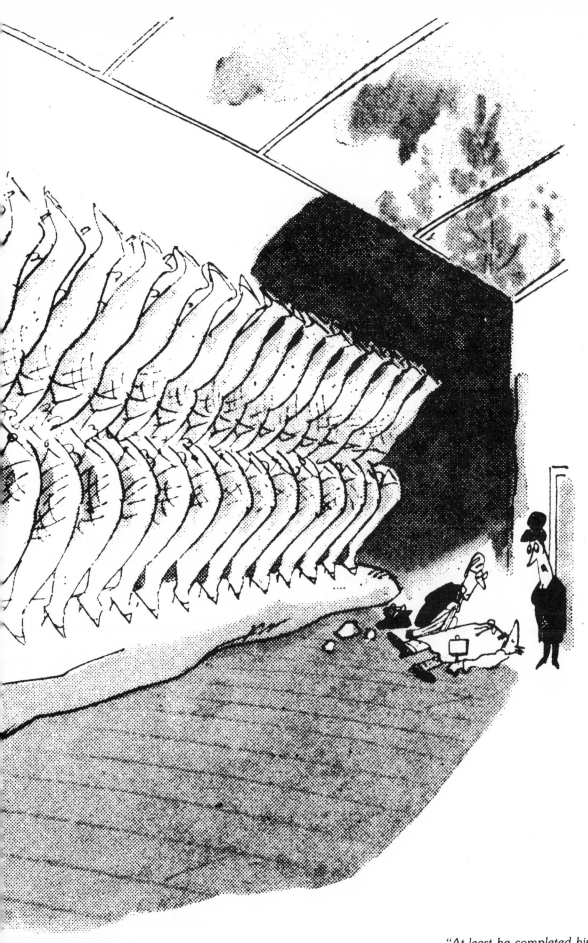

"At least he completed his life's work."

IF YOU DON'T LOVE THE AUDIENCE THEY WON'T LOVE YOU
Harry Secombe

There was once an American night-club comedian who used to come on stage, glare at his audience and begin his act with the immortal phrase, "Good evening, opponents." It takes a brave man to do that, believe me. Those of use who spend our lives trying to coax laughter from reluctant throats might often feel like using similar tactics, but we would have been lucky to leave the stage of the Empire, Glasgow, on a Friday night second house in one piece.

We comedians *have* to love our audiences just as much as we want to be loved in return. In the dressing room before I go on I always pace up and down wondering how they are going to be out there. I think of them crouching in the darkness waiting for me to appear, hoping that they are going to love me as much as I want to love them, and at the same time asking myself why I took up performing in the first place.

What makes us go on stage and make fools of ourselves? It's not just the money. Let us examine the reason for anyone choosing acting as a profession. It has to be exhibitionism in some form or another—a desire to show off, to be noticed, to be loved—and it usually reveals itself at a fairly early age.

A budding comedian is the child who likes to dress up in his father's clothes and wear a lamp-shade on his head at family get-togethers. (The boy who prefers to put on his mother's frocks and lipstick has a different kind of problem with which we should not concern ourselves here.) He draws attention to himself in this way and if he is lucky he will be rewarded by laughter and a little light applause. This spurs him on to greater efforts and he begins to seek wider horizons and larger lampshades. The four walls of the front parlour can no longer contain him and his desire for acclamation might drive him on to the stage of the Church Hall.

If his lamp-shade act goes down well there he will be so excited by the applause that he is usually hooked for life. "All those people out there are laughing at *me*," he thinks. "I love them, I love them." He spends all his pocket money on lamp-shades for his act, and when he grows up he becomes a light comedian. It's as simple as that. A clip around the earhole from his father when he first donned a lamp-shade might have stopped the rot, but once he has heard that laughter and applause there is no turning back.

It sometimes happens that love of an audience can take hold of a person quite late in life. I know a theatre manager in his fifties who had never been on stage in his life until one day he had to make a live announcement. It earned him such a roar of approval that he forsook his own side of the business for the acting side. Unfortunately he never met with the same success again because, naturally, it's not every day that we get Germany to surrender.

Constant television appearances mean that someone with as large a figure as I possess is instantly recognisable and I find that I have an audience wherever I go. It is a compliment, of course, to be asked for one's autograph, although sometimes it can be rather inconvenient. I was once spotted entering the gents' toilet in one of the motorway garages and was forced to sign pieces of paper thrust under the door by a party of children on a school outing. Some of them were girls.

In Mallorca, where we have a holiday home, I was once having my hair cut in a barber's shop in the main street of Cala Millor. There was no-one else in the place and I was having the full treatment—shampoo, massage, and the bit where they put a net over your head and dry your hair with a blower. Rather decadent but very relaxing. The shop has a large plate-glass window and people were wandering about the street outside. Out of the corner of my eye I saw passing a middle-aged man and his wife, wearing the unmistakable British holiday gear—short-sleeved Celanese shirt, sandals with socks and khaki shorts. He was wearing a mac. They walked out of sight and after a short pause they came back

again. The woman peered at me through the glass and nodded to her husband. He in turn shook his head. She then called to someone out of vision and suddenly the window was full of people, some nodding their heads, others shaking them. They seemed to reach a decision and delegated one of their number to open the door. He was a short, bald man with an aggressive manner. Putting his face up against mine he scrutinised me carefully and then, without saying a word to me, he called back to the others who were now crowding the door—"It *is* him!" I waved feebly at them.

The barber, who was at first non-plussed by this invasion, carried on with his job while I tried to look unconcerned. The crowd outside began shouting encouraging remarks to him as he swivelled my neck this way and that. Slowly he began to respond

to his unexpected audience and he put on a show for them. His success went to my head. He removed the net, flourished his comb and scissors and snipped away at my nostril hairs, getting a round of applause for his delicacy of performance. Powder and hair oil flew in all directions as he completed his ministrations. By this time I too became involved and sang a little snatch from *The Barber of Seville.* "Bravo!" cried our audience. He whipped the sheet from around my neck like a matador doing a fancy pass with his cape, whisked the hairs away with a brush and we both bowed to the storm of applause.

It was one of the most bizarre experiences in my life. It was also one of the worst haircuts I have ever had, but that's neither here nor there. The audience loved it and that's all that matters, really, isn't it?

INDEX
OF
WRITERS
AND
ARTISTS